Forming
Thinking
Writing

SECOND EDITION

Forming
Thinking
Writing

SECOND EDITION

Ann E. Berthoff

with
James Stephens

BOYNTON/COOK PUBLISHERS
HEINEMANN
PORTSMOUTH, NH

BOYNTON/COOK PUBLISHERS
A Division of
HEINEMANN EDUCATIONAL BOOKS, INC.
361 Hanover Street
Portsmouth, NH 03801
Offices and agents throughout the world

Second edition

Library of Congress Cataloging-in-Publication Data

Berthoff, Ann E.
    Forming, thinking, writing / Ann E. Berthoff, with James Stephens.
  — 2nd ed.
      p. cm.
    ISBN 0-86709-238-6
    1. English language—Rhetoric. I. Stephens, James (James W.)
II. Title.
PE1048.B485 1988   88-15626
808'.042—dc19   CIP

Printed in the United States of America
92   9 8 7 6 5 4 3

ACKNOWLEDGMENTS

The following have generously given permission to reprint copyrighted material in this book:

BERTOLT BRECHT. "The Buddha's Parable of the Burning House." Reprinted from *Bertolt Brecht: Poems 1913-1956* with permission of the publishers, Routledge, Chapman & Hall, New York, and Methuen London, London.

HENRI CARTIER-BRESSON. From *The Decisive Moment*. Copyright ©1952 by Henri Cartier-Bresson, Verve and Simon & Schuster. Reprinted by permission of Simon & Schuster, Inc.

EDWARD KOREN. Cartoon from *The New Yorker*, February 16, 1976. Copyright ©1976 by The New Yorker Magazine, Inc. Reprinted by permission.

GEORGE KUBLER. From *The Shape of Time*. Copyright ©1962 by Yale University. Reprinted by permission of the publisher, Yale University Press.

M.R. MONTGOMERY. "Measure Mine the Old-Fashioned Way, Please." From the *Boston Globe*, July 25, 1985. Reprinted courtesy of the *Boston Globe*.

KIMON NICOLAÏDES. From *The Natural Way to Draw*. Copyright ©1941 by Anne Nicolaïdes. Copyright © renewed 1969 by Anne Nicolaïdes. Reprinted by permission of Houghton Mifflin Company.

JAMES THURBER. Copyright ©1931, 1959 by James Thurber. From "Ladies' and Gentlemen's Guide to Modern English Usage," in *The Owl in the Attic*, published by Harper & Row. Originally printed in *The New Yorker*. Reprinted by permission of Rosemary Thurber.

DEREK E. TILL. "Innovation Revisited," from *Opportunities for Innovation #6*, Arthur D. Little, Inc. Reprinted by permission of Derek E. Till.

CONTENTS

Special Features

Schemata, Diagrams, Checklists, Guides

Paragraph Sequences

Sentence Structures

Charlotte's Composition

FOREWORD

Forming/Thinking/Writing is a textbook whose time has come. It has worked very well for four years as the rhetoric text in the freshman English course at Marquette University, stimulating the kind of healthy argument – both for and against – that marks the arrival of a force which, on the one hand, is innovative and even experimental, yet, on the other, obvious, even elementary, in its clarity and thrust. Ann Berthoff's method for teaching composition may or may not be well explained in the first edition of *F/T/W*; her illustrations and "assisted invitations" may or may not be appropriate for the 1980s and the students we now serve; her style of address may appeal to readers as philosophical and personal at the same time, or as muddled or indirect. What remains, at the end of any debate about the merits of *F/T/W,* however, is the simplicity and beauty of the method of composing which is outlined and illustrated there.

We at Marquette did feel the need to supplement the text with a teacher's guide we developed. At first, we feared that the mix of instructors – beginning teaching assistants, experienced assistants, part-time faculty, full-time faculty, and graduate faculty, some sixty people, all teaching freshman English – would make the adoption of this text impossible. After all, experienced teachers may not find either "chaos" or "back-and-forthness" as useful or dependable as the traditional rhetorics can seem to be. What we found, of course, is that teachers of composition care most about their students, and that most are willing to try *anything* that gives promise for improvement in classroom atmosphere, student performance, and teacher morale.

With the help of a practical, day-by-day guide to *F/T/W,* much of which is incorporated in this revised edition, and with the added benefit of a supplementary text – the *Norton Reader,* in our case – Marquette University has developed a writing program that works for the great majority of its students and instructors. Teachers have to be learners, and most of us have learned – from preparing the instructor's manual, from logging the results of our classes and the gains of student writers, from using the heuristics in our own writing and in class preparations – that the method works for everyone involved. You will get the best writing you have ever had, and you may begin to see how much more original your own writing is and how creative your assignments have become.

To date, approximately 6000 students have been enrolled in our process-oriented composition sequence (two courses in the freshman year) and most have profited greatly. At least 125 instructors have been involved. And most of us have learned something new about students: as Ann puts it, "Students like to think if they think they can." We have seen young writers respond to concepts they have never grappled with before: the dialectic, generation of chaos, the double helix – naming/opposing/defining – forming concepts, and, of course, forming/thinking/writing. Our students have learned about that mysterious branch of knowledge called "heuristics" (or, more simply, "ways in" to writing), and they have discovered the "ways out" of chaos, too, which is to say that they do learn to oppose, define, classify, describe, and argue as occasions demand. On the first day of a writing course, we hold up the textbook, with its spine towards the students. The spine says simply: FORMING · THINKING · WRITING; the three activities are inseparable.

When our writing program was formally evaluated by the Council of Writing Program Administrators (WPA), it was commended for choosing an approach which assumes that composition courses should not be merely remedial, or service, courses, but rather major parts of the college curriculum, in which students learn to see writing as a way of learning. The focus is not so much on the written product or its mode as it is on the students and the process of composing. The shift in focus from *what* is written to *how* students write is consistent with most recent theories and practices in composition and "suggests a syllabus shaped not by nouns" (*organization, diction, thesis statement*) "but by verbs" (*thinking, planning, drafting, revising*). "Berthoff's *Forming/Thinking/Writing* is an appropriate textbook for such a verb-centered, process-centered course."

The corps of teachers at Marquette University probably knows more about *Forming/Thinking/Writing* than even Ann Berthoff does. We have lived with it, some of us for the entire four years, and few would make any drastic changes in a book that works so well. What we all want to do, however – to use Ann's own words – is "aerate the thing," so that it can work even better, communicate even more straightforwardly, and in more contemporary terms, to the students. To that end, we have added many new materials, including readings and exercises – "kitchen-tested," of course – that are designed to give student writers opportunities to improve their powers of critical thinking about the world they inhabit. Our experience has shown, too, that individual instructors always supplement the readings and exercises with selections chosen for particular classes, which we are happy to encourage.

Some practical notes: this method works best when students are required to keep dialectical notebooks. Instructors usually take up portions of the notebooks every three weeks or so. Some look over the complete notebooks; others check them over in class; and some ask students to choose a few entries to turn in for the instructor's comments. To alleviate the physical burden of carrying around so many notebooks, we recommend that all students use loose-leaf paper and submit, in a folder with pockets, only those pages which are requested. Throughout the first half of this book, incidentally, we have included portions of one student's notebook for a 1200 word paper on women in advertising. Instructors might inform their students that this notebook is among the better examples of its kind; that it deviates from our method on occasion; that it is offered as an illustration of what can be done, not as a model to be imitated in detail. A final note on practice: we offer an index to "assisted invitations" in this edition, having found that many instructors move around in the book and need a guide. We hope you find it useful.

I should use this space to name the dozens of people who have helped Ann and me over the past four years. They know who they are, of course, and I will name just those to whom we owe the major debts for suggestions and contributions of student writing: James Balestrieri, Brooke Barker, Stan Blair, John Boly, Joanne Cutting-Gray, Edward Duffy, Donna Foran, Michael Goddard, Paula Gillespie, Matthew Herrick, Verda Jaroszewski, Mark Kamrath, David Krause, Patricia Lantier, Michael Mikolajczak, Shannon O'Laughlin, Paul Reuteman, Julie Smith, Beth Sokolowski, and James Swearingen.

J.S.

INTRODUCTION

In the first edition of this book, published ten years ago, there was a lot I wasn't clear about, a lot I didn't make explicit – not because I was trying to camouflage difficulties, but because I didn't recognize them. I was committed to avoiding the condescending tone of the rhetorics of the day, either the "there, there" approach or the "WOW-POW! ISN'T this exciting?" approach. My title was probably the first to include *thinking;* I'm certain it was the first (and may still be the only one) to include *forming.* I believed – and I still do – that students like to think if they think they can, and it was my chief aim to offer them assistance in discovering that they could. But I was unsuccessful in making clear that learning to think systematically, learning a method of composing, is a matter of developing certain habits over a period of time. One response I cherish came from a Harvard freshman who wrote in an evaluation his instructor asked for: "If you had a paper due Monday morning and somebody gave you Berthoff's book Friday night, you'd break out in a cold sweat."

Many teachers had the same response. They often told me that they loved the book, that they photocopied the section on definition and the one on paragraphs and the discussion of generalization, but that they couldn't teach the book because it was much too difficult for their students! What they meant was, I think, that the book scared them. *Forming/Thinking/Writing* was itself not a course in composition, nor did I intend that it should take over a course in which it was used. Its weaknesses were defects of this virtue: the ellipses and non sequiturs, the sketchy explanations and missing demonstrations resulted from an unwillingness to seem prescriptive.

For all its faults, *Forming/Thinking/Writing* nevertheless found a place in various taxonomies and was awarded several seals of approval, sometimes by people who had never followed out any of the "assisted invitations" and in some cases had not read past "Introduction: Philosophy and Pedagogy." The central concept of the book – the idea that by looking at *what* we are doing we can find out *how* to do it – was not widely discussed, but a technique introduced there with minimal fanfare has certainly caught on: I mean the double-entry journal, which I call a *dialectical notebook*. Looking and looking again, thinking about your thinking, observing your observations is so fundamental a capacity of mind that any technique which helps us develop this power is immediately adaptable to many different purposes.

There have been three influences which have led me to undertake a radical revision of *Forming/Thinking/Writing* to remedy its faults and to make more accessible what it had to offer. The first came when Dixie Goswami showed me what had happened when the teachers in her seminars at the Bread Loaf School of English had used the dialectical notebook in their reading and writing. This notebook is described in the text, but the defining character is that each page is divided by a vertical line making a wide left- or right-hand margin. On one side are written first responses, reading notes, initial apprehensions and, on the other side, comments about those notes and observations. In the notebook Dixie displayed, the right-hand side with the initial responses was, in the first week or so, full of uninterrupted quotation; on the left-hand side appeared comments like "I don't understand a word of what is being said." "So what?" "I don't agree." Towards the end of the second week, the balance began to shift, and by the end of the summer term, there were only a few lines on the right, whereas the left-hand side contained substantial questions, "yes, buts," and continuous discourse in real sentence form. The teacher-student had begun to listen in on her inner dialogue and to represent it in the form encouraged by the format of the dialectical notebook. This particular notebook became an emblem of how to reclaim the imagination as the forming power of mind. The success other teachers had with the dialectical notebook – notably Rae Iverson, Sheila Koff, and Ann Raimes – persuaded me that it was indeed a powerful pedagogical instrument because it allowed students to do as writers what they already do simply as human beings – to recognize and to represent, to interpret and to revise – and to do so continually.

The second influence which led to this revision has been the success of James Stephens' enterprise at Marquette University, where *Forming/Thinking/Writing* was adopted as a text for freshman English. Jim has described that experience in some detail in his Foreword, so I will say here only that I was very gratified to know that what I characterized as a method of composing was found to be pertinent for the work of a course based on the reading of literature. Furthermore, the fact that young, inexperienced teachers learned to let it guide their teaching validated my conviction that those who teach composition well are necessarily learners.

The third influence has been the experience of meeting with writing staffs all over the country, addressing conferences, and offering workshops in universities and colleges of many sorts. It seems to me that everywhere I go the problems and dilemmas are the same; that what I have to say to teachers is as appropriate in one place as it is in another. Energy given to testing and evaluation and a concern for addressing the special needs of contemporary students can obscure the fact that all students come to us as language animals, as makers of meaning, and that the social construction of knowledge is in a necessary dialectic with personal knowledge. I believe that the new *Forming/Thinking/Writing* can help teacher-researchers transform their classrooms into "philosophic laboratories" – as I.A. Richards has it – for the study of the making of meaning – always remembering that as we ask *what* that transformation would be, what it requires, what it entails, we will be discovering *how* to bring it about.

Finally, there has been the influence of Robert Boynton, whose encouragement was responsible for my writing the book in the first place and whose continuing faith in what it could accomplish has kept it alive and in print, even when it languished.

What *Forming/Thinking/Writing* attempts to do can best be explained by a consideration of the chapter titles, but let me begin with the book's title. Here are my working definitions:

- *Forming* is what the active mind does all the time, as a matter of course.
- *Thinking* is seeing relationships.
- *Writing* is representing recognitions of sames and differents. The slashes are meant to suggest not that they are all the same but that they are all correlative and that as we are writing, we are simultaneously forming and thinking.

The first three chapters introduce forming/thinking/writing:

1. *Looking and Looking Again* exhibits and explains observation as a useful habit for any composer and shows how perception, taken as *forming,* provides a natural point of departure for thinking and writing.

2. *Construing and Constructing* claims that reading and writing go together and that whatever is learned about one can be useful for the other. The dialectical notebook is introduced as a way of auditing the making of meaning.

3. *Naming/Opposing/Defining. Composing as a Double Helix* suggests that three operations go on throughout the composing process. "Oppositions" is a word for *relationships:* forming oppositions is the way to get from naming to defining.

The next three chapters recapitulate and develop what has been explored so far about the composing process:

4. *Forming Concepts* demonstrates particularizing and generalizing at work dialectically in forming ideas.

5. *Articulating Relationships* demonstrates how drawing inferences and establishing warrants enable us to explain. Students are invited to deploy certain skills which they might not have known they already possess, e.g., discovering and inventing analogies and using them to guide forming/thinking/writing.

6. *Gathering/Sorting/Gathering* shows how glossing and paraphrasing work to keep the composing process spiraling without getting out of hand. It shows how forms of language work to help us discover the forms of thought. (Language is itself the great heuristic.) It explains various techniques for revising, which is very much a matter of forming/thinking/writing, and for editing, which is not.

7. The concluding chapter, *Academic Writing,* offers observations about academic purposes and constraints, and suggestions for how a method of composing can be adapted to academic purposes.

James Stephens has worked with me on this new edition, providing new student writing, suggesting many ways to correct structural weaknesses, and contributing new assignments and explanations. The result is that teachers and students alike can now see how the method we are describing can be put to work. Students are shown learning the uses of chaos and exercising a number of heuristics to emerge from chaos towards order. One student composition is followed throughout the composing process, demonstrating the role of the dialectical notebook in both reading and writing.

As before, the "exercises" in this book are called "assisted invitations." "Exercises" suggest aerobics and Nautilus; all such metaphors drawn from motor activity are consonant with the view of language as "verbal behavior," a notion that runs counter to the principles of *Forming/Thinking/Writing*. Here's the explanation of "assisted invitations" from the first edition:

> This book embodies a philosophy of composition, but it centrally concerns actual acts of composing, not just thoughts about composing. It offers not rules and exhortations but *assisted invitations* to students of composition to discover *what they are trying to do and thereby how to do it*. This language comes from I. A. Richards, who once claimed that what we need in teaching reading and writing is "not so much some improved philosophic doctrine, though no one should despise that, as sets of sequenced exercises through which...people could explore, *for themselves,* their own abilities and grow in capacity, practical and intelligential, as a result. In most cases, perhaps, this amounts to offering them *assisted invitations* to attempt to find out just what they are trying to do and thereby how to do it."*

Not all the assisted invitations here are for everybody, but we have not identified which ones are which because, for one thing, it has sometimes turned out that a problem whose solution seemed self-evident has been found to be perplexing, and some considered very difficult have been found delightful. The assistance we offer should, of course, be supplemented by a teacher's own experience, his or her own ideas and assignments, explanations, and demonstrations.

The consequences of what Paulo Freire calls "conscientization" – thinking about thinking, being conscious of a consciousness that you are making meaning – I have explored in two books published since the first edition, *The Making of Meaning* and *Reclaiming the Imagination*. Certain pedagogical consequences were sketched, however, in the Introduction of 1978 and I would like to restate them here.

> The assisted invitations to write experimentally are intended to teach that "pre-writing" is writing; that getting started is as important a phase of composing as getting it

Design for Escape (New York: Harcourt, 1968), p. 111. Italics in the original.

together and getting it finished; that in all phases, composing is forming. A composition is a bundle of parts: students are invited to explore for themselves how discovering the parts and developing ways of bundling them are interdependent operations. The ambiguities and complexities of composing are right there from the beginning because I believe that elements of what we want to end with must be present in some form from the first; otherwise we will never get to them. Furthermore, in these suggestions for composing practice, I have included both critical and creative writing, since both exercise the forming power of the active mind: the imagination is engaged in a process of making meaning, which may take the form of image or argument, story or discursive demonstration. I don't believe that students should have to wait until graduate seminars to learn that storytelling and exposition have a lot in common or that finding forms of feeling exercises the mind....

Any exercise – perceptual, grammatical, expressive, rhetorical, logical – can have heuristic value only if students know what they are trying to do. Discovering how to work is contingent on exploring what is to be done: a method of composing should continually ensure that the *how* and the *what* and the *why* are seen and experienced in dialectical relationship. There are two consequences of this methodological principle: one is that the exercises will be carefully limited in scope; the other is that, since what is being presented is "everything at once," there will be lots of repetition.

The first consequence – short writing assignments – means that teachers can afford to encourage students to compose continually, habitually. The fact that short "papers" – single paragraphs, selected sentences – are easier to read than 500-Word Themes means that there can be more time for conferences; more time for considered responses; more energy to give to an ongoing review of writing careers. Teachers don't have to read everything that students using this book produce; indeed they *shouldn't* read everything. Students reading one another's work is the best alternative, especially if it's combined with discussion in small groups. Knowing that there is an attentive reader whose critical questions you can learn to make your own ahead of time is an experience every writer should have. But whether papers are read by the instructor or not, they should not be "graded."

Measurement is appropriate to what can be measured. Apples and eggs are graded according to their dimensions, freshness and soundness being presupposed. Compositions can be factored and judged in terms analogous to those used in judging apples and eggs, but the price is high: we begin to attend to the factors and not to the process. But to say that writing should not be graded is not to say that it should not be evaluated. I prefer a system in which progress reports prepared in conference with the student, a final review of the folder or notebook made by the instructor, and a review of papers from other courses or an extra-course competency exam read by the instructor and his/her colleagues form the basis for an assessment ideally expressed in terms of *pass* or *incomplete....*

The second consequence of teaching a method of composing in which everything is happening simultaneously is that every principle of composing gets presented and re-presented – explained and demonstrated and explained again. Every teacher I know agrees that the fundamentals of composing have to be presented, analyzed, demonstrated over and again. The first of several explanations of classification, say, might take two weeks, but the next time around, when classification shows up again as an aspect of paragraphing, it might be handled in a single class. The challenge is to make that repetition have a cumulative effect by having students see how principle and practice are related.

The new *Forming/Thinking/Writing* is adaptable to different writing courses and to writing-intensive courses across the curriculum. I believe that we should foster the composing imagination, no matter what the level, K-35: the real difference is in pacing. This book can be used in any freshman English course – the first three chapters during the first semester, the following three in the second semester. Or the whole book can be covered in one term and returned to in the second. It can be the central or adjunct text for intermediate or advanced composition courses. What all readers will need is Chapter Two, which explains the dialectical notebook and sets the scene for integrating reading and writing.

The chief aim remains what it was in the first edition: to offer students the chance "to explore, *for themselves,* their own abilities and grow in capacity, practical and intelligential, as a result."

A.E.B.

Forming Thinking Writing

SECOND EDITION

I

LOOKING AND LOOKING AGAIN

1. Exploring the Composing Process

This book teaches a method of composing that focuses on the ways in which writing is related to everything you do when you make sense of the world. This method is meant to serve both the inexperienced writer and the student who has written many papers but who finds the next one as difficult as the first. Here are some things about composing which this book can teach you:

- How to get started writing.
- What to do next.
- How to get started again when you come to a dead end.
- How to repeat yourself on purpose with effects that you are controlling.
- How to describe, define, limit, expand, eliminate, argue, amalgamate, coordinate, subordinate, and recapitulate.
- How to know when to stop and how to stop.

A method of composing isn't a set of rules, but it does provide guidelines and procedures. A method helps you find your way around, but it isn't like a map, since a map for one territory is not much use in another – and there's no such thing as a general map. But if you have a method, you can make your own map according to the terrain and the nature of transport, depending on where you want to go and how far you want to travel. A method of composing is a critical method, a way of getting thinking started and keeping it going. The more you can learn about composing, the better able you'll be to argue with yourself and others; to take notes and study for exams; to read poems and textbooks; to think through problems and to formulate questions that almost answer themselves. The main justification for learning a method of composing is that it can help you think clearly.

This book offers down-to-earth, practical suggestions as well as general principles; theory and practice need one another because principles are easily forgotten unless they're put to the test, and practical suggestions can't be counted on to help you more than once, unless they're grounded in principle. Invitations to explore what's involved in the composing process, how it's related to the everyday use of your mind, are indicated by this little sign: ◆

They are *assisted invitations;* that is to say, all exercises and suggestions for composing practice are accompanied by explanations and analyses: you're *invited* to form and think and write; you're offered *assistance.*

Whatever you really learn, of course, you teach yourself. If you learn only what you're told, then you're only keeping in mind, for a longer or shorter interval, what was put there by somebody else. What you really learn is what you discover – and you learn to discover by questioning. This book offers you many invitations to question what it is you do when you compose and thereby how to do it better – more easily, more quickly, more confidently than you've ever done before.

Nothing in this book is important only for itself: everything here is intended to encourage you to adapt the method of composing to your own needs and talents. This method takes advantage of the fact that, when you do anything, the *what* and the *how* depend on one another. The more you learn about what goes on when you compose, the more you'll learn about *how* to compose. In order for that to happen, the composing process has to be slowed down and observed. In this book, everything gets repeated. Our hope is that the repetition will have an enlightening, not a deadening, effect, but we can't be sure. Just as something that you find perfectly obvious can be obscure to us, so some things in this book which we think are self-evident and accessible might seem confusing or pointless to you. Bear with us: if you remember that there is a *what* and a *how,* you'll learn a method of composing that will stand you in good stead long after you leave the classroom.

Developing a method of composing means explaining your explanations, writing about your writing, thinking about your thinking; sometimes that can make you dizzy. But as you read this book, when you find a sentence that makes no sense, don't reread it until you've finished the paragraph. Then, if things are still obscure, go back and reread. The second time around, rereading a sentence can be useful, but you should avoid backtracking until you see what's ahead. Learning to read and write critically means, for one thing, finding what it is that you don't understand.

You don't suddenly become another person when you sit down to write, though that may be what it feels like sometimes. Composing means putting things together – and that's something you do all the time. When you take in a scene or an event or a piece of news, you are interpreting, putting things together to make sense. When you see what is happening or understand what has happened or imagine what might happen, you are composing. You are figuring out relationships, working out implications, drawing conclusions. What is currently called "getting it together" used to be known as "composing yourself."

When we think, we compose: we put this with that; we line things up; we group and classify and categorize; we emphasize or pass over, start and stop and start up again, repeating ourselves, contradicting, hedging, declaring and questioning, lying and denying. Even in dreaming we are composing, although for different purposes and in a mode different from the ones common to waking hours. When we read, we *re*-compose, juxtaposing, or *opposing,* this character with that character, the theory with the supporting evidence, the argument with the alleged facts, and so forth. We compare premises and conclusions, ifs and thens, the beginning of the story with the ending, seeing what goes together to make up the whole, seeing how the composition is put together, enjoying it, learning from it.

You may, for example, read an essay opposing vigorously the presence in our society of "latchkey children," but you may also see that *nowhere* does the author take note of the fact that a majority of mothers in our society, whether single parents or married, must work, whether they want to or not. You are recomposing that essay. Again, you may read an essay that urges the development of mandatory testing for AIDS and other infectious diseases, but you may find yourself thinking: "No one in this country is *required* to do anything that may invade his or her privacy." You have recomposed that essay as well.

Composing, putting things together, is a continuum, a process that continues without any sharp breaks. Making sense of the world is composing. It includes being puzzled, being mistaken, and then suddenly seeing things for what they probably are; making wrong – unproductive, unsatisfactory, incorrect, inaccurate – identifications and assessments and correcting them or giving them up and getting some new ones. And all these things happen when we write: writing is like the composing we do all the time when we respond to the world, make up our minds, try to figure out things again. We're not born knowing how to write, but we are born knowing how to know how to write.

Although writing has a lot in common with that composing we describe simply as *consciousness,* writing doesn't just happen as a matter of course; the writer has to make it happen. Writing is not a "natural-born" capacity that we normally and necessarily develop, the way a child learns to walk and talk. Nor is learning to write like learning the facts in an anatomy text or making a Shaker footstool out of a kit. When you write, you do not follow somebody else's scheme; you design your own. As a writer, you learn to make words behave the way you want them to behave and to say what you want them to say and to mean what you want them to mean. You want to look at *what* you're doing so as to discover *how* to do it with language you control. Language and thought are not the same, but they depend on one another. You don't think something up and then "put it into words"; as you're thinking, you're *languaging.*

Up to a point, writing can be explained and taught as a skill. And it can be demonstrated, as dovetailing the joints of a drawer can be demonstrated. Composing means working with words, and, in some ways, that is a skill comparable to working with wood. But woodcraft is not just assembling some pre-cut forms, nor is wordcraft merely a matter of gluing statements together. Composing is more than a skill, though the writer must be skilled with words and syntactic structures, just as a cabinet-maker has to know how to use a gimlet and an auger. Composing is more than craft, and it requires more than skill, because working with words requires working with meanings, and meanings are not like walnut planks or golfballs or bulldozers or typewriters, or anything else that simply requires skilled handling. Learning to write is not a matter of learning the rules that govern the use of the semicolon or the names of sentence structures, nor is it a matter of manipulating words; it is a matter of making meanings, and that is the work of the active mind.

Writing, as it's discussed in this book, involves you in thinking about thinking and the making of meanings by means of language. That doesn't mean that you must have a detailed knowledge of neurophysiology and linguistics any more than a swimmer needs a theory of hydrostatics. But having some knowledge of how the mind makes meanings is the way to understand how writing has to do with making sense of the world and thus to take advantage of the fact that the composing process is a continuum, an unbroken and continuing activity. The work of the active mind is seeing relationships, finding forms, making meanings: when we write, we are doing in a particular way what we are already doing when we make sense of the world. We're composers by virtue of being human.

You don't have to philosophize or master psychological theories in order to learn to write, but it's important and comforting to know that the means of making meaning which you depend on when you make sense of the world and when you write are in part made for you by your brain and by language itself. You don't have to reinvent English grammar when you compose a sentence (though you may have to learn to adjust your ways of using it to those of your reader) any more than you have to take grammar lessons to learn to talk. What you do within the limits provided by language and perception, how you use them to make meanings, is up to you, but you don't begin from scratch.

2. Observing; Observing Your Observations; Observations on Observing

What you do when you make sense of the world involves the same acts of mind as those involved when you write: that's what it means to say that the composing process is a continuum. Keeping a journal of observations is one way to see how your mind works; since the active mind is a composer, there is something to be learned by observing it in operation. (*Journal* comes from the French word *jour,* day; a journal is a daily record.) Poets are often addicted to journals, because they know that the composing process is going on all the time and that they need a record of the dialogue between them and the world. Of course, a journal has the practical value of teaching concentration and account-taking. A poet I once knew was hired as a research assistant to an anesthesiologist. The job was to observe the appearance, reactions, speech, behavior, etc., of children before and after surgery, and she got the job, not because of *A's* in biochemistry (she had no pre-med courses), but because the doctor guessed correctly that her powers of observation were highly developed.

Deliberately observing your observations and interpreting your interpretations sounds like being *self-conscious* and, in a sense, it is: you're the one who is aware of what's going on and you're also the one responsible for the going on; you're the do-er, the agent. To be deliberately aware of what you're doing is a consciousness of self. But thinking about thinking is not the same kind of operation as thinking about how to serve in a game of tennis or what to do with your lips when you're learning to play an instrument or what to do with your feet when you're learning to dance. In such cases, self-consciousness is what you have to get over. Learning a skill involves immersing yourself in the rhythm of the activity so that you "think" with your whole body; concentrating on what-the-agent-is-doing is therefore a distraction. For the student of composition, however, concentration on what you're doing in making meanings is the best way of learning to write.

Here's the procedure we're suggesting for keeping a journal of observations. Get yourself either a small notebook or a folder with an ample supply of paper (preferably law-ruled paper with a left-hand margin of one-third the page's width). Such paper allows you to observe and comment on your observations at the very point where they were first recorded. For about a week, write in the journal for ten minutes a day in response to some natural object. This object shouldn't be something you're familiar with. Instead of an apple, for example, take a pomegranate or a Seckel pear. And it shouldn't be a rock or a pebble, since they're not *organic,* and one of the points of this looking/seeing exercise is to learn something about *organization.* Address yourself to the object; ask it questions; let it answer back; write down the "dialogue." Record your observations and observe your observations. Follow your mind in its course: the composing process rather than a composition is your concern, but if what you're composing seems to have a will of its own, follow its lead; you may be surprised to see where it takes you. At the end of a week or so, see if you can compose a couple of paragraphs setting forth the meanings you've made.

If the observing becomes tedious (and it will), stay with it, regardless; if it become intolerable, get yourself another object. I offer my students a choice from several cigar boxes full of bird feathers, crab legs, shells, dried seaweed, seed pods, various weeds, pine cones, two or three puff balls and oak galls, bits of bark with fungus; but they sometimes prefer their own twigs and bones and parsnips. Some teachers offer organic objects that change during the week: fresh flowers, vegetables, and fruits: branches with leaves, or even apples or berries, on them; fresh herbs are especially good. There's nothing like a little basil or dill to give character to your desk or backpack!

❧ To get started, here's an assisted invitation to learn to observe carefully by drawing. This lesson on contour drawing comes from Kimon Nikolaïdes's *The Natural Way to Draw,* which has been called the best "how-to" book ever written about anything.

Sit close to the object you intend to draw and lean forward in your chair. Focus your eyes on some point, any point will do, along the contour of the model. (The contour approximates what is usually spoken of as the outline or edge.) Place the point of your pencil on the paper. Imagine that your pencil point is touching the model instead of the paper. Without taking your eyes off the model, *wait* until you are *convinced* that the pencil is touching that point on the model upon which your eyes are fastened.

Then move your eye *slowly* along the contour of the model and move the pencil *slowly* along the paper. As you do this, keep the conviction that the pencil point is actually touching the contour. Be guided more by the sense of touch than by sight. *This means that you must draw without looking at the paper,* continuously looking at the model.

Exactly coordinate the pencil with the eye. Your eye may be tempted at first to move faster than your pencil, but do not let it get ahead. Consider only the point that you are working on at the moment with no regard for any other part of the figure.

Often you will find that the contour you are drawing will leave the edge of the figure and turn inside, coming eventually to an apparent end. When this happens, glance down at the paper several times during the course of one study, but do not draw while you are looking at the paper. As in the beginning, place the pencil point on the paper, fix your eyes on the model, and wait until you are convinced that the pencil is touching the model before you draw.

Not all the contours lie along the outer edge of the figure..... Draw "inside contours" exactly as you draw the outside ones. Draw anything that your pencil can rest on and be guided along. *Develop the absolute conviction that you are touching the object.*

This exercise should be done slowly, searchingly, sensitively. Take your time. Do not be too impatient or too quick. There is no point in finishing any one contour study. In fact, a contour study is not a thing that can be "finished." It is having a particular type of experience, which can continue as long as you have the patience to look.... A contour drawing is like climbing a mountain as contrasted with flying over it in an airplane. It is not a quick glance at the mountain from far away, but a slow, painstaking climb over it, step by step.

If this exercise seems to have little apparent purpose in a writing course, consider this comment by an art teacher about the relationship of naming and identifying, drawing and defining.

To put a line around something is to name it and to attempt to enumerate its characteristics. It is a form of definition. Children arrive at the same time at a stage when they draw objects and when they name them. It is difficult for any of us to draw in line something which we cannot name – that is to put a line around something which we cannot separate intellectually from its surroundings. If we draw a nameless thing, we automatically ask what it is while we draw it, and attempt to see a likeness in it to something which we can name. Both to draw things and to name things are attempts to identify and understand objects, situations, conditions and relationships. A particular function of line in drawing is (like naming) to define objects. With a line we first draw nouns. Later we describe relationships: physical situations, the geometry of space, psychological situations, movement. In the traditional European school of drawing (the heritage from Masaccio, through Raphael to Ingres), contour defines objects and gives them their precise structure and character, while tone (shading) is largely used to state generalities of form – the physical characteristics which all objects share alike – planes and structural relationships, space, lighting conditions. A cube or a cylinder may be given solidity by tone, but it is defined as a cube or a cylinder by line. Whenever we wish to give individuality, precise definition and character to a figure in life drawing or to a head or anything else which we put in a drawing, we find that we must pursue the contour ruthlessly and search out the form by means of outline. The more particular we wish to be, the more ruthless we must be. The characteristic shape is in the contour. If in a painting we see a line which is enclosed, we presuppose an object and try to recognize what it is.

Frederick Gore, *Painting: Some Basic Principles*

The key terms in this paragraph on drawing are also the key terms in a writing course: *name, enumerate, see a likeness, define, describe, state generalities of form, search out the form by means of outline, recognize.*

Now read some recent examples of student journal entries, a meditative essay based on a journal, and a feature article for a newspaper written after such journal practice. They're offered not as models but as authentic responses to encourage you in your own observations.

Steve's Rose Bush Stem

9/7 How many people have you poked or stuck? How beautiful an object were you, at one time, in your glorious days? But now, you are alone, sitting on my desk, and your thorns are not jagged or frightening anymore, just dry and brittle. I still wonder about how many days that dead rosebud lived on you and whether any blossoms ever came from you. Did those blossoms get attention?

9/9 I really don't feel like looking at this stem for two more days. It has been sitting here on my shelves next to my *Cosmos* by Carl Sagan all afternoon. I hope it likes stars! I wonder if the stars have anything to do with the way certain plants are formed during their growth. They have to, because cosmic rays, beta particles, gluons, muons, photons, and neutrinos are constantly bombarding the earth. So plants receive radiation in all these forms. Maybe every thorn on this thing knows all the secrets to the creation of the universe? Maybe not, though. I wish I knew.

Christine's Cucumber

9/7 I have always loved cucumbers but now I am thinking that I don't. Carrying a vegetable around is a sure sign that I am a Freshman; I guess I'll hide it in my back pack for a week. Thank God I don't have one of those big branches or sticks! I have never seen anything so *damned green or juicy!* This is the slickest, most elegant, shapeliest thing in the universe. It feels waxy and all shined-up, like new shoes, but also like a tube of toothpaste before you bend it or a tube of lipstick. I can't wait to cut it open and see what's inside.

9/8 A cucumber is definitely masculine. I won't say why. It also seems human to me. It has different personalities depending on how you look at it. It has too many eyes, little spiky ones that never stop staring, but, if you turn it on its side, the eyes stare at the walls and that suits me fine. My cucumber has entered middle age, I'm sure, because it is getting soft in the middle and it does not have the texture or slickness that it had yesterday. How can such beautiful things fall into semi-ugliness in just one day? It reminds me of my mother and how she told me about her arms falling. They just *got fat and fell* one day. My high school physics teacher had a chin that did the same thing. We were all amazed. Tomorrow, I'm going to cut this open. Maybe I'll make a salad for Jeff or saute the slices in some kind of cheese and oil.

9/9 I did make a salad today. I had fresh, strong broccoli pieces and cauliflower pieces and some bad tomatoes. I bought a new cucumber to go with the one I have for class. The new one fell into perfect round slices with the same shape as the onion I cut. My old masculine cucumber has "lost it" in a way but he does taste good and he did cut up fairly well. His seeds fell away immediately though and the whole delicious white middle parts of the slices were soft and not appealing. I covered all this with parmesan and homemade dressing and Jeff never noticed the difference between a new and a really old cucumber. I hope he doesn't notice how girls grow old.

9/10 This morning I confess I tried to re-write my journal for the whole week. I am embarrassed to turn this in because I see now that my parents were right about how I don't concentrate on anything but Jeff and how it's getting ridiculous. Unfortunately, my cucumber is gone but it did teach me a lesson. Please burn this. I'll do better next time.

Joanna's Hawthorn Branch

9/7 Yes, I have seen you before, but never on my desk in a classroom and never in the weird, broken form you're in now. Yes, your name reminds me of Nathaniel Hawthorne, but, the truth is your body reminds me of my favorite man, Mikail Barishnikov (sp?), because you are in the perfect pose of ecstatic leaping. Drawing you is easy and pleasurable, but I can't believe you'll stay this beautiful. I can see the hawthorn tree out the window with all the branches on it, your family, and can see where you got your spirit and beauty and loneliness. My cruel teacher ripped you right off the tree on his way into the class. How would he like it if someone ripped one of his arms off casually on their way to work? I wonder if Mikail's appeal has anything to with his being an exile from Russia? Lonely, maybe, ripped from his family and friends.

9/8 Today I am detached from this branch the same way it is detached from its tree. It has lost a leg and is miserable to look at. I hate it. It is leaning against the wall. Its berries are on the floor and my roommate's pepper is looking at it with scorn. I can't believe that a practical person like me is getting upset, or even writing about a broken branch for ten minutes. Let's see. A dictionary definition. Its name means little hedge thorn. Its definition is "any of a group of spiny shrubs and small trees of the rose family, with fragrant flowers of white, pink, or red berries (called *haws*)." What is a haw? Same page: a haw is four things. It is the third eyelid of certain animals (I wonder what animals have three eyes. Sounds like science fiction). It is a "hesitation in speaking, a groping for words, a faltering as in *hem* and *haw*." Now I really know why I got a hawthorn branch. I hem and haw just the way I am doing now. I am hemming and hawing about hawthorns, ho ho. What else is a haw you ask? A haw is also a "word of command as to a horse or an ox, etc." My teacher commanded me, a slave animal who pays tuition, to hem and haw about hawthorns. Yes a haw is also the berry of the hawthorn and sometimes it is used as shorthand for hawthorn. This day is over! Tomorrow, if I can't stand looking at my branch, I'll think about what it has in common with roses (same family) or about Nathaniel Hawthorne, writer of the terrible Scarlet Letter book I had to read twice, or about a town in Calfornia, suburb of Los Angeles, population 33,000, named Hawthorne.

9/9 Today has been fantastic. The weather was great, summery and breezy. I walked to Lake Michigan and, believe it or not, thought about this assignment. I have been doing a good job of avoiding it by writing about some other things, though I did define hawthorn and compared it with something. It is true that writing is like drawing. It requires tremendous concentration because you can't write about anything, even a branch, if you can't see it completely.

Tim's Dahlia

9/7 I picked this dahlia from my teacher's basket because I have seen these flowers before, though I never knew their names. This flower and long stem come from a very tall plant that blooms in the fall and late summer and that has a lot of huge flowers in bright colors like red, orange, purple, yellow, and pink. The stem of my plant is totally hollow but the outside is thick and slick, like a bamboo pole. My flower is very bright red. On different smaller branches there are three buds, a big one about to open up, a middle sized one, and a pea-sized bud. Just like Poppa, Mama, and Baby bear. My flower is seven inches wide and about seven inches long (a circular form) and it has a lot of petals. The petals are shaped like hundreds of little cups or mouths all open to receive water from the sky. Guessing at how many petals would be like guessing on how many jellybeans are in a bathtub full of jellybeans. I would say 750, but it is hard to tell because the petals are close together and tight. They flair out and make a shape that looks like what a rose does with a lot of layers of petals. It really is amazing when you think of how much effort and food and rain and sun went into the production of this useless but beautiful plant with close to a thousand separate petals. This flower came from my teacher's garden but I can't picture him out there watering it or feeding it even though he has a suntan and looks like he spends time outdoors.

9/8 Using the dictionary really gets your mind going. My dahlia is named after an 18th century Swedish botanist, which makes me think about how strange some names are. Rose and tulip and daffodil and daisy are great names for pretty flowers, but *dahlia??* My dahlia can be defined. It is "any of a group of perennial plants of the composite family, with tuberous roots and large showy flowers in various bright colors." I knew that, except that "perennial" and "tuberous" don't mean anything to me. With the help of my trusty dictionary, I am now classifying my dahlia. Some plants are annual, which means they are planted and grow in only one year. Some, like mine, are perennial and keep coming back. Some plants are tuberous – the dictionary names dahlia as an example. They grow from tube-shaped roots that don't have buds or scale leaves but are thick and fleshy like sweet potatoes. Now imagine the dahlia's home. Looking at it in a garden in Chicago, you would think it belonged there. Maybe though it belongs in Sweden, since it was named after A. Dahl. If you thought either one you were very wrong. Read this from "World Book." "Dahlia, DAL yuh, is the name of a popular group of flowers cultivated from the original dahlia of Mexico." Now we can picture it in its home. It grows in the fields and in the yards of senors and senoritas. It sits on tables where people with bright clothes eat, sometimes with their sombreros on. The sombreros are shaped like dahlias and the clothes are the same colors – yellow, red, orange, pink. "World Book" says to see also Fall Blooming Flowers and Flower, but I haven't got time. *Adios.*

9/9 I realize now that I did not look at my dahlia yesterday, just did research on it. It is standing in a beer can full of water on my window sill. The petals around the outside rim have withered up and the thing is beginning to smell wrong. One of the buds has fallen off and the big flower is drooping like a sad old lady. Yesterday I liked the idea that dahlias are sometimes called pompoms, which reminded me of pretty cheerleaders and football games in the fall, but today it would look better on a lady at a funeral. I could get poetic and talk about how flowers remind us of people and of how we bloom and then we die but I don't see the comparison. Anything dies when you cut it off or pull up its roots. I am going to just hang on and try to live more than three days. If anybody comes near me with garden cutters, watch out! So long dahlia. It's been good knowing you.

In these notebook entries you can see individual minds focusing – sometimes sharply, sometimes just casually – on one object. Since the writers *must* write something, their minds go to work, and it is interesting to watch those minds in operation. Like a painter, they put lines around their objects by naming them and by enumerating their qualities. All the writers, as they grope for meaning, compare or juxtapose their objects to something else. A rose bush stem reminds Steve of stars; a cucumber makes Christine think of a new tube of toothpaste; Joanna thinks of a ballet dancer when looking at her hawthorn; and the petals on Tim's dahlia are like cups or mouths. Further, these writers all make attempts at definition and description by generalizing about form, and re-cognizing, or re-seeing, their objects each day. What the human mind does when it composes it does naturally in response to a new situation, assignment, or scene. It perceives form, takes perspectives, asks questions and guesses at answers; and it draws lines around its subject or object. Students like Steve, Christine, Joanna, and Tim are making every effort to be honest with themselves and us, and they do some thinking every day, even if it seems not to lead anywhere.

〜 Here's Italo Calvino telling us about Mr. Palomar's discovery. What do you imagine Steve and the others would have to say to him? What would you say to him? (And why is he called "Mr. Palomar"?)

It has always happened that certain things – a stone wall, a seashell, a leaf, a teapot – present themselves to Mr. Palomar as if asking him for minute and prolonged attention: he starts observing them almost unawares, and his gaze begins to run all over the details and is then unable to detach itself. Mr. Palomar has decided that from now on he will redouble his attention.

Mr. Palomar tries staring at everything that comes within eyeshot; he feels no pleasure, and he stops. A second phase follows, in which he is convinced that only some things are to be looked at, others not, and he must go and seek the right ones. To do this, he has to face each time the problems of selection; he soon realizes he is spoiling everything, as always when he involves his own ego....

But how can you look at something and set your own ego aside? Whose eyes are doing the looking? As a rule, you think of the ego as one who is peering out of your own eyes as if leaning on a window sill, looking at the world...So, then: a window looks out on the world. The world is out there; and in here, what do we have? The world still – what else could there be? With a little effort of concentration, Mr. Palomar manages to shift the world from in front of him and set it on the sill, looking out. Now, beyond the window, what do we have? The world is also there and in this instance has been split into a looking world and a world looked at. And what about him, also known as "I," namely Mr. Palomar? Is he not a piece of the world that is looking at another piece of the world?

Whatever your assignment or task may be, you can benefit from the habit of keeping a journal. Here's a week's record of observations from a journalism major who was familiar with many kinds of writing assignments but not with inspecting a weed. You can observe how he develops a method in the course of his observations of himself as an observer.

David's Milkweed Pod

Thursday, Sept. 2 I have set the milkweed pod on top of my digital clock and my minutes of observation are very neatly numbered for me. The first thing I notice is the damage incurred to the pod while it got carried around in the pocket of my coat. It has split slightly at the end of its seams, and its fur is slightly matted and worn. Its shape is similar to the shape of a large, fat goldfish. Its color is a nice light brown, the color of a mouse. In rereading that sentence I notice that "nice" is a totally unnecessary word that doesn't tell anybody what color brown the milkweed pod is.

This exercise is going to make me babble, I can see. I can observe my observations ahead of time so that they will come out in ordered, "literary" paragraphs.

Friday The first thing I observe is that in plugging in my typewriter, I have unplugged my clock. That seemed like an awfully long minute. I tell myself to look at the pod, to center myself around it, so that at least my babble originates its drifting there. I stare at the pod, making associations; thinking about a book I read called the *Psychology of Meditation* that talked about meditating on objects. Then I think about a poem I read that used a pod as a sexual metaphor.

Saturday "Hello pod," my brain says to itself, feeling already a degree of familiarity. I notice faint lines running the length of the pod, like the grooves on smooth bark. Little bumps and nodules interrupt the grooves at random points. Short, white hairs stick out the seams. I realize I haven't really touched it to see what it feels like, and so I reach out and stroke it and it is very soft.

Sunday I think about the milkweed pod in terms of time. Probably no observable changes will happen in the week or so I observe it, but I know it's changing, drying out and transforming. It seems sterile and devoid of purpose, sitting there on my shelf. I get the urge to open the window and throw it out. For awhile the pod seems to be less an inanimate object and more a part of ongoing process. I think about the hundreds of potential milkweed plants contained inside the pod, and then remember when I was a child my father breaking open the stem of a milkweed plant and squeezing the milk onto a wart on his hand. He claimed that it cured warts, but I don't remember if it did or not.

Monday It occurs to me to smell the pod. Nothing very distinct, but then my sense of smell was never very acute. I can be in the same room with a hundred pieces of toast burning and never quiver a nostril. In this particular instance, however, I do not feel too deprived, since what I do smell has the faint odor of the dust bag in a vacuum cleaner. What I have really observed here is the limitations of my observational powers.

I realize also that this journal would probably be different if I was writing it just for my private self. I am aware of the audience, mainly you, Mrs. Berthoff, and try to picture you reading this by the fireside of some Concord home.

Tuesday I set the pod out on the kitchen table so I could type there, and when I came back one of my roommates had picked the pod apart. I was already feeling overwhelmed at the possibilities of what there was to write about, and this made it seem like an infinity made more infinite. All there really is time to do in the 5 or 10 minutes that I look at it is to pull a few sentences down out of the brain static that gets generated. This gets me to thinking about what thought is like before it becomes sentences, which would be very hard to express in sentences. I've been thinking and writing for 5 minutes, and I've hardly said a word about the pod.

Wednesday I think I'll start off with more description. Dark, oval seeds cover a thick body of very light silken material, like cornsilk only more fragile. The seeds are overlapped in a pattern exactly like shingles on a roof. My thoughts spread out in associational chains from this fact. First of all I note that I would probably not make this comparison if I hadn't worked on roofs. Then I wonder if most people notice the pattern of shingles, and wonder if that comparison would reach the mind's eye of most people. I feel that it is important for a writer to worry about that.

Another chain began with noticing the pattern, and was concerned with function. I realized that I knew the function of the pattern on a roof (to prevent leaks) but that I didn't know the function of the pattern on a seed pod.

Thursday All the seeds are falling off from the silk. I can't figure this out, because it seems to me that the seeds should be firmly attached, each to its own tuft of silk, so that they can float on the wind. The only explanation I can think of is that because the skin has been torn off, the inside is drier than it should be. Or maybe as the seed dries out on the wind it drops to the ground like a parachuter jumping out of an airplane. I doubt it, but the idea sounded good.

The following late-in-the-semester meditations on an earlier assignment show that we make meanings out of our writing experiences for a long time after they've occurred. And, of course, we find new meanings.

Martha's Bit of Branch

Here's a bit of branch, long since broken from its tree. All the juices have drained from this husk, but if you look closely at the core you can see the channels where they ran. The pith has splintered vertically, not across the stump; that tells you something about the direction of transport. Up and down food and drink were carried, from root to leaf and back again. (How water can be pushed so high, no one quite knows. The laws of hydraulics are broken by the tree, which follows secret laws of its own.) Nothing runs here now and there is no sign of root or leaf. Dried out like this, you might think such a fragment had been fixed and preserved forever – were it not for the sprinkling of fungus along its length, invisibly reducing organic back to inorganic stuff. Life is chewing away at death, reclaiming immortal matter.

There's a paragraph, a bundle of words split off from experience. Could a reader tell which way the currents that fed it ran? To one who knows the history of its composition, it seems impossible that any clues could be found in those splintered ends. See, the process of criticism is already starting to pull it apart. I wait to discover what new shapes will spring from its decomposing.

Suzanne's Crab Leg*

What am I looking at? What are these particles of shell, lying broken on a sheet of paper? And what are these dried filaments? Are they connective tissue, transparent and fragile, encrusted with sand, no longer able to bear the wrench and pull of the living, moving crab inside? Why is it that the upper part of the crab's leg is shattered, while the claw itself is nearly intact? Does the tubular, curved, tusk-like shape give the claw strength, or is it thicker and more resilient? I wonder – do those evil little teeth on the inner edge of each "jaw" of the claw contribute to its unbreak-ability? And why, in the drying-out and aging process, does the upper leg lose its resiliency so much more than the claw?

And what is there to see when I focus in close? Is it a process of close focus that reveals the complexities of surface and blurs the perception of forms? Why am I now more conscious of the play of orange toward the tip and cream toward the upper part of the claw? Is the ability to notice a shiny streak along the ridge (how is it I never *noticed* the ridge along the outside of the claw?) a function of concentrating on surface to the exclusion of form?

And now what happens when I move back again? Why am I conscious, now, as I wasn't before, of the arrangement of these forms on the white blue-lined sheet of paper? What roughness of claw teeth, fineness, abrasiveness of speckles of sand, what hungry, cave-like space interior to the claw's joint, bereft of its contiguous parts do I see? What happens to my mind as it moves in and out and over these forms, surfaces, textures, spaces?

What statement can I make that means as much as a query?

What mental process, what level of perception does the question keep pushing me toward, what statement would it close me off from, forcing a false start with each sentence? What happens when I touch these fragments, turn them over, rub my finger over the sand deposited inside, meditate on the salty, watery, sandy, sea-grassy life these forms belonged to when they were whole? What part of the whole is a crab, after all? What does it know of a windy afternoon in early summer, of the glassy slick of water on sand that its motions disturb only slightly? Does it feel and sense its structural wholeness, fresh and pungent flesh protected by

*Note that the sentences are all in the form of questions.

a hard but resilient outside bone? Doesn't it know it belongs there and not here, dry and fragmented on my paper, in my electric-heated, sun-filled winter bedroom on Waltham Street? Why did it get there in such a broken condition, if not due to the detached curiosity of Ann Berthoff, if not to the indifference and pocketbook-disorder of Suzanne Lynch, if not to the testing and naughtiness of my son's friend Thomas? Did you break it, Ann and Suzanne and Thomas, or was it broken already, when the water level went down and left it drying and dying in last summer's sun?

This feature for the campus newspaper shows that the writer has developed the habit of careful, active observation followed by observing those observations.

Robin's Fish Trip

Why didn't somebody tell me? Why didn't you tell me? During the 7 years I've lived in Boston, I've been dragged to concerts, coerced into buying various record albums, and had my sanity questioned for not seeing certain films. But in all that time, no one has ever insisted that I visit the New England Aquarium. If I hadn't been sent there on a writing assignment, I might have missed out forever on the most involving museum in this area.

The Aquarium is such an exciting visual experience that I was talking to myself in wonder before I got off the first floor. You must go and see for yourself. The Aquarium opens at 9 A.M. It's important to arrive early before the endless busloads of schoolchildren disrupt the silent and intimate setting created by the very low lighting. The Aquarium uses the concept of theatre and entertainment in its interior layout. In the semidarkness, as in a theatre, one's sense of both privacy and involvement are heightened and a very personal experience is possible. Tanks of varying sizes are mounted into the walls and lighted from behind. Like small stages they present a particular view of aquatic conditions or explain the complex relationships of sea plants and animals to one another and to us. In each tank there is at least one creature whose brilliant colors or fantastic shape stand out wonderfully, luring us through the half-light to the next tank.

The Aquarium manages to present an enormous amount of information and a great variety of exhibits in a simple direct manner. I learned about underwater sounds (the ocean, it turns out, is a pretty noisy place), and got some static from an electric fish when I pushed the button in front of its tank. I was warned against poisonous stingrays, man-eating sharks, and the dangerous shellfish-out-of-season! Printed information is mounted in colored letters, along with photographs, on plexiglass and then illuminated from behind. Some exhibits have recorded information which plays when you press a button. All the tanks are placed on opposite ends of each floor. The side walls are either left in shadow or have pictures of whales and sharks painted in large, outline form.

The real first floor is actually a wide, shallow pool in which penguins and sharks live in apparent harmony. Around this pool runs a slightly elevated walkway, and from its center rises the three-story, cylindrical glass tank. Another walkway spirals right around the sides of this enormous tank until it reaches the top floor where you can look down into the water and realize just how broad the tank is. Going up this ascending walkway is just like walking through Harvard Square on any warm Sunday afternoon. I just couldn't believe what I saw. Giant sea-turtles with shells like batiked leather, the world's fattest fish, sharks with quick, subtle movements, and hundreds of fish of every size, including a deflated blowfish and one poor creature with a healed-over bite taken right out of its back. Every hour a diver goes to the bottom and feeds the turtles and smaller fish, while the sharks turn terrifying arcs through his rising air bubbles. This feeding procedure became a strange water ballet, which set off for me a chain of associations on our relation to the sea and our place with these creatures in the evolutionary chain.

All these musings were lost when I got back down to the first floor exit and came upon the sea otters. These little animals have the same effect on order as the Marx Brothers, tearing about their area and bathing pool in a total frenzy. The glass boundary was the only reason I was able to keep from picking one up and taking it home. The otters actually seem to wave as they swim on their backs and perform series of difficult underwater somersaults, squeaking all the while. If their appeal isn't enough to encourage you to visit the Aquarium, go anyway! I promise that you will find yourself wondering, as I did, why no one ever told you about the New England Aquarium.

3. The Auditor and the Sheepdog

Observing, thinking, writing: these are all forming activities. If you consider the composing process as a continuum of forming, then you can take advantage of the fact that you are born a composer. The way you make sense of the world is the way you write: how you construe is how you construct. You can set about learning to write, confident that composition is not a matter of hammering together words and phrases, sentences and paragraphs, according to standard patterns that somebody else tells you to superimpose. This book will never insist that you put together a definition, a system of classes, a narrative or an argument, according to any formula other than your own. It *will* ask you to develop your own formulas, but of course, you have been defining, classifying, narrating, arguing for, and with, yourself for years now. This book will invite you to test and then, if necessary, alter and improve your patterns of communication and concept-forming. It will encourage you to experiment with new methods. It will explain those methods and offer invitations to employ them profitably.

How you construe *is* how you construct; how you understand is how you compose. To "construe" is to interpret or make meaning, as in "His statements about the President were construed as hostile." In grammar, "construe" means to analyze a clause, sentence, or paragraph for both construction and meaning. "Construct" is defined as a verb meaning "to build" or "to put together systematically." The acts of mind which allow you to construe meaning from a host of sensations and data also allow you to put that meaning together in a grammatically accurate, coherent series of sentences and paragraphs. Construing and constructing are both acts of forming.

Thus, writing is a matter of learning how to use the forms of language to discover the forms of thought, and vice versa. By conceiving of meanings not as things but as relationships, you can avoid the futile question of which comes "first" – the chicken or the egg, the thought or the language – and explore instead the mutual dependence of choosing and limiting, identifying and differentiating, finding and creating forms. You can discard the faulty notion that when you compose, you figure out what you want to say before you write; you formulate a thesis statement, you write an outline, and then you write the paper. This formula has never worked for writers, and no professional writer has been known to use it. It may be frightening to work without the trusty thesis statement and outline, but try to accept this helpful slogan: *You can't know what you mean until you hear what you say.* Or as the poet, W.H. Auden, asked, "How can I know what I think until I see what I say?"

The point is that form finds form; the thought finds the language, and the language finds the thought. At the heart of the composition process is the fact that ends and means are mutually dependent. Though it's difficult for young writers to find this formula comforting or trustworthy at the beginning of a composition course, experience has shown that writers *do* find the forms they need – the definition, the cause-effect chain, the story – *when* they need to find them; and, similarly, when the forms are available and understood, the language to express their content and meaning will become available as well (though not easily, any more than chemical formulas, psychological models, or historical theories are instantly grasped and retained). You'll find the language or the form when you need it because you can't have developed the one in your mind without having developed the other.

If, for example, you have formulated for yourself an explanation of why the inner cities of the Northeast and Midwest have been allowed to decay as they have, the language will come back to you and you'll be able to express that understanding so that another can share it. If the contrast between the "rust belt" and the "sun belt" is clear to you, you can make it clear to others by means of language and the forms it takes. Studies by professors in mathematics, chemistry, psychology, computer science, physics, and biology, incidentally, have recently shown that students who can explain an equation, a formula, a natural phenomenon, or the results of a laboratory experiement in paragraph form – rather than in fill-in-the-blank or multiple-choice or some other shorthand method – have a much stronger grasp of the material than those who can't. That seems obvious. If you've apprehended and retained a concept, however abstract it may be, you can express it in words and sentences. Form finds form.

Studying the composing process can teach you that ideas are not floating in the air, waiting to be brought down to earth; thoughts are not nonverbal butterflies that you catch with a verbal butterfly net; meanings are not lying out there like Easter eggs, waiting for you to find them. The relationship between thought and language is dialectical: ideas are conceived by language; language is generated by thought. (*Conceive, generate:* sexual metaphors are indispensable in describing the life of the mind unless you want to consider the mind a machine and speak of *products*.) Composing, in this book, is considered as an organic process, not a mechanical one.

A composition is a bundle of parts. When you compose you "get it together," but the "it" is not a matter of things or "words"; what you get together in composing is relationships, meanings. In composing, you make parts into wholes; you compose the way you think — by seeing relationships, by naming what you see, by defining or classifying (if necessary) what you see, by articulating the relationships implied in what you see. What makes it hard is that you have to do two things at once: you have to bundle the parts as if you knew what the whole was going to be and you have to figure out the whole in order to decide which parts are going to fit and which are not. The only way to do that is to keep everything tentative, recognizing that getting the parts together, figuring out the whole is a *dialectical* process.

Dialectic is the term used throughout this book to name the mutual dependence of language and thought, all the ways in which a word finds a thought and a thought, a word. The most useful definition comes from I.A. Richards, who calls dialectic *a continuing audit of meaning.* Just as a bookkeeper has to account for income and expenditures in order to balance credits and debits, an audit of meanings would have to balance what one sentence seems to say against what others seem to say; how one way of saying something compares with another; what one word seems to refer to in a certain context with what it seems to refer to in another. Of course, *audit* also has to do with listening. In composing, you have to be your own auditor in both senses: you have to listen in on the inner dialogue, which is thinking, and you have to be able to balance the account of what you've been hearing against what is set down on paper.

In all its phases, composing is conversation you're having with yourself — or *selves*, since, when you're writing, you consciously play the roles of speaker, audience, and critic all at once. You do the talking; then you do the answering; and you listen in to the dialogue between the speaker and the respondent. When you're making meaning in sentences, gathering sentences to compose paragraphs and paragraphs to construct arguments, you're doing the same kind of thing you do when you carry on a conversation. But then why is it, generally speaking, more difficult to write than it is to talk? ("Generally speaking," because all of us find occasionally that putting something on paper is a lot easier than saying it, speaking it right out to an actual person.) What is there about conversation that's missing when we write? An actual audience, of course.

From an audience, we get "feedback," a response that lets us know the effect of our words, a response that helps determine what we say next. Furthermore, in conversation we depend on slang and informal expressions; we're uninhibited except by our sense of propriety about what our audience should hear or could stand to hear. If we get stalled, we can hem and haw, and stutter and gesture until we find the words we need; we can count on lowering our voices or raising them to make a point; we can take back anything we wish we hadn't said. When we talk, we stop, wander, get off the track, get back on again. All of this oral composing is easier for most of us most of the time because our sense of the audience keeps us alert to what needs to be said or re-said or un-said.

Learning to write means learning to listen in on the inner dialogue. When students read this statement, they sometimes say that there *is* no inner dialogue: "I have no opinion; I couldn't care less; I don't find it interesting; I need another topic." Learning to compose is in part learning to invent the dialogue, as we do daily in unplanned conversations. And when you are really listening to a lecture or a discussion, you feel involved; you are recreating the discourse – what is being said – in your head. When you are really listening, you are silently thinking. As a writer, you listen in on your own thoughts; you are both the "lecturer" and the one who hears the "lecture": learning to write is learning to hear and to re-present your own inner dialogue.

In composing, you must be able to be your own auditor in both senses: you have to listen in on the inner dialogue – your own thinking – and you have to be able to balance the account of what you have been hearing against what is set down on paper. A law-ruled tablet makes it possible to audit your meanings both as a listener and as a "bookkeeper."

The method of composing that's set down in this book is dialectical. The words *dialogue* and *dialectic* are *cognate,* which means "born together." Each names a linguistic activity or process in which a "twoness" is made one. The following chapters are intended to help you develop a *dialectical* method for making the inner *dialogue* make sense to others. It allows you to take advantage of the fact that every operation involved in composition – naming, opposing, defining, and all the rest – involves all the others. A dialectical method of composing helps you avoid making hard and fast decisions about what to say ahead of time. As Herman Melville remarked, "There are some enterprises in which a careful disorderliness is the true method."

Composing by our method is not like plodding down one row and up the next with a mule, and it certainly is not like a tractor tearing along making beautiful, entirely regular patterns. Our method works like a Scottish sheepdog bringing in the sheep: she races back and forth, driving the flock in one direction signaled by the shepherd, but acting in response to the developing occasions, nudging here, circling there; rushing back to round up a stray, dashing ahead to cut off an advance in the wrong direction. When you compose, you're the shepherd *and* the sheepdog and it's up to you to decide whether you want the sheep in fold, fank, or field and to know how to get them there.

II

CONSTRUING AND CONSTRUCTING

1. A Dialectical Notebook

Once you've started developing the habit of observing your observations, you can put it to further use in thinking about your thinking. The way to adapt your journal of observations to academic use is to keep a double-entry notebook, what we will be calling a *dialectical* notebook. The pages of this notebook all have wide margins at the left. You use one side of the line for your notes and observations; the other side is for your notes on these notes. If your college bookstore doesn't stock "law-ruled" note paper, you can draw in your own wide margin, about one third of the way across. The point of this double-entry system is that it encourages you to think about your thinking and to carry out an audit of the meanings you are making. The important thing is to separate your notes from notes about notes so that you can carry on a dialogue between you-as-listener and you-as-reviewer, the One Who Listens and Looks Again.

Sometimes your instructor may ask you to summarize during the closing minutes of class; if not, you should do so on your own. Learning to summarize a lecture in a sentence or two will save hours when it comes to reviewing for an exam. It will also alert you to the inadequacies of your note-taking techniques in time for you to do something about them. A director of a cell biology lab has her scientists sign out with a "sentence for the day" in which they try to state what happened in their experimentation and study. Practicing summaries improves your note-taking by alerting you to possible shortcuts and ways of representing in your own shorthand, but it also helps you learn to anticipate. *What is likely to come next?* is a question which helps you listen and observe by focusing your attention.

Keeping a dialectical notebook develops the habit of looking and looking again. Law students use the margin to annotate cases which have been discussed in seminar or lecture: you can do the same thing in reviewing. Embryologists of the nineteenth century drew their specimens on one side of their notebooks and posed questions about the significance of one or another structure or feature or formation on the facing page. You can do the same. Notebooks kept by geologists and archeologists in the field generally have this dialectical feature: scientists, like artists, train themselves to look and look again.

The dialectical notebook is also adaptable to your needs as a critical reader. Discard all those fancy highlighters, those pink and green markers, and instead learn to audit your meanings as you're making them, whether you're reading a short story or a chemistry textbook. It will take more time at first, but the time spent will pay off. There are several specific techniques you can learn right away and others which will take some practice: they are all ways to make reading easier and more interesting, ways to help you remember – and to remember what to remember; to help you look and to know what to look for.

Whether it's put to use in lecture hall, laboratory, or library, what makes this dialectical notebook especially valuable is the double-entry format. Of course, it's also adaptable to your needs as a composer: a writer developing your own topics, working on assignments, preparing your own papers. On the right side (or left, if you choose) will go the random materials: the reading notes, the direct quotations, the details of your observations, names, fragments, lists, images – verbal and visual – dictionary definitions, questions you might have, and all manner of other immediate material (no matter how unconnected it may seem with your topic). On the opposing side of those entries will go all your notes about notes, your revisions, comments on comments, personal observations, and summaries or paraphrases. The reason for the double-entry notebook will become apparent to you as you begin to see that you are conducting the continuing audit of meaning that is at the heart of learning to write critically. The two columns of your notebook pages will be in dialogue with one another.

Charlotte, who was a first year college student not long ago, took as her topic for one paper the image of women in advertising. After a week of observing and thinking about this topic, her dialectical notebook looked like this:

"Women in Advertising"

10/4

educated woman,
professional
skilled

Wall Street Journal
women in dark suits with
white blouses standing by
computers that print in
colors. Many men, much
older, standing by them.

IBM
2 banks
"I know where I'm
going and
how to get there."

women described in ads as
having "much on the ball"
and "in the swim"

MBA?

"Are you a displaced
homemaker with a college
degree? Do you seek
employment?"

A.M. Television: NBC

Cascade
On-Cor Lasagna
Spray and Wash
Jergens
Bran Flakes
Sure
Midol
Bounce

The ads are for dish
detergents, dishwasher soap,
floor waxes and cleaner
gasoline, makeup, face
cream, microwave food, dog
food, insect repellent, cereal,
sink cleaners, cures for
menstrual pains and
headaches, and fabric. Men

People
feed Twinkies
to their kids?

and children are excited to
find their clothes so fresh
and they get very worked up
over how Mom removes the

High fiber diets
are important.

sweat marks from pants and
the oil stains from Dad's
work clothes. One little boy
goes nuts over the smell of

fabric softener and one husband is having exultations about how clean the sink is. Some others talk about how good microwave food can be, far better than homecooking or restaurant food.

Movie stars

Big porches

rec rooms

The woman in these ads is always pretty, well-dressed (no sweatpants, bathrobes, shorts, or bowling jackets). They have dresses on and high-heeled shoes, and they wear jewelry. Their houses are very nice, full of good furniture and with no clutter, no dirt, no clothes on the furniture, no magazines or newspapers lying around. Outside their houses we see long fields and lots of trees.

10/5

Foreign names:
couture
Giorgio Amani
Lancome
L'Oreal
Marciano
Chloe
Cache
Hermes
Piaget
Jean Patou
Dior
Cellini
Erno Laszlo

Vogue *magazine: at least ¾ advertisments.*
I counted about 80 women in ads and they were all very, very thin; very beautiful; lots of makeup; wearing clothes with big pricetags (blouses at $400; underpants at $65; scarves at $200; some socks for $20).
Also has interviews with movie stars and famous models, health tips, horoscopes, and advice on relationships with men. A good mix.

Charlotte got her list of possible topics on a Monday and has done this much in four or five days. It is not much – she has not looked at her three sources closely, much less looked again – but, as we shall see, the seeds of a good essay have already been planted in this notebook. We will return to it later. You should note, though, that she has already made some meanings, even though none of them is very interesting at this point in the composing process: the *Wall Street Journal* includes women in its ads and portrays them as professionals, young and educated and savvy. Daytime television also shows women positively: as clean, attractive, excellent family people, highly concerned with the environment and the general well-being of both themselves and those they love. *Vogue* magazine, though different from the other two, offers a "good mix," even if it is "¾ ads" (which are this writer's topic). A fair beginning.

A notebook like Charlotte's illustrates the practice of writing. Here it shows that composition begins with random notetaking, observations, lists, and questions. Writing in it every day can become tedious, but it may also become essential to your understanding of what you're doing and thinking. Joan Didion speaks of keeping a notebook as a way of remembering experiences: *"How it felt to me:* that is getting closer to the truth about a notebook." Charlotte will probably remember that she was surprised at the emphasis television put on food, and especially on the opposition between good food that is bad for your health and bad food that is good for your health. Gail Godwin, another prominent writer, uses her notebook to "organize the clutter of too many details into some meaning" and because writing in a journal every day "keeps my mind fresh and open." A mind that is fresh and open is a *critical* mind. By keeping this double-entry notebook, you'll learn to read for meaning and to write to make meaning. The dialectic, the give and take, between your reading and your writing will be revealed on the pages of your notebook, a visible record of your thinking and critical interpretation.

As an example, here's one of Charlotte's notebook entries on *Vogue,* the same issue discussed in the entries above. At this point, she is *looking again* and is engaged in a real dialogue with herself.

| Topics: managing money, grown up love, shaping up now, fit at forty, food additives, drinking water, entertaining. | 10/10 |

Sections:
Fashion, People Are Talking About, Beauty and Health, Special Report (Who's Who in American Style), Living, Travel, Horoscope (mine: take a chance on love, gamble, show your spirit of adventure, chance to change careers when Jupiter contacts the sun in the third week).

Ads: glossy, excellent photography, beautiful women but a lot are my mother's age, haven't counted but it seems that these are the main ads – fur coats, makeup, dresses, perfume, nail polish, luggage, stockings (hosiery), shoes, lipstick, underwear, sunglasses, hats, purses.

Articles: "Grown-up Love" is an interview with an MD. She recommends being flexible and tough in love relationships. "Life is tough and love is hard to come by" – p. 58.

"Managing Your Money" is about IRAs, financial planning, buying stocks and bonds.

Very interesting, long article on "The Success of American Style."

"We are talking about a whole new society of rich," concurs Bill Blass, "not just in New York but from coast to coast." (174)

This is for high-income people with good taste and good bodies.

Speaking of stars, this book is chock full of them – Liza Minnelli, Elizabeth Taylor (one article and 5 or 6 pages of ads), Linda Evans, Catherine Deneuve – older stars.

You don't have to be brilliant to see that these ads try to make you want to change yourself and spend money. They say things like "There's another you underneath" and "Teach your old hair new tricks." About ten of these ads have nudity in them and three have naked men – Greek God types.

Charlotte is now in the position of having some material for a composition but not having much to say about it. Her details, examples, facts, and images don't, so far, produce any interesting concepts related to women in advertising. It's at this point in the composing process that you can learn most from the simple truth that meanings are relationships.

You can use a dialectical notebook when you respond to the assisted invitations in this book – the exercises which ask you to think about your thinking. It will help you be your own audience if you use one side of the page for notes, quotations, drawings and what we will be calling *chaos* and *oppositions*. Use the other for putting sentences together and for composing paragraphs.

Sometimes you're invited to write on a particular topic in a particular way, to compose within narrow limits; in other instances, you're invited to discuss certain conventions or to consider one point or another, with no particular writing suggested. But that doesn't mean that you therefore do no writing: developing your own topics is part of your job as a writer and you'll have opportunities to practice that skill. When the discussions are carried on in class, it's a good idea to save time for everybody, including the instructor, to write. After a 15-minute discussion – or argument – there is generally plenty to write about, to write with and from.

All the assisted invitations are meant to help you bridge from theory – the *what* and *why* – to practice – the *how*. The exercises offer you a chance to practice on a small scale, but the whole point of a method is that it should help you in real writing – that is, papers and exams for other courses, letters and essays and job resumes, reports and explanations, and all the other writing that life will "assign" you. Our assumption is that you'll be working on papers required in other courses, perhaps even when you're studying this book, and that you'll adapt what is offered here to all those exercises in composing.

A technique which works for reading and writing, for observing your own observations and those of others, is *glossing*. A gloss is a restatement in summary form and it's most useful to you if you can formulate it as an opposition – if you can note *what* is said about *what*, or name whatever is being juxtaposed to something else. We'll discuss its uses in writing at a later point; here's how it works in reading.

Whether you're reading a single paragraph or an entire chapter, you should first read it through in order to get your bearings. You should read quickly so that you can be ready to reread: that's where the action is. In an essay or article or chapter, you should reread by the paragraph: glossing is a way of telling yourself what you've just read. You can think of a gloss as a headline – the big typeface – plus the secondary head – in medium-size type. Writing headlines for newspaper stories is excellent glossing practice. Here's one from the *Wall Street Journal* that tells you exactly what you're going to read:

RIDING IT OUT
Economy Fares Well
In Wake of the Crash,
Leading Experts Say

Slump More Likely in the
Next Year or So, But None
See a Depression

Worries About Overreactions

Another from the *New York Times:*

SENATE APPROVES $4 BILLION
AID TO FARMING BANKS

Revising Credit System

Joint Budget Panel Working to Resolve
Disputes Blocking Catchall Spending Bill

You can think of a gloss as a title plus a subtitle. In some editions of complex essays, you'll find marginal summaries: these are glosses. But the glossing you'll be practicing is somewhat more substantial than most marginal annotations. When you gloss a paragraph, you don't just name the subject or the topic: you include the *so what?* It isn't just a few key words: it's more like a telegraphed message; or a certain kind of advertisement:

• Arriving tomorrow. Missed plane.
• Have gun. Will travel.
• Things are getting desperate. Please send chocolate.

A gloss represents the way you read the paragraph: the reason for glossing is to learn to make your reading critical. When you read critically, you analyze how the parts are bundled to make the whole: the fundamental question for the reader, as for the writer, is, "What goes with what?" Critical reading is simply the reverse of composing and we could call it "decomposing," except for the fact that that word suggests organic deterioration. *Critic* derives from a Greek word that meant *to judge, to discern, to be able to discuss* – all capacities necessary to forming concepts and making meanings in both reading and writing: how you construe is how you construct.

Here are four styles of glossing. Note that all are oppositional: they set one point over against another.

1. orientation: adaptation (animals) transformation (man)
2. humanizing/ adapting
3. man's sense of history value, "project"/ animals' adaptation, instinct
4. Man transforms; animals merely adapt.

If, for animals, orientation in the world means adaptation to the world, for man it means humanizing the world by transforming it. For animals there is no historical sense, no options or values in their orientation in the world; for man there is both a historical and a value dimension. Men have the sense of "project," in contrast to the instinctive routines of animals.

Paulo Freire,
The Pedagogy of the Oppressed

ᘒ Use your dialectical notebook to practice glossing. For instance, copy a whole sentence from anywhere in a paragraph and then on the left, write your own version of what you think the sentence says. Practicing interpretive paraphrases of single sentences can help you grasp the whole paragraph in a gloss. Here are some sample paragraphs to work with.

A work of (whatever) art can be either "received" or "used." When we "receive" it we exert our senses and imagination and various other powers according to a pattern invented by the artist. When we "use" it we treat it as assistance for our own activities. The one, to use an old-fashioned image, is like being taken for a bicycle ride by a man who may know roads we have never yet explored. The other is like adding one of those little motor attachments to our own bicycle and then going for one of our familiar rides. These rides may in themselves be good, bad, or indifferent. The "uses" which the many make of the arts may or may not be intrinsically vulgar, depraved, or morbid. That's as may be. "Using" is inferior to "reception" because art, if used rather than received, merely facilitates, brightens or palliates our life, and does not add to it.

C.S. Lewis, *An Experiment in Criticism*

Avoid fried foods which anger the blood. If your stomach disputes you, lie down and pacify it with cooling thoughts. Keep the juice flowing by jangling around gently as you move. Go very light on the vices such as carrying on in society – the social ramble ain't restful. Avoid running at all times. Don't look back. Something may be gaining on you.

Leroy (Satchel) Paige

We rode in quiet down the valley, whose waters hardly reached its mouth before vanishing in the importunate desert. I wondered restlessly what it is in dry mud ruins, the speech of alien people, the mixed drabness and gay colors of a caravanserai, the smell of camels in a camp in the desert that makes a struggle in one between the richness of the present vision and the vague offer of the next horizon, that leads one to the noble aspiration and perpetual renunciation of travel. I think myself that the real ritual of travel is a sort of processional celebration of the mystery of life.

Owen Lattimore, *High Tartary*

Everything appears differently to the man habitually on horseback. It raises him up, makes him wear different clothes, makes him a centaur. In the *Politics,* Aristotle attributes the strong oligarchy that always ruled in Thessaly to the horses, to the advantage, moral and physical, they gave to richer people. The continual use of horses is a barbaric splendor – in the Greek sense of bar-baric – a meaning which suggests extravagant or miasmic horizons as if Space moved, or, instead of being the medium in which things stand, could be devoured like Time. Certainly the horseman feels that he devours Space. The ground totters past him. He is an upstart creature, the lover of princes and gaunt ceremony. The poor man is, to him, a biped, a dust-treader. The horseman takes his nobility from the horse. The mountains rear for him, they do not stand. He scatters the stones or curses them.

Adrian Stokes, *The Stones of Rimini*

One of the chief purposes of glossing is to help you identify conceptual terms – words whose definition requires more than the dictionary. Explicitly identifying a writer's "key" terms is good practice for reading documents and other texts in which concepts don't jump off the page. For instance, if you're giving the Bill of Rights a careful, critical reading, there's no signal to tell you which terms are conceptually complex, calling for something more than a lexical definition. Take the Second Amendment:

> A well-regulated militia being necessary to the security of a free state, the right of the people to keep and bear arms shall not be infringed.

Practice in identifying conceptual terms can alert you to the fact that any central name or word or fact should be carefully examined and interpreted; thus *militia* sounds like a down-to-earth name for *local citizens with guns,* but once you have developed a historical context, you can see that it does not belong in the same class with *Americans protecting private property with firearms.* The meaning of "the right of the people to keep and bear arms" has nothing to do with the claims of the National Rifle Association.

In reading essays, articles, or any text in which technical language is necessary in forming the concept, it's a good idea to prepare a *lexicon,* which is a list of words serving a special purpose. A gardener's *lexicon* would include names of equipment and processes as well as the names of plants. Preparing a lexicon is essential in keeping track of a complicated terminology, but it also has its uses in helping you keep familiar terms carefully differentiated. If you're reading about the economics of energy, for instance, it would be useful to include in your lexicon the terms *fuel, energy, power, resources,* along with examples of their use. They are all familiar, of course, but each is used to indicate a different function or state. Coal in the ground has one name; coal in the furnace or in a statistical table has other names. Developing a lexicon prepares you for naming the classes accurately and appropriately, an act that is essential to forming concepts.

Naming conceptual terms – underlining or copying them in the margin – is preliminary to recognizing them in grammatical transformations (if *variation* is a key term, it is likely that *vary, invariant,* or *varying* will occur somewhere in the passage); and it is also essential for an understanding of the ground of analogies or images. It can be disconcerting to be reading along and suddenly find yourself in the midst of something that seems to have nothing to do with what you thought you were reading about. ("What in the world does plum pudding have to do with epic diction?" See paragraph by C.S. Lewis, pages 126-127.)

2. Seeing Relationships

All of the paragraph sequences in this book (see Special Features) concern the process of *thinking* – the process of *forming* impressions and opinions and ideas and arguments. Each emphasizes a different aspect of this process, though of course there are overlaps: remember the sheepdog. Nevertheless, aspects of thinking can be differentiated as we consider it from different angles. (An *aspect* is the appearance something has from one or another angle.) In this sequence, the comment is by poets and philosophers, artists and psychologists; the paragraphs all concern how we see relationships, how we make sense of the world.

Each paragraph is followed by a brief comment which relates the points made by the writer to the composing process itself. You are then invited to do some experimental thinking and writing of your own. Again, these assisted invitations to think and write are indicated by the little sign ∿ : sometimes a particular exercise is suggested; sometimes we simply say "consider," although you might, of course, be asked to write out your "consideration." The experiments do not increase in difficulty; in fact, they may become simpler. There are no right answers. The experiments are ways of exploring the composing process as an ongoing operation, which includes getting ideas, seeing the point, thinking something out, inventing, arguing, dreaming – writing things down all along the way. Keeping everything together will enable you to return to an experiment and rediscover what it is about and, perhaps, to give it another go. Anything your instructor wants to read can be handed in, but this is *your* notebook, a way for you to listen in on the inner dialogue you carry on when you are thinking.

Sensory Knowing: Muir's Girnel

Our diet was a curious one by town standards. We went without many necessaries, or what are considered necessaries – beef, for instance – and had a great number of luxuries which we did not know to be luxuries, such as plovers' eggs, trout, crab, and lobster: I ate so much crab and lobster as a boy that I have never been able to enjoy them since. Our staples were homemade oat bannocks and barley bannocks, butter, eggs, and home-made cheese, which we had in abundance; white bread, bought at the Wyre shop, was looked upon as a luxury. In the kitchen there was a big girnel with a sliding top; inside it was divided in two, one compartment being filled with oatmeal and the other with barley-meal. The meal had to be pressed firmly down, otherwise it would not keep. The girnel, when the top was slid back, gave out a thick, sleepy smell, which seemed to go to my head and make me drowsy. It was connected with a nightmare which I often had, in which my body seemed to swell to a great size and then slowly dwindle again, while the drowsy smell of meal filled my nostrils. It is from smell that we get our most intense realization of the solidity of things. The smell of meal pressed tightly down in the girnel made me realize its *mass,* though I could see only its surface, which was smooth and looked quite shallow. My nightmares probably came from an apprehension of the mere bulk of life, the feeling that the world is so tightly crammed with solid, bulging objects that there is not enough room for all of them: a nightmare feeling powerfully conveyed in the stories of Franz Kafka.

Edwin Muir, *An Autobiography*

Human beings learn in childhood to read the book of nature. You come to understand what to expect when you tease a cat or toss a pebble in a pool or touch a hot stove. You don't have to go to school to learn how to judge distance or to tell whether it's early or late afternoon (assuming that you aren't suddenly transported to a different latitude). We learn in terms of the space things take up, the time things take to happen. We live in a world of space and time because it is of such a world that our senses give report. Learning to make sense of that world, discovering physical dimensions and the psychological limits of experience, is the work of childhood. It can be the happiest work we ever do – or the grimmest; more and more frequently for American children, it is simply missing. Watching a television program about burrs and frogs can't give you the same experience as exploring a vacant lot; seeing a documentary about life in an inner city slum is not the same thing as the remembered experience of being cold and hungry.

        ↪ Write paragraphs in response to some of the following invitations:

1. Muir observes that it is smell which gives us "our most intense realization of the solidity of things." What sense, would you say, gives us our most intense realization of the fluidity of things? Tell about how you know from your own experience.
2. Can you remember an early occasion when you were conscious of *space,* as well as of something small or large *in* space? Describe the experience.
3. The environment of the country and the environment of the city are different: the world of space and time is the same. What do you think a city child might find strange about the country? A country child about the city? What might either find familiar in the unfamiliar environment and why?

Physiognomic Knowing: Gombrich's Ping/Pong

...What is called "synesthesia," the splashing over of impressions from one sense modality to another, is a fact to which all languages testify. They work both ways – from sight to sound and from sound to sight. We speak of loud colors or of bright sounds, and everyone knows what we mean. Nor are the ear and the eye the only senses that are thus converging to a common center. There is touch in such terms as "velvety voice" and "a cold light," taste with "sweet harmonies" of colors or sounds, and so on through countless permutations....Synesthesia concerns relationships. I have tried out this suggestion in a party game. It consists of creating the simplest imaginable medium in which relationships can still be expressed, a language of two words only – let us call them "ping" and "pong." If these were all we had and we had to name an elephant and a cat, which would be ping and which pong? I think the answer is clear. Or hot soup and ice cream. To me, at least,

ice cream is ping and soup pong. Or Rembrandt and
Watteau? Surely in that case Rembrandt would be pong and
Watteau ping. I do not maintain that it always works, that
two blocks are sufficient to categorize all relationships. We
find people differing about day and night and male and
female, but perhaps these different answers would be reduced to unanimity if the question were differently framed:
pretty girls are ping and matrons pong; it may depend on
which aspect of womanhood the person has in mind, just as
the motherly, enveloping aspect of night is pong, but its
sharp, cold, and menacing physiognomy may be ping to
some.

E.H. Gombrich, *Art and Illusion*

Elephants, Rembrandt, and soup have nothing in common
except that when they are placed in opposition with something
else of a certain kind to be symbolized by "ping," they are
"pong." It's hard to see if an elephant could ever be a *ping,* but if
you put a cold soup—*gazpacho*—in opposition with chili, soup
might then be *ping.* Rembrandt's shadows help make him *pong,*
but shadows in a summer grove could be *ping* if they are in
opposition to a stormy sea.

All of this categorizing has to do with how the interior of
your mouth is shaped when you say *ping* or *pong* and how the
sounds those words make are associated with objects. In making
sense of the world, we use all our senses and associate one sense
experience with another. But we also judge character and temperament and develop our expectations about feelings and ideas
on the basis of those experiences. This game can teach you a lot
about the interaction of sensory experience and thinking, which
is seeing relationships.

☙ Write paragraphs, lists, or
dialectical oppositions in response to the following
invitations.

1. Categorize as ping or pong any of the following oppositions: the U.S.S.R./the U.S.A.; blue jeans/blue serge
   suits; Toyotas/BMWs; McDonald's/Burger King; *Play-
   boy/Esquire*; compact discs/stereos; basketball/foot-
   ball; fishing/hunting; high school/college; conservative/
   liberal.
2. When most people say "I feel," do they mean the same
   thing as "I think"? What differences and similarities
   are there between the two statements, if any?

3. If you have ever felt in one of the following ways, explain that feeling as fully as you can: blue, seeing red, in the pink, yellow, blacked out, green with envy, white hot.

Sensory Education: Welty's Moon

Learning stamps you with its moments. Childhood's learning is made up of moments. It isn't steady. It's a pulse.

In a children's art class, we sat in a ring on kindergarten chairs and drew three daffodils that had just been picked out of the yard; and while I was drawing, my sharpened yellow pencil and the cup of the yellow daffodil gave off whiffs just alike. That the pencil doing the drawing should give off the same smell as the flower it drew seemed part of the art lesson – as shouldn't it be? Children, like animals, use all their senses to discover the world. Then artists come along and discover it the same way, all over again. Here and there, it's the same world. Or now and then we'll hear from an artist who's never lost it.

In my sensory education I include my physical awareness of the *word*. Of a certain word, that is; the connection it has with what it stands for. At around six, perhaps, I was standing by myself in our front yard waiting for supper, just at that hour in a late summer day when the sun is already below the horizon and the risen full moon in the visible sky stops being chalky and begins to take on light. There comes the moment, and I saw it then, when the moon goes from flat to round. For the first time it met my eyes as a globe. The word "moon" came into my mouth as though fed to me out of a silver spoon. Held in my mouth the moon became a word. It had the roundness of a Concord grape Grandpa took off his vine and gave me to suck out of its skin and swallow whole, in Ohio.

This love did not prevent me from living for years in foolish error about the moon. The new moon just appearing in the west was the rising moon to me. The new should be rising. And in early childhood the sun and moon, those opposite reigning powers, I just as easily assumed rose in east and west respectively in their opposite sides of the sky, and like partners in a reel they advanced, sun from the east, moon from the west, crossed over (when I wasn't looking) and went down on the other side. My father couldn't have known I believed that when, bending behind me and guiding my shoulder, he positioned me at our telescope in the front yard and, with careful adjustment of the focus, brought the moon close to me.

The night sky over my childhood Jackson was velvety black. I could see the full constellations in it and call their names; when I could read, I knew their myths. Though I was always waked for eclipses, and indeed carried to the window as an infant in arms and shown Halley's Comet in my sleep, and though I'd been taught at our diningroom table about the solar system and knew the earth revolved around the sun, and our moon around us, I never found out the moon didn't come up in the west until I was a writer and Herschel Brickell, the literary critic, told me after I misplaced it in a story. He said valuable words to me about my new profession: "Always be sure you get your moon in the right part of the sky."

Eudora Welty, *One Writer's Beginnings*

Sensory knowing is our first way of making sense of the world. In childhood, we see and feel one thing in terms of another. We believe that certain aspects of life go together naturally: "The new should be rising." Eudora Welty suggests that artists rediscover this early way of knowing, of looking at the world. In our dreams, all of us have access to this kind of knowing, but of course it must be corrected, adjusted, and supplemented in our waking hours. And sometimes dreams usefully edge out reality.

 ∾ Respond, as suggested, to the following observations.

1. As children, we develop our vocabularies by naming sensory experiences, opposing them with other sensory experiences, and defining them in the contexts of our own perspectives. Write a paragraph on one of your early experiences with flat and round, up and down, or vertical and horizontal. What concepts did you form?
2. Write a descriptive passage that captures your early perceptions of the sky, the stars, or the sunset. Has the study of science changed those perceptions at all?
3. In the passage quoted above, Welty says that when she reads, she both *sees* the words and *hears* them. The voice in writing gives it movement. Can you explain in a paragraph, using experiences of your own, what Welty means here?
4. Try to describe in a paragraph how a telescope or microscope alters previously held perceptions.

Interpretation: Arnheim's Droodles

Visual knowledge and correct expectation will facilitate perception whereas inappropriate concepts will delay or impede it.... A Japanese reads without difficulty ideographs so small that a Westerner needs a magnifying glass to discern them, not because the Japanese have more acute eyesight but because they hold the *kanji* characters in visual storage. For similar reasons, bird watchers, hunters, mariners, physicians or microbiologists often seem endowed with super-human powers of vision. And the average layman of today has no trouble perceiving human figures or animals in Impressionist paintings that looked like assortments of meaningless color patches eighty years ago.

It should be noted that the effect of such "preperceived" images depends not simply on how often their prototypes have been met in the past but also quite importantly on what the nature of the given context seems to call for. What one expects to see depends considerably on what "belongs" in that particular place. The perception of familiar kinds of objects, then, is inseparably related to norm images the observer harbors in his mind.

Rudolf Arnheim, *Visual Thinking*

We construe – figure out what we're hearing or seeing – on the basis of what we've seen, but also according to what we think we might be seeing or hearing. (Once, in the days before jet travel when transatlantic planes had to make fueling stops, I found myself in Iceland. After three months in Europe hearing very little English, I had expected that customers at the coffee bar in Reykjavik would be speaking Icelandic. I took in with fascination the strange and wonderful sounds of a language I associated with stirring epic and wild, primitive song. As I listened, it became clear that what I was hearing was my native language spoken by two young men from the Bronx. I tell this story to remind you that, in composition, we often make the mistake of seeing what we expect to see and refusing to see what we do not expect. A.E.B.)

ᖇ Write in your dialectical notebook on the following questions and then compose paragraphs interpeting what you've entered.

1. Name one of the times in your life when your expectations were completely different from what you found out was true. What did you learn from that experience?
2. Arnheim suggests that "droodles," which are "playful examples of visual paradoxes ingeniously exploited,"

can provide "good study material for any explorer of visual perception." One of his students created this droodle, captioned "Olive dropping into martini glass" or "Closeup of girl in bikini." Another student saw it as "Hip roof with a paint bucket on the porch." Can you see it as something else? Draw your own droodle. Ask your friends for captions.

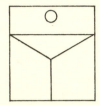

Re-cognition: Barfield's House

A little reflection shows that all *meaning* – even of the most primitive kind – is dependent on the possession of some measure of this power [the capacity to recognize]. Let the reader imagine for a moment that he is standing in the midst of a normal and familiar environment – houses, trees, grass, sky, etc. – when, suddenly, he is deprived by some supernatural stroke of every vestige of memory – and not only of memory, but also of all those assimilated, forgotten experiences which comprise his power of *recognition*. He is asked to assume that, in spite of this, he still retains the full measure of his cognitive faculty as an adult. It will appear, I think, that for the first few moments his consciousness – if it can bear that name – will be deprived not merely of all thought, but even of all perception – unless we choose to suppose a certain unimaginable minimum, a kind of panorama of various light, which he will confront with a vacant and uncomprehending stare. It is not merely that he will be unable to realize that that square, red and white object is a "house," and to form concepts of an inside with walls and ceilings – he will not even be able to see it *as* a square, red and white object. For the most elementary distinctions of form and color are only apprehended by us with the help of the concepts which we have come to unite with the pure sense-datum. And these concepts we acquire and fix, as we grow up, with the help of words – such as *square, red,* etc. On the basis of past perceptions, using language as a kind of storehouse, we gradually build up our ideas, and it is only these which enable us to become "conscious," as human beings, of the world around us.

Owen Barfield, *Poetic Diction*

The osprey dives from a great height above a broad river and takes off again with a fish in its talons; the boy runs after the ball, dodging cars in the busy street, snatching it just in time from in front of a truck. Are the two acts of the same kind? A cat about to give birth to her first kitten looks pained and perplexed, but the minute the first kitten pops out, she licks it, nudges it into place by a nipple, eats the afterbirth and gets ready for kitten No. 2; the pianist looks over the score for a minute or so and then plays it through without pause. Are the two acts comparable?

Re-cognition means *re-knowing* – but what is *knowing?* For a student of composition, it is instructive to keep asking that question: How do I know? What do I know? How do I know I know? Do I know my knowledge?

Barfield's difficult book is about the making of meanings by all those who use language; that's you and me and the poets, but not cats or fish hawks or even cute chimpanzees.

~ Write speculative paragraphs in response to some of the following invitations. Use your dialectical notebook to help you think about your thinking.

1. What does "coming to your senses" mean in the case of regaining consciousness after fainting? How is that different from suddenly seeing that you've been mistaken about something important?
2. Have you or somebody close to you been handicapped in a way that alters or impairs perception? If a blind man can't see, what do we mean when we say that blindness alters his *view* of the world?
3. Look up an account of a person who, having been blind or deaf since birth, is by surgical means given back that sense. How do their experiences tally with what Barfield imagines would happen if we lost our power to recognize?
4. Read an account of one of the following and write on how it compares with the way the human mind works: fish finding schools, rats finding packs, wasps finding their homes after a day of buzzing around.

5. What role does re-cognition, in Barfield's sense, play in science fiction? Choose one illustration from a favorite example of yours and show how the re-cognition of twentieth-century readers is what the author counts on.
6. As Barfield says, we "acquire and fix" concepts in our minds "with the help of words." Explicate this short passage from the notebooks of Gerard Manley Hopkins, a poet who took his notebook with him when he went for walks in the country. How many words did you have to look up? How does Hopkins' "storehouse" of words enable him to "acquire" a concept of the oak?

July, 11 (1867).... Oaks; the organization of this tree is difficult. Speaking generally no doubt the determining planes are concentric, a system of brief contiguous and continuous tangents, whereas those of the cedar wd. roughly be called horizontals and those of the beech radiating but modified by droop and by a screw-set towards jutting points. But beyond this since the normal growth of the boughs is radiating and the leaves grow some way in there is of course a system of spoke-wise clubs of green – sleeve-pieces. And since the end shoots curl and carry young and scanty leaf-stars these clubs are tapered, and I have seen also the pieces in profile with chiselled outlines, the blocks thus made detached and lessening towards the end. However the star knot is the chief thing: it is whorled, worked around a little and this is what keeps up the illusion of the tree: the leaves are rounded inwards and figure out ball-knots. Oaks differ much, and much turns on the broadness of the leaf, the narrower giving the crisped and starry and catherine-wheel forms, the broader the flat-pieced mailed or shard-covered one, in wh. it is possible to see composition in dips etc., on wider bases than the single knot or cluster. But I shall study them further. See the 19th.

July 19.... I have now found the law of the oak leaves. It is of platter-shaped stars altogether; the leaves lie close like pages, packed in and as if drawn tightly to. But these old packs, wh. lie at the end of their twigs, throw out now young shoots alternately and slimly leaved, looking like bright keys. All the sprays but markedly these ones shape out and as it were embrace greater circles and the dip and toss of these makes the wider and less organic articulations of the tree.

Forming: Langer's "Things"

Our merest sense-experience is a process of formulation. The world that actually meets our senses is not a world of "things," about which we are invited to discover facts as soon as we have codified the necessary logical language to do so; the world of pure sensation is so complex, so fluid and full, that sheer sensitivity to stimuli would only encounter what William James has called (in characteristic phrase) "a blooming, buzzing confusion." Out of this bedlam our sense organs must select certain predominant forms, if they are to make report of *things* and not of mere dissolving sensa. The eye and ear must have their logic – their "categories of understanding," if you like the Kantian idiom, or their "primary imagination," in Coleridge's version of the same concept. An object is not a datum, but a form construed by the sensitive and intelligent organ, a form which is at once an experienced individual thing and a symbol for the concept of it, for this *sort of thing.*

. . . Mental life begins with our mere physiological constitution. A little reflection shows us that, since no experience occurs more than once, so-called "repeated" experiences are really *analogous* occurrences, all fitting a form that was abstracted on the first occasion. *Familiarity* is nothing but the quality of fitting very neatly into the form of a previous experience. I believe our ingrained habit of hypostatizing impressions, of seeing *things* and not sense-data, rests on the fact that we promptly and unconsciously abstract a form from each sensory experience, and use this form to *conceive* the experience as a whole, as a "thing."

Susanne K. Langer, *Philosophy in a New Key.*

In the daily entries in your journal of observations, you can begin to test the truth of Langer's argument. Perception, which is a process of composing, involves differentiation and selection, amalgamation and elimination. As you describe your "thing," you are selecting and differentiating, saying what it reminds you of, setting it apart from others of the same kind. You can listen in on your own thoughts to find out how it is that what you see becomes familiar.

ॐ When you're studying a difficult passage like this one, it's a good idea to read it straight through first. Then compare the final sentence with the opening sentence and see if you recognize a common point. Then reread. Finally, look up the words you still can't figure out (*hypostatizing?*) and reread again. How does the first sentence relate to the last?

1. Can you rephrase and explain, in terms of your own experience, the statement that "the eyes and ears must have their logic"? What about the nose or the toes or the tongue?
2. Though Kant and Coleridge say the same thing in the quotations Langer takes from their works, there are shades of difference in what they say. Consider.
3. You know the old story of how the blind men described the elephant: can you describe the object of your observations in terms only of touch?

Thinking about Thinking: Burke's Trout

All living organisms interpret many of the signs about them. A trout, having snatched at a hook but having had the good luck to escape with a rip in his jaw, may even show by his wiliness thereafter that he can revise his critical appraisals. His experience has led him to form a new judgment, which we should verbalize as a nicer discrimination between food and bait. A different kind of bait may outwit him, if it lacks the appearances by which he happens to distinguish "jaw-ripping food." And perhaps he passes up many a morsel of genuine food simply because it happens to have the character which he, as the result of his informing experience, has learned to take as the sign of bait. I do not mean to imply that the sullen fish has thought all this out. I mean simply that in his altered response, for a greater or lesser period following the hook episode, he manifests the changed behavior that goes with a new meaning; he has a more educated way of reading the signs. It does not matter how conscious or unconscious one chooses to imagine this critical step; we need only note here the outward manifestation of a revised judgment.

Our great advantage over this sophisticated trout would seem to be that we can greatly extend the scope of the critical process. Man can be methodical in his attempts to decide what the difference between bait and food might be. Unfortunately, as Thorstein Veblen has pointed out, invention is the mother of necessity: the very power of criticism has enabled man to build up cultural structures so complex that still greater powers of criticism are needed before he can distinguish between the food-processes and bait-processes concealed beneath his cultural tangles. His greater critical capacity has increased not only the range of his solutions, but also the range of his problems. Orientation can go wrong. Consider, for instance, what conquest over the environment we have attained through our powers of abstraction, of generalization; and then consider the stupid national or racial wars which have been fought precisely because these abstractions were taken for realities. No slight critical ability is required for one to have as his deepest enemy a people thousands of miles away. When criticism can do so much for us, it may have got us just to the point where we greatly require still better criticism. Though all organisms are critics in the sense that they interpret the signs about them, the experimental speculative technique made available by speech would seem to single out the human species as the only one possessing an equipment for going beyond the criticism of experience to a criticism of criticism. We not only interpret the characters of events (manifesting in our responses all the gradations of fear, apprehension, expectation, assurance, for which there are rough behavioristic counterparts in animals) – we may also interpret our interpretations.

Kenneth Burke, *Permanence and Change*

Kenneth Burke's disquisition on how a trout responds to the world makes the point that it is language that enables nontrouts to go beyond the interpretation of signs to the interpretation of interpretations. The trout lives in a world of stimuli and responses; nontrouts live in a world of meanings. Even if it is called "verbal behavior" in an attempt to bridge the worlds of animal and human life, *language* as a mediation differs profoundly from *language* as a system of signals. The retinal cells act according to certain codes that are stored neurologically, but when we look at something, when we see relationships, there are numberless other intervening acts by which the brain/mind transforms signals into symbols. Throughout this book there are passages from the writings of psychologists and philosophers about the nature and character of those transformations; for now, what we need to note is that interpreting our interpretations is made possible because language gives us a means of making meanings.

〜 1. "No chimpanzee thinks he thinks": that is the poet W.H. Auden's way of putting the point about the world of meanings in which we live. Thinking about thinking; observing our observations; interpreting our interpretations: How would you explain these formulations?
2. What's the difference between Kenneth Burke's trout and a trout in a Walt Disney animated cartoon? What does *animation* mean?
3. How would you explain the difference between Morse *Code* and a *code* of ethics?

3. Form Finds Form

When you're faced with a blank piece of paper, what you need in order to get started is not philosophy but a method; nevertheless, if a method is not going to degenerate into a set of do's and don'ts, it must have a philosophical foundation. A method should be grounded in certain principles that can account for what you do when you compose. Those principles all concern the making of meaning. Here they are in summary form.

1. *The composing process by which we make meaning is a continuum.* We don't take in the world like a camera or a set of recording devices. The mind is an agent, not a passive receiver; experience is not poured into it. The active mind is a composer, and everything we respond to we compose or re-compose.

Things are "really" there, but what is "really" there we can't see. For instance, you look in front of you and see a solid object – say a table, which is usually the philosopher's favorite example. Modern physics tells us that this table is really an event, but we don't see electrons moving in that frenzy of activity that makes the table an event. We do not have eyes that can take in that scene; if we did, it would be quite a focusing job to move from submicroscopic levels to those required to see objects in space. An electron microscope, which transforms in an exceedingly complex manner, could give us a picture of one infinitely small portion of that excited mass, but it would be in no way relevant to the experience or knowledge we have of the piece of furniture we put the cups and saucers on. We don't have x-ray eyes, because human life does not require such vision and indeed would be impossible if we saw inner structure rather than contour and color. We can judge dimension and mass and depth of field because the space in which we move requires such perception. The brain puts things together, composing the percepts by which we can make sense of the world. We don't just "have" a visual experience and then by thinking "have" a mental experience: the mutual dependence of seeing and knowing is what a modern psychologist has in mind when he speaks of "the intelligent eye." That is very ancient wisdom: our word *idea* derives from a Greek word that originally meant both *I have seen* and *I know*.

2. *Meanings are relationships.* Seeing means "seeing relationships," whether we are talking about seeing as perception or seeing as understanding. "I see what you mean" means "I understand how you put that together so that it makes sense." The way we make sense of the world is to see something *with respect to, in terms of, in relation to* something else. We cannot make sense of one thing by itself; it must be seen as being *like* another thing; or *next to, across from, coming after* another thing; or as a *repetition* of another thing. *Something* makes sense – is meaningful – only if it is taken with *something else*.

Now, just as the retinal cells and the rest of the brain compose the relationships we see/perceive, so the active mind composes the relationships we see/understand. These relationships, based on what we see, become what we call ideas, or what we know. Relationships, whether perceptual (I see) or conceptual (I know), are compositions. Note how Hopkins, in the passage above, claims to know "the law of the oak leaves" because he can see in them "composition in dips, etc." We perceive and understand relationships in terms of space and time and causality. The way we *know* reality, the ways we have of seeing relationships, are encompassed by those three terms – space, time, causality: they are what Immanuel Kant called the "categories of human understanding." We see/know outline, contour, color, texture; we judge size, volume, distance, rate of speed, direction; we apprehend succession, whether it is a chain of happenings, or a complicated story or play or joke; we can figure out the cause if we see the effect, and we can guess the effect if we know the cause. Of course, we will be frequently mistaken (Is it a man or a bird?); having the capacity to understand means having the capacity to misunderstand. The categories of understanding are not guarantors of the truth; that is why we need to be critical in our thinking, to learn a method that will guide us in interpreting our interpretations. The illustrations from student notebooks that you encounter throughout this book will show you that all of us, not just great philosophers, compose by seeing relationships.

3. *There must be a means of making meaning.* One of the chief meanings of "meaning" is "mediation," or the "means by which." We can neither apprehend (take in, gather, seize upon, make sense of) reality nor express an idea without a means of doing so. Everything we know, we know in some *form;* there is no *im*mediate knowledge—that is, knowledge without mediation or form. We do not "have" meanings that we then put into words. Language is not a set of pigeonholes into which we put things, ideas, feelings. We discover meanings in the process of working and playing with the means language provides.

4. *Language is our readiest means of making meaning.* Linguistic forms correspond to perceptual forms. Seeing that the circles move out from where the stone is tossed is comparable to saying/thinking: "If I toss the stone in the pool, it will then mark the center of a series of expanding circles." Or, more simply, "Look what I can make happen!" Making meanings with language is like making sense of the world. Telling left from right is like telling beginnings from ends, both when we watch something happen and when we tell a story about how it did happen. Differentiating dark from light, figure from ground, the shore bird from reeds and grasses may take practice and experience, but it involves the same acts of mind as are involved when we follow an argument or answer a question.

The way meanings are put together by means of language matches our experience of how things are related in time and space and the way causes and effects reflect and control one another. *Form finds form* is a shorthand way of saying all this. It's a way of representing both *feedback*—the guidance we get from the means we are using—and *feedforward*—the capacity to formulate the choices we make when we are putting things together, seeing relationships, interpreting our experience, making meanings.

To show you that we all make meanings in these ways, not just great thinkers like Aristotle and Kant, let's look briefly at the third stage of Charlotte's journal on women in advertising.

10/12
Describe the women in the *Vogue* ads –
The poses are mystical and sexy, and a little bit exaggerated. The legs are stretched and the lips are pressed together in a pouty or a far-away manner. Liza Minnelli is doing three looks in her Revlon ad, and her eyes are looking out at us. Her lips are parted and her teeth are beautiful. Her hair is perfect and her neck and breasts are mostly bare and beautiful. In one pose, she looks like Cinderella at the ball but in the next one she is a star, ready to take on New York and then the world. The last one shows her in a thrilled mood. Other ads here are clever too. One shows a clock on a woman's face (Ultima II makeup). It "assumes new responsibility" for your face and makes this promise because it has an "exquisitely refined molecular color system" that has "successfully married color to treatment." This "anti-aging firming foundation" is "so total" that it "could be perceived as a separate category of cosmetic." Linda Evans models "Ultress Gel Colourant" (English spelling). This product makes "anything else ordinary" because it "is the ulitmate in luxury." It ends: "be the best you've ever been." What I

ideas to develop – glamor, beauty, sexiness.
Stereotypes of women – what about Peace Corps ad on p. 324 and essays on the environment, AIDS, art, books?

Liza Minnelli is supposed to be plain and orphany. I saw her in *Arthur*. This shows that many woman can be glamorous? Is that the point, because she has it all here?

Think of better examples here. Who knows how Cindy looked at the ball? She's a fairy-tale character. She looks like a romantic young girl who has never been anywhere or been in love, but wants all that.

"exquisitely" – carefully done or elaborately made, beautiful, lovely, delicate, of highest quality, admirable, sensitive, refined, fastidious.

A product for the refined woman with a big vocabulary.

French, Italian, English are the big things to be in America. 90% of everything in here is one or the other.

like about this assignment is that it makes me read the words in these ads and I have never done that before. The women in these ads are described as unique, stunning, exciting, fun, burning, brilliant, beautiful. Daytime television ads usually show family scenes, either in the kitchen or the bathroom, sometimes in the bedroom. These are women in their private lives, but looking glamorous. What do they have in common? Families: almost all these ads show beautiful, well-dressed children with beautiful, well-dressed mothers. Ore-Ida sells microwave fries using puppies, babies, pretty kitchens and very attractive mothers. You can bet that none of these "mothers" eats french fries. In a Nutra-Sweet ad, a mother is on a bicycle and behind her are about five children on bicycles. The children sit quietly in a row while the mother sells NutraSweet. One great ad opens with a mother sitting at her kitchen table. Her hair is messed up and her face shows exhaustion. She says that she has 2009 ways to fix chicken but needs another one because the family is sick of chicken. An announcer then plugs Applause, the new Kraft

Generalizing about family life in America and about how women deal with it, the TV ads seem to be saying that most families have to be very attractive looking, with children who are adorable and homes that are very clean. We also see that the American mother has a lot of headaches, sinus congestion, "face aches" (according to Exedrin ads), and problems with hair and skin.

Ads during two hours of daytime TV:

Microwave cakes by Pillsbury: man kisses woman when he sees the cake. She smiles blissfully.

Cover Girl Replenisher: Jennifer O'Neill shows that all women need to have their faces replenished, so that tiny lines disappear and people notice how much they glow.

Tilex shows that mildew, the big bathroom problem in family life, can be conquered.

Dubuque Ham: "Welcome to Iowa," where Sunday dinners with the family are important. The announcer talks about family and product, that lets you do exciting things with chicken. The ad ends at the dinner table – where else? The whole family is giving mother a round of "Applause" for thinking of barbecued chicken. The mother has her hair fixed and her makeup on now, and she is smiling. "Bring on number 2010," she says joyfully. Another good ad has a pretty mother in the kitchen and about to make a batch of Pillsbury Instant Chocolate Chip Cookies. A little boy with a snowsuit on then starts out the door, saying he is running away forever and the mother says, "Well I guess I don't need to make these Pillsbury Chocolate Chip cookies today, then." The little boy perks up and says, like Cookie Monster on Sesame Street, "Coookies." He races into the kitchen and says, with a great smile on his face: " I missed my plane." This ad is good because the camera stays on the little boy's eye level the whole time, so that we never see the mother's whole body, just the cookie dough and the little boy's face. How many mothers would make these cookies if they thought it would thrill their children so much and make them behave?

Another thing we see in these ads is that the fathers friends while we see a long shot of a country scene with fields, a pretty small town, and church steeples, like a Christmas card. Dubuque hams are made in this atmosphere and therefore taste very good.

Folger coffee – "the freshness hits you" the same way it does the yuppy couple at the breakfast table. Interesting that the man is dressed for work and the woman is in her beautiful robe and nightie.

The kitchen is a designer's kitchen.

In one ad, I thought for once a working woman would be the star. Maybe even a divorced or single woman or one who has children but no husband. The woman is dressed in a suit in the first closeup. She talks about her worst headache of all time and how she has too much to do to stop for the pain of it. Fortunately, she took Excedrin just a few minutes ago, and now she feels great. The camera backs up and what do we find? The woman is in a department store. I think she is shopping, probably for makeup or for her family! What a disappointment. I watched at least 25 daytime commercials and have seen only one woman doing a job outside the home: that was a professional weight-loss

of these perfect families tend to be a little dumb, even though they have perfect families, nice homes, and white-collar jobs. The mother, even the kids, are much more intelligent than the father. In the Liquid Dial ad, a husband keeps saying that all soaps have germ killers because that is what soap is about. As he puts on his tie, he argues (in the bathroom) with his wife, who claims that only this product has germicides. Finally, their beautiful, curly-haired, blue-eyed, blond little boy (about five) tells father once and for all that only Liquid Dial kills germs, and the father accepts it. In another ad, two fathers go running and brag stupidly about how good their sweat clothes smell, thanks to some detergent with a fabric softener. We also have an ignorant man complaining about absorbency in paper towels (his wife points out how cheap he is and how much better expensive towels can be. He is amazed.) Other losers in these commercials are the guy who applauds his wife at the dinner table, the one who brings flowers so he can have a piece of microwave cake, and the one exulting over NyQuil, the
nighttime
sniffling

advisor who used to be very fat (and still looks a little chunky to me).

Quotation from Bartlett's:

"You can tell the ideals of a nation by its advertisements." (Norman O. Douglas, *South Wind,* Ch. 7).

Another one: "It pays to advertise" (Anonymous).

Helen Reddy: "If I have to, I can do anything. I am strong, I am invincible, I am woman" ("I Am Woman," 1972).

Basically these are a mother's jobs: dishes, child-care, home cleaning, baking, staying beautiful, grocery shopping, car pooling, scouting out the newest ways to soften sweat clothes, kill mildew, change chicken, pick up spills, get rid of wrinkles and so on. I didn't see any ads for interesting things like beer, car, clothes, trips, computers, records, books, restaurants, or even television sets or VCRs. This implies that the daytime watchers, which are probably mostly women, are not in charge of the big things families do, or the enjoyable things. They have the grocery budget, and the husbands (dumb?) pick out cars and stereos? There is an

sneezing
coughing
aching
stuffy head
fever
so you can rest
medicine.

If it is true that you can find out the ideals of a country by its advertisements then I guess American ideals include health, beauty, a typical surburban family with some kids and a non-working wife, a successful husband, a beautiful home, possibly a cat or dog, definitely a station wagon, lots of good food and *no* stains, mildew, athlete's foot, spills, wax buildup, wrinkles or bad hair.

Some statements from TV ads in the daytime:

"Hair's the ticket."
"The big tough towel."
"Let the freshness hit you."
"Welcome to Iowa."
"I haven't got time for the pain."

The language on television is definitely different from *Vogue* or the *Wall Street Journal*. Different audiences? Or is this because the products are just different? Or are fashions marketed differently because they have to be made interesting. They are not necessities like cereal and paper towels and medicine.

ad for Lee Jeans ("Made for a woman's body") and one for a movie (about flying saucers).

The women in these ads do not bring home the bacon and fry it in a pan. They buy the bacon with the husband's earnings and feed it to everyone, to much applause. They are somebody's ideal, but how can this be an American ideal in the 1980s?

Anybody who has lived in a family knows that it is good to have somebody who knows how to get stains out, cook good food, keep the house organized. Why in this time, when practically everybody works, is it the wife and mother only who can do these things?

Advertisers seem to know that family women worry a lot and get a lot of headaches. They are afraid of being fat, cooking bad food, having wrinkles, and having hair that looks bad ("Hair's the Ticket" and with Jhirmak you can buy your way to beauty). Yes, advertising pays. It makes us all worry. Which came first, the ad or the worries?

Charlotte's mind is, by now, engaged: her thinking is becoming active and critical as she thinks about her thinking, composing her ideas about the role of women in American advertising. You may have noticed, too, that her thinking has included, quite naturally, all those ways of knowing that we've discussed in this chapter. Sensory knowing, for example, is evident in her response to the elegance, luxury, and freedom implied by the ads in *Vogue,* while physiognomic knowing of a kind is demonstrated in her interpretation of the poses and facial expressions of models. She seems to be doing her own version of "ping" and "pong" when she speaks of the vocabulary of both magazine and television ads ("exquisite," "the hair's the ticket," "Colourant"). Charlotte is also doing elementary interpretation throughout her notebook, as she examines scenes and people for information. What *does* Liza Minnelli seem to be communicating in those three professional photographs? Is she a transformed Cinderella, a world-celebrated star, a "mystical" or "thrilled" woman who "has it all"? What of that woman in the "Applause" ad? Is her first face more indicative of the modern housewife's life than that "blissful" look she has as her family applauds her barbecued chicken? Maybe the large number of ads for headache remedies implies that her first expression is the more accurate one; after all, she is alone then.

Charlotte is construing as she constructs; her constructions, so far, are at the level of dialectical oppositions, as represented by her many questions and by the page itself, still with a line down the middle; they are just now becoming clearly important to her thinking. She notes that *Vogue* appeals to older, wealthier, more elegant women than most magazines and that it seems to encourage shallowness, but at the same time she sees that it carries serious articles on AIDS, the Peace Corps, the environment, art and books. What can be made of a magazine that features both horoscopes and environmental studies? She has similar trouble with the opposition between the American ideal, as portrayed on television, and the American reality of working mothers, broken families, and children who do not always behave well or look attractive. As for "re-cognition," Charlotte's journal is full of interesting examples of how that process works; she judges what she is observing now in terms of what she has observed many times before. She knows that the children in television ads are unreal, that the fathers who do well at work but are stupid about soap are unlikely figures, that the words used in cosmetic ads in *Vogue* are not common words used by ordinary women, that the slim and elegant women who serve french fries probably never eat them themselves.

As she begins to listen in more acutely to her own thoughts, as she encounters and re-encounters her "things," what she sees and thinks will become familiar enough for her to write clearly about them. She's beginning to do what Susanne K. Langer calls "forming." Perhaps the best example is her ability toward the end of the day on October 12 to perceive that the language of the three sources she's studying differs in important ways. She's beginning to make sense of the "blooming, buzzing confusion" she has created in her journal. She has formed some very good arguments already from the dialogue she has been having with herself. She is *composing,* though, at this point, she doubts it!

᭡ 1. What examples can you find in Charlotte's notebook of renaming, redefining, re-composing what she sees?

2. Where is it most clearly seen that Charlotte understands that an "intelligent eye" is the key to both seeing and knowing?

3. Has Charlotte shown any awareness yet of the fact that meanings are relationships? Where do you find examples of relationships seen in terms of space, time, and causality?

4. Charlotte knows that "there must be a means of making meaning." Where does she impose form on her data: that is, where does she begin to organize by means of definition, narration, selective description, classification, cause-effect analysis, questions, comparison, contrast? Do her oppositions make any meanings?

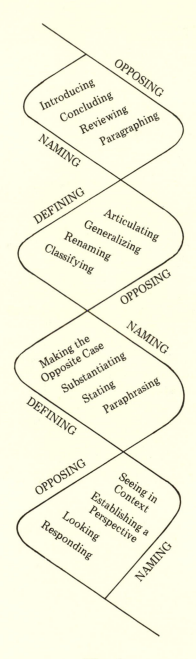

Fig. 1.

III

NAMING/OPPOSING/DEFINING
The Composing Process
as a Double Helix

1. Allatonceness

In composing, everything happens at once – or it doesn't happen at all. We make new meanings by means of old ones; we discover what we want to say as we say it and tell ourselves what it is that we are saying; we continually identify relationships and how relationships relate to one another. And all that thinking and languaging is going on as we are trying to construct sentences and paragraphs. When you learn to write, what really happens is that you learn to let thinking help writing and writing help thinking. The chief reason for learning a method of composing is so that you can learn to take advantage of this allatonceness which, otherwise, is only a source of trouble.

         ༦ How would you say *allatonceness* in any other language you may know? German-speaking friends gave me these translations: *Allgemein-totalität, Gleichzeitigkeit, Auseinandersetzung.* Translated back into English, you'd have something like *altogether-totality, at-the-same-timeness, out-of-each-other-ordering.*

We can represent the allatonceness of the composing process by a model borrowed from biology – the double helix, which is the structure the DNA molecule takes. The chief feature of this model is that at any one twist of the spiral, we meet certain activities

61

over and over: wherever we cut a section, the same things are going on. Whether you're just starting a paper or are about to finish or are right in the middle, there are three things you're doing with language and in your thinking. Call them *naming, opposing, defining:*

- You *name:* you tell, say, show, identify what it is you want to express and convey.
- You *oppose:* you see relationships, you put this with that. An *opposition* is any way something is related to something else.
- You *define:* you say what it is and what it isn't, what it's like, what it goes with, what doesn't go with it. As you define, you get things together and set limits so that what doesn't belong is sent someplace else.

If you look at the model (Fig. 1), you can see how the three activities of naming, opposing, defining hold everything together: the process is itself a sort of structure. The model is meant to be read from the bottom up, but within each space, at every turn, these particular activities can be read as a list either up or down. There's no set sequence because, generally speaking, each one brings the other along with it. Thus you can't actually *respond* without *looking* and when you look, you do so from one or another point of view, in this or that *perspective.* And what you see is in a *context.*

          ❧ Look back over your journal of observations and see if the first turn of the spiral includes everything you did when you started.

One way to see how naming/opposing/defining are all going on at the same time is to look at listmaking – to look again at what happens when you make a list.

2. Listing and Classifying: Purposes and Presuppositions

A list of names is a composition: it presents simple information in simple form. A list names the *contents* or it names the *members of a series.* The table of contents in a cookbook; a label on a paint can; a line-up of ballplayers; a program telling us that the pianist will play first the Haydn E Major Sonata (Hoboken 52) and then the Mozart B Major Sonata, K. 570. These are all lists whose function is to tell us what's *in* something or what comes *before* what.

Such lists don't make very good reading; only compulsive readers study the breakfast cereal box. Most lists are not meant to entertain us, but only to inform. However, a list can become an expressive composition if the form it takes is predominant. If we sense rhythm and balance, an opening out and a gathering in, then we have no mere catalog. The difference between a paint can label and Leporello's list of Don Giovanni's conquests; between a stock clerk reading the shelves and a child's counting game; between a chronicle of "begats" and a creed; between a recipe for fish chowder and a litany, is the predominance of form – the balance, order, rhythm that gives us the sense of a lively whole.

The only use most of us have for a formal list is to help us remember certain items by memorizing their names. Medical students pass on to those who come after them dozens of obscene rhymes whose sound patterns lighten the task of learning, say, the vessels and tissues of the wrist cross section in the proper sequence. In *mnemonic* devices (Mnemosyne is the mother of the Muses and goddess of Memory), the role of rhythm and pattern is to fix the names in mind. The form of the list may please us, but that is not its chief purpose. Other kinds of formal lists might help us remember, but their chief function would be to make us feel part of a ceremony, to lift us out of our private selves and give us a sense of being a member of a community.

To see how a writer goes about creating a form by means of which he can assemble various items is to learn something very important about composing. Lists are composed; they don't just happen.

Isaak Walton's *The Compleat Angler,* written in the seventeenth century, concerns everything you ever wanted to know about fishing and aren't afraid to ask your old friend *Piscator* (Fisherman). Walton's book is about the sport of angling, but it's also a meditation on Man and the rest of Creation, on the beauties of the Earth, the fact of mortality and the promise of eternal life. Walton can go with no strain from a short discourse on the soul to a recipe for carp (stuffed with oranges and anchovy butter). He writes in dialogue form, one of the oldest forms in which philosophy can be written; it's an inner dialogue being brought out into the open. The novice fisherman, who gets hooks caught in his thumb and can't tell a pike from a pickerel, asks leading questions which Piscator then answers with directions and explanations – and recipes. A great deal of information has to be set down, but in a pleasing form. The modern procedure would be to publish the anecdotes in one volume and the "how-to's" in another, but *The Compleat Angler* was written to provide both instruction and delight and to show how they are related. Here is Piscator's catalog of trout flies:

> And now, good Master, proceed to your promised direction for making and ordering my Artificial Fly.
>
> PISC. My honest Scholar, I will do it, for it is a debt due unto you by my promise. And because you shall not think yourself more engaged to me than indeed you really are, I will freely give you such directions as were lately given to me by an ingenious Brother of the Angle, an honest man, and a most excellent fly-fisher.
>
> You are to note, that there are twelve kinds of artificial-made Flies to angle with upon the top of the water. Note by the way, that the fittest season of using these is a blustering, windy day, when the waters are so troubled that the natural fly cannot be seen, or rest upon them. The first is the Dun-fly, in March: the body is made of dun wool, the wings of a partridge's feathers. The second is another Dun-fly: the body of black wool, and the wings made of the black drake's feathers, and of the feathers under his tail. The third is the Stone-fly, in April: the body is made of black wool, made yellow under the wings, and under the tail, and so made with wings of the drake. The fourth is the Ruddy-fly, in the beginning of May: the body made of red wool wrapt about with black silk, and the feathers are the wings of the drake; with the feathers of a red capon also, which hang dangling on his sides next to the tail. The fifth is the yellow or greenish fly, in May likewise: the body made of yellow wool, and the wings made of the red cock's hackle or tail. The sixth is the Black-fly, in May also: the body made of black wool, and lapped about with the herle of a peacock's tail; the wings are made of the wings of a brown capon with his blue feathers in his head. The seventh is the Sad-yellow-fly in June: the body is made of black wool, with a yellow list on either side, and the wings taken off the wings of a buzzard, bound with black braked hemp. The eighth is the Moorish-fly: made with the body of duskish wool, and the wings made with the blackish mail of the drake. The ninth is the Tawny-fly, good until the middle of June: the body of tawny wool, the wings made contrary one against the other, made of the whitish mail of the wild drake. The tenth is the Wasp-fly, in July: the body made of black wool, lapped

about with yellow silk; the wings made of the feathers of the drake, or of the buzzard. The eleventh is the Shell-fly, good in mid-July: the body made of greenish wool, lapped about with the herle of a peacock's tail, and the wings made of the wings of the buzzard. The twelfth is the dark Drake-fly, good in August: the body made with black wool, lapped about with black silk; his wings are made with the mail of the black-drake, with a black head. Thus have you a jury of flies likely to betray and condemn all the Trouts in the river.

This list-maker knows what he's talking about and he knows what he wants to say – a happy state of affairs for any composer. Piscator gets across the general idea of a trout fly by describing in minute detail the materials that it is to be made from and where they are to be obtained, how the parts are to be assembled, and when each fly is to be used. One fly after another is described according to a pattern which makes it easy for the reader to refer to the list to find out *which* fly to use *when* and *how* to make it out of *what*. The list is designed for easy reference and the metaphor that closes it neatly reminds us of the purpose of these twelve flies.

Composing a list involves organizing names according to some purpose. The act of drawing up the list is also a way of discovering purposes. If your shopping list is arranged by stores in the order in which you pass them on the street, then that order will itself suggest items for your list. Remembering that the bookshop is next to Eastern Mountain Sports where you intend – an *intention* is a purpose – to pick up the backpack you've ordered might lead to adding a book to your list; the listing process helped you discover a further purpose: *Pick up backpack* led to *Get spy novel for Shep*.

Purposes generate lists and listing helps discover purposes. Here are some assisted invitations to see how that works.

         ✺ If you know a lot about cars, make a list of what you would want to remember to check or ask about when you shop for a secondhand car. Then make a version of your list for someone who doesn't know anything about cars except how to drive. Compare the two lists: Which is longer? Which was harder to compose? Why?

๛ Everybody makes lists of things to get done over the weekend or on their day off. How do you organize yours? Do you cross off items as you go? Do you *use* the list — or is the list*making* enough? Why make one if you don't use it?

๛ Draw up a Christmas list. Is there any order to it? What purposes have determined that order?

You can think of a list as answers to a set of questions: *purposes* answer *needs*. Here are some lists in the form of a record. They're taken from the pocket diary of a farmer and surveyor living in Dubuque County, Iowa, over a century ago. (He was my great-grandfather and the family legend is that he was not a lovable man, a notion that is perhaps suggested by this record. A.E.B.) From these lists, what can you tell about the needs and purposes of William I. Anderson? Of any prairie farmer in the mid-nineteenth century?

January   Saturday 10   1857
Killd old Dice

Sunday 11
out hunting a dutch gal
got none

Tuesday 13
cheese & crackers   20
staid all night at A.D.A.
Bot corn of Boss Straton   25
Took ADA the 3d load of wood
made 9 dolars

Wednesday 14
Bot lamp & fluid & can   370
Pair of shirts silk   400   Baskett   50
figs   10 cents   Patent leather   25 cents
Ink of Ratory   50 cents   Hood & flannel
for Baby   245   corn of Straton   25
at home   Gerry is off at some
fooll affair at Mikes
went to see Hibrid Woman monkey   25

Thursday 15
off to Moores to swap
otter for corn

January   SATURDAY 10   1857

Killed old Dia

SUNDAY 11

out hunting a dutch gal
got more

MONDAY 12

January   TUESDAY 13   1857

cheese & crackers 2c 20
Staid all night at A.D.H.
Bot cow of Sim Straton 25
took A D H the 3rd load
of wood   make 9 dolars

WEDNESDAY 14

Bot lamp & fluid & can 370
Pair of shirts silk 400 Basket 50
figs 10 cents Patent luther 25 cents
Ink of Ratary 50 cents Hood & flanel
for Baby 2 45 corn of Straton 25
at home Gerry is off at some
ball affair at M Kees
went to see Hibraid woman monkey 25

THURSDAY 15

off to Moores to swap
Otter for corn

January   FRIDAY 16   1857

Bot Davis Pain Killer 25
got the surynge mended 25
corn at Dubuque teak a small
load of curly sugartree wood & Dot
got Dubuque staid at Neely
Aniversary of the Mark
degree for N Wm I A

SATURDAY 17

got mares shod 135 cents
Bot shoes for susand 140
Paid Stouts & co for lumber 1080
Coffee Paid 200 Bbl of Basel
10 gal Molasses 950 & 50 lbs
of sugar 600 dollars did not pay
got home from Nase a little

SUNDAY 18

January   MONDAY 19   1857

TUESDAY 20

WEDNESDAY 21

helpd to bury G Duglass
Bot nails to fix roost
for hens & fixed them

Friday 16
Bot Davis Pain Killer   25
got the suryinge mended   25
corn at Dubuque   took a small
load of curly sugar maple wood   ADA
got Dubuque staid at Neebys
Aniversary of the Mark   degree for Wm IA

Saturday 17
got mares shod   135 cents
Bot shose for Susan   140
Paid Stants & co for lumber   1080
Coffee Paid   200   Bot of Brecht
10 gal Molasses   950 & 50 lbs
of sugar   600 dollars did not pay
got home froze Nose a little

Wednesday 21
helpd to bury G Duglass
Bot nails to fix roost
for hens & pend them

(*Note:* "Ink of Ratory" is shorthand for "Bought ink from Ratory." A.D.A. stands for Andrew D. Anderson, William I.'s brother. The "dutch gal" refers to a servant; anybody who didn't speak English was called "dutch." He found such a young woman eventually to whom he paid $24.20 for working from April 6 to September 25. The "degree" mentioned is a Masonic honor.)

Studying how lists are drawn up and considering the principles by which they are organized can teach a writer some very important things about the composing process.

       ∿ Make up a grocery list and keep it on hand for use during the discussion to follow.

Grocery lists are highly personal compositions. They are often written in a kind of shorthand, a code that saves time but that could cause confusion. A 25-year study of grocery lists abandoned in shopping carts convinces me that few people make out a list which anybody else could safely use.

- Why did you get this flour?
- You said to get flour. That's what the list said.
- I didn't say Pillsbury's.
- I got flour; you said flour.
- Don't you know I always get Gluten Beauty?

- The list said flour.
- Well, I didn't mean just any flour.
- You didn't say that.
  Etc.

A list is a composition even though it's composed with just words, not sentences and paragraphs. The list-maker knows the relationships that those words stand for, the groups and classes and sequences that the list indicates in a succinct and economical way. Each item of a list could be expanded to a sentence:

Rice
Carrots
Green peppers
Tea

"If there are going to be 20 people for supper and I have only $10.00 for groceries and if the cupboard is bare, which it seems to be, I'd better get out the regimental rice cooker and make vegetable curry; tea would be the thing to go with the curry and since I have only a little leftover Lapsang Souchong, I'd better get a quarter pound of spiced Indian: that'll fill them up."

We've found that the composition students who draw up the most efficient grocery lists are householders. An experienced shopper knows how to save time not only in making the list but also in using it. Efficient lists are often schematized according to the area in the store where certain items are to be found; indeed, some lists could serve as floor plans. *(Scheme* or *schema* derives from the Greek word for *shape* or *plan.* Note that these words are both nouns and verbs.)

lemon	p. chips	Thuringer
P.E.I.	gerk	
B. lettuce	kidney beans	hamburger
leeks	coffee	o j
tom	sugar	milk
red onions	spaghetti	Monterey J
	marinara	
pie cr		bread
Ital gr b		

You can read the schematized list as you would a map, orienting yourself at the entrance. If you read up from the bottom right-hand corner and from right to left across the top, with side trips into the center and then down the left-hand column, you will have done a tour of the store, ending at the checkout counter. Here is the list again as a floor plan:

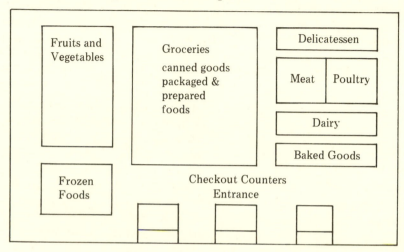

The schematized list/map represents the order in which the merchandise is displayed. And, of course, that order is determined by various requirements and needs, physical and psychological: food that must be refrigerated will generally be along the walls since this is where the pipes and electrical lines are; advertising specials will be placed at various eye-catching points, etc. The merchant/architect/planner organizes the store with various purposes in mind, just as you organize a list with purposes in mind. We find something more easily if we know what we're looking for; both the list and the layout of the store are meant to facilitate that. You can see how this works if you consider how the order of various names on the list offers clues for decoding certain items that are not intelligible by themselves: *lemon, leeks, red onions* help us make sense out of *tom (tomatoes); P.E.I.* is harder, but if you find yourself among the leeks and tomatoes you might catch sight of a bag of potatoes from *Prince Edward Island.*

ॐ Using the floor plan as a guide, decode the other mysteries in our list.

Each of the groups of items is a *class:* when you compose a list, you are *classifying.* A parsnip is a parsnip is a parsnip, but it is also a vegetable. Classifying is *renaming* so that one item can be grouped with others of the same kind. *Vegetable* is a class name given to certain edible plants. A parsnip has characteristics in common with carrots and potatoes and all "such like" that grow not on vines but underground; they form a subclass called *root vegetables.* When carrots and potatoes are grouped not only with lettuce but with pears and raspberries and apples, they are seen as members of a larger class, *fruits and vegetables.* The more kinds that can be included, the more general the class.

Degree of generality	Class-name
general	merchandise, groceries produce
specific	fruits and vegetables vegetables root vegetables
particular	parsnips "this parsnip"

In any kind of list, one word suggests another; one name joins another and another until you have a class that you then name: you rename the names. A class is a form that finds forms — not only members that belong to that class but other classes as well. One thing leads to another, we say; one thing makes you think of another; one class finds another class, not just other members. "Produce" finds not only pears and raspberries, eggplant and acorn squash, but "meat" and "dairy." That is to say, we not only move up and down from particular to general and back down to particular, but we also go from one to another class. Thinking moves in both vertical and horizontal planes.

The names you choose for your classes will depend on the *context of situation.* When you look for parsnips in the produce department, that name is appropriate to the situation: you are buying an item that the grocer finds convenient to keep with other fresh *products* that need to be kept cool and ventilated and sometimes watered. The names listed on a menu, on the other hand, would be entirely different. You would write *salad,* not *produce; creamed parsnips,* not *root vegetables; radishes,* not *fruits and vegetables.*

The reason why a menu doesn't make a very good shopping list is that it belongs to a different context of situation. Suppose that you shop with a menu as your guide: if the menu reads "Hamburger," you first have to translate that shorthand to "dill pickles, catsup, sliced tomatoes, sliced onions, mustard, hamburger rolls – and hamburger." Then you have to disregard terms that are relevant to cooking and preparation only, eliminating any items you already have or adding quantities needed.

      ∿ Translate the names of these menu items into names appropriate for a shopping list:

> Green Salad
> Lasagna
> Ice Cream
> Coffee

You can see that the menu determines the shopping list, but shopping can in turn determine the menu. If the menu calls for hamburgers and you discover when you get to the meat counter that the ground beef is sold out and that steak is $2.99 a pound, that situation could force revision of the menu and, hence, of the shopping list.

      ∿ How can you use the situation (the hamburgerless meat department), the schematized list, and the need for a revised menu to help you save the picnic?

      ∿ For what context of situation would such class names as *protein, minerals, carbohydrates,* etc., be appropriate?

      ∿ Here's a list composed by a student named Rick. How much revision do you think it would need to be ready as a sales guide or a memo to salespeople?

I have to try to sell compact discs to somebody who knows nothing about them, and this is going to be very difficult.
What, dear buyer, will you be wanting to know?
Rick, I want to know why these gadgets are improvements over ordinary stereos and cassette players that I already have.

So, that means, first, that I will discuss the improvement in materials and quality, the tremendous sound improvement, exactly how they work to create a more realistic sound, and the economics of the purchase. I will show:

1. how the plastic and vinyl materials are superior
2. how the manufacturing of these discs, with layers of vinyl, will last for a long time and cannot be scratched
3. how the laser beam is used to split the piece into different layers and the pits in the materials are used, with laser beams, to create different musical effects
4. how the difference between stereo sound and CD sound can be compared with a farmer whistling on his tractor; a bystander could not hear it over the tractor noise but, if it is recorded on CD, with the right adjustments of friction, it could be heard.

For economy, I will have to talk about strength, durability, storage capacity, sales figures, and sound noise ratios. Where did I get that quote: "The CD is the densest storage medium available to man"? Yes, from Julien Hirsch in *Stereo Review* (1986), 52-55.

When you draw up a list, you are addressing yourself to certain needs that can be stated as questions. Thus, *baking soda* on a grocery list is an answer to these questions: "Do I need baking soda? Does that cake recipe call for baking powder or vinegar and baking soda? Is there any baking soda left from last summer when I used a lot on bee stings?" But *baking soda* on the grocery list does not answer questions that are not raised in the context of situation, which is shopping for kitchen and household supplies. It is not, for instance, an answer to the question, "What is the common household product whose chemical formula is HCO^3?" A shopper would have to be able to differentiate baking soda from washing soda, but he wouldn't have to know the chemical formulas to do so.

Any one list answers only certain questions, not all possible questions about all possible purposes it may serve. If we had to take into account every need, we would be fated to draw up an endless list and we might never get anything done because we would never get the list ready. (For some compulsive list-composers, this is precisely the point: lists substitute for actions.) You need to eat, but that need is not part of the context of situation in which grocery lists are composed; it's a presupposition, an assumption that does not have to be proved or argued or deliberately considered.

Leon looked again at his grocery list and noted what it was that he'd taken for granted. Here's his list of the presuppositions of his shopping list.

- that I will be living
- that I will go shopping to purchase these items
- that I will want or need these items
- that I will not be shopping for another week after this trip
- that I am the only one who will be eating the foods listed
- that I can pay for these purchases
- that I will eat three meals per day, plus snacks
- that the amounts purchased are sufficient for my intentions
- that the items listed are available

The presuppositions of a list can be obscure or fairly self-evident. Here, of course, the analyst is the list-maker, so he has more to go on than the list itself in reconstructing the context of situation.

Sometimes you can tell just from a list what sort of person the list-maker is. You don't have to be a Sherlock Holmes to read the items of a list as clues to the character of the list-maker and the circumstances in which he or she lives.

♋ Using your powers of detection, write a characterization of this list-maker.

Shop for supper (scrapple, syrup)
Ask for scraps for Wicked Willie
Renew subsc to *The Friendly Agitator*
Write letters about the bombing
3:30 silent vigil, P.O.
5:00 Chiropractor (phone Marilyn about ride)
Start green afghan for Dan

♋ Mystery story writers have to invent clues to the identity of victims, criminals, witnesses, etc. Make out a list of activities planned for the day so that a detective could deduce three things about the list-maker.

♋ What are the presuppositions of these mnemonic lists? What do you need to know to make sense of these lists?

- *Market, Arch, Race,* and *Vine*
  Chestnut, Walnut, Spruce, and *Pine*

- *Every Good Boy Does Fine*
- *Mark's Very Extravagant Mother Just Sent Us Nine Parakeets.*

∾ Write out the directions for getting someplace by car or public transportation. Assume that the list will be used by someone who is familiar with the area.

Then write out the directions for the same trip assuming that the list will be used by someone from out of state.

Compare the lists: what presuppositions can you identify in list No. 1?

One meaning of meaning is *purpose*. To ask what a list *means* is to ask what it says and what it's for, what purposes it serves. A list can be used to remind you of what's to be done or to record what has been done. When you check off a list, it's like making another list. The composing process involves this kind of comparison between intention and achievement, between purposes that have been fulfilled and those that are still unrealized.

∾ Suppose that you're the chief organizer of a public meeting. You have four committees reporting to you. What are they? Compose the lists they submit to you. Then compose the master list that will guide your organizing efforts. Would anyone else be able to use your master list? Why or why not?

Drawing up a list requires *naming,* of course. As you see relationships and discover further purposes, your list expands. One name/word on the list follows another, suggests another, cancels, supplants, modifies, corrects another: all that renaming involves you in *opposing* – putting things together, seeing them in various contexts. Your list selects and orders and classifies – and all those activities are required in *defining*.

3. Naming and Opposing: Chaos and Dialectic

Listing is the composing process in a nutshell. Composing a list may seem a simple act, something we do rather thoughtlessly; nevertheless, virtually every aspect of composing is represented in listing: naming, grouping, classifying, sequencing, ordering, revising. Each of these operations can involve the others, which is why it's so difficult to talk about composition: everything leads to everything else. There's no linear progress from one step to another in the early stages and no sequential movement is possible at first. A good course in composition could be entitled "Related Everything," because naming implies grouping, grouping implies classifying, which, in its turn, implies sequencing, ordering and revising; revising, of course, suggests renaming, and there we are, beginning the process again. The term we are using for the interdependence of all the operations involved in composing is *dialectic.* Your job as a composer is to guide the dialectic, *just as the sheepdog guides the sheep.* If you can remember that composing begins with naming, which is a kind of defining, and ends with definition, which is a kind of naming, you will have a slogan that can help you keep the dialectic lively.

Getting started in composing means getting names. They don't come out of the air: you generate them in responding to pictures, images, objects, arguments, ideas, questions, answers, statements – to what you see and read and hear and feel. One student got started in a composition course by carrying around a potato for a week and writing about the experience for ten minutes each day. His list: McDonald's, Idaho, world hunger, the potato famine in Ireland, cheap, nutritious, easy to grow, Wisconsin State Fair, salad, root, microwave. This writer is responding, not just to his experiences with golden french fries and potato salad, but to something he read about an effort to make potatoes a staple food in countries where hunger is a serious problem. He even recalls vaguely old family stories about the potato crop's failure in Ireland in the mid-nineteenth century, the beginning of a long and successful history of mass emigration. In one instance, he remembers his dog, left behind when he entered college, and writes testily that "dogs, cats, people, fish, etc. are companions, but not potatoes. Death to this potato."

The names generated for any assignment provide the essential source for a writer; they provide chaos. If this student *had* to do a 500 word essay on potatoes, he might do well, because he already has an argument for potatoes as one solution to the global disaster of famine, and he has a platform too: they are nutritious, easy to grow, and delicious, even if they are bad companions.

Chaos, as your dictionary will tell you, is a state of disorder. As a "thing," the word, in both English and Ancient Greek, means "formless matter." It is *matter,* however, not the nothingness that you find on an empty page. For centuries, chaos has been praised by creators as the "material" necessary for invention of any kind. One author, Tom Peters, in *Thriving on Chaos,* argues that the business world needs chaos in order to move forward. Continual stock market surprises, mergers, new products, technological feats, stiff competition, and unpredictable demand and supply have combined to make business not only a popular major in colleges, but a genuinely-exciting career, full of surprises and opportunities for creative contributions. Other recent studies have shown that science and engineering, too, thrive on chaos. More and more bright young people are choosing careers in those fields because they recognize disorder and formlessness as invitations to an interesting intellectual life.

Here's a good description of chaos from Mary Shelley, the author of *Frankenstein,* who explains in an introduction to a later edition of that famous tale just where it came from.

> Everything must have a beginning...and that beginning must be linked to something that went before. The Hindus give the world an elephant to support it, but they make the elephant stand upon a tortoise. Invention, it must be humbly admitted, does not consist in creating out of void, but out of chaos; the materials must, in the first place, be afforded*: it can give form to dark, shapeless substances but cannot bring into being the substance itself. In all matters of discovery and invention, even of those that appertain to the imagination, we are continually reminded of the story of Columbus and his egg.† Invention consists in the capacity of seizing on the capabilities of a subject and in the power of moulding and fashioning ideas suggested to it.

Invention requires chaos, which is generated by naming, the primary act of creation or composing. In the Biblical account of Creation, the Lord God commands Adam to name the newly-

---

*"Afforded" means "on hand"; the materials must be "there."

†"When Columbus' friends taunted him, saying that discovering America was really easy since one only had to point west and keep going, he asked them to stand an egg on end. They tried but failed. Then Columbus took the egg, flattened one end and stood it up. Naturally his friends protested that they had thought the egg could not be damaged. His friends had assumed for the egg problem limits which did not in fact exist. But they had also assumed that it would not be possible to point west and keep on sailing. This feat of navigation seemed easy only after Columbus had shown that their assumptions were imaginary." [Edward de Bono, *The Use of Lateral Thinking* (London, 1967), pp. 88-89.]

created beasts; it's a way of saying that language and creation enter the world at the same time.

You get started by naming, but remember allatonceness: when and as you name, you are composing; when you work out oppositions among the names, you are forming; when and as you form, you are making meanings. Naming gets you started, but it also keeps you going. Your ideas grow and develop with naming and opposing; defining comes as you rename. Allatonce you are making meanings, which are your means of making further meaning.

Some writers who compose on a word processor feel liberated when they discover software that allows them to note and keep track of what comes to mind, whether or not it belongs in the main drift of what is being "processed." But they didn't have to wait for the computer to liberate them: a dialectical notebook is the best software you could find, because it helps you teach yourself to generate chaos without fear that you'll never get out of it.

                        ℧ Here's an invitation to explore the uses of chaos.

Fig. 2.

Step 1. Write down at least twenty words at random in response to Fig. 2. In your inner dialogue, you can ask, "What do I see?" and "What does this figure make me think of?" Take five minutes.

Step 2. Across from each noun, set down a verb appropriate to the figure; e.g., *tree...grows.*

Step 3. Choose one of your words and see if any of the other words cluster around it. What context of situation is being developed that allows this clustering to happen?

Step 4. What is the most general name (other than "thing"), the one which could include other names, the way "produce" includes parsnips, pears, lettuce, apples, etc.? If there is no such word in your chaos, can you develop one by combining two or three words which are there? Can you add a new one?

Step 5. Choose two words from the chaos of names that seem farthest apart and write one sentence in which they both appear. Does this sentence create a context of situation or is it nonsense? Why?

Step 6. Can you form two — and *only* two — classes that include *all* your names? (The names needn't be equally distributed.) How would you rename these sets?

Step 7. Using any of your original chaos and any new names generated as you grouped and sorted, write a few sentences in which you consider the figure.

The ways we order a chaos of names are the same as those by which we make sense of the world: we see and know in terms of space, time, and causality. If you check through the words in your chaos, you'll find that every one of them names Fig. 2 as a *spatial* form or a *temporal* form or as something that *causes* something or is itself an *effect*. The spatial form of Fig. 2 is obvious: it has a shape; it occupies space. What kind of spatial form depends on who's looking and what kind of setting the figure is given. The words you set down in your chaos probably include names for that shape like *tree* or *river mouth;* if you have a word like *lightning,* you can see that the spatial form takes on a temporal dimension. A picture or a drawing of lightning records its shape, but it also captures a moment in the passage of time. You can represent a streak of lightning by means of an arrangement of lines, but that pattern also stands for the moment in which the lightning flashed across the sky, the happening itself. Whether the spatial or temporal aspect of a figure is emphasized depends on how you look at it, how you construe it.

Here's Irene's comment on Fig. 2:

Assuming, for the moment, the tree-like qualities of this grouping of lines, the point of convergence (the trunk) is not grounded; it is in a suspended state of imbalance. If incomplete, then this "down" design might be more apropos as:

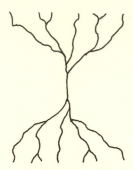

(Grandma Moses was asked how she painted. She answered, "Down. I paint the sky, then the trees, then the land.")

The way you look at something creates a context, and once a context is supposed, further particulars are suggested; that's the dialectic in operation. Matching verbs with nouns is a first step towards tentatively setting up a context. *Tree/grows* suggests, perhaps, other trees. You can set one tree next to another – and another and another; the line of trees is being inspected by a man (or is it a bear?) in a Scout hat with a chin strap; there's a little camp fire smoking in the foreground: pretty soon, you'll have a poster warning of forest fires.

Here are some assisted invitations to construe and construct.

❧ Add lines (all straight) that convert these two lines to a sketch that represents something you could name and that would be recognizable.

❧ What happens to the way you see the figure above when you name a location? How many events can you think of that this figure could represent?

꙼ Whenever you watch something happening, you are seeing/knowing in spatial, temporal, and/or causal terms. Consider how you interpret the trajectory of a baseball; the flight of a broad-winged hawk; the track of a spaceship.

꙼ The more things a figure could represent, the more generalized it is, just as *"produce"* is a more general term than *"fruits and vegetables,"* which is more general than *"apples and carrots."* See if you can develop a term – a word or a phrase – that is general enough to include Figs. 3 and 4 and specific enough to exclude Figs. 5 and 6. Is the term you decide on the same as the one you identified in Step 4, page 79?

Fig. 3.

Fig. 4.

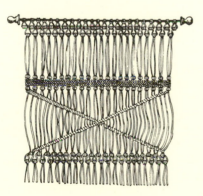

Fig. 5.

Fig. 6.

If you look at a tree in winter, you see both the bare branches and the pattern they make. That pattern is what the tree has in common with anything else that has that shape and structure. The pattern is the figure the tree makes, and you see it precisely because you see resemblances in shape and outline and structure between the bare tree and similar forms. Sometimes the pattern will be more emphatic than the object. If you look down from a high cliff or an airplane and see the mouth of a river, it may look like a triangle; from that perspective, the design the river makes is more apparent than the particular details of mudcracks, marinas, and waves. Indeed, the characteristic shape of a river mouth is called a *delta,* after the Greek letter of that name: △

A bare tree might not look like a triangle because the linear pattern of its branches is more apparent than the outline, but a bare tree does look like a river mouth in which tributaries, however faint, are discernible. The bare tree and the river mouth both have a central element with subsidiary elements going off from it – *branching* off. The class name that gathers these examples and everything else that is organized in this way is *branching system.*

Charlotte, our student writer, might agree with the artist Paul Klee: "I begin logically with chaos; it is the most natural start. In so doing, I feel at rest because I may, at first, be chaos myself." Charlotte is certainly chaos herself at the early stages of her composition on "Women in Advertising" (pp. 28-29). It's not until she generates names by responding to pictures, to texts, to scenarios, to movie and television stars, to assumptions, and to her own responses to her responses that she is in any position to write coherent sentences or paragraphs, much less to invent an entire essay of her own. It's interesting that she avoided reading the texts of ads, preferring the pictures instead, until she found the word "exquisite" and had to look it up, thus beginning a line of thinking that will prove very creative.

Having a chaos of names on hand can save you from neatly ordering a few names into a strict "outline" and starting to "write it up" before you have done any real exploring. If Charlotte, for example, had stopped investigating on 10/5, she would have produced a shallow, and, yes, boring, five-paragraph theme, with three points to make: The *Wall Street Journal* features professional-looking women who probably have MBA degrees, while television likes to show women in nice homes feeding lasagna and Twinkies to their families; *Vogue* is a "good mix" of ads, fashions, features, and entertainment that appeals to the stylish, probably wealthy woman. Her points would have been neither interesting nor accurate, because she simply had not by then done enough naming. By 10/10 (p. 30), you may have noticed, she has come up with some names that are certain to be useful in the future: "glossy" photographs, taste, good bodies, Elizabeth Taylor, "there's another you," "a whole new society of rich," "you don't have to be brilliant." The point is that you should not commit yourself to one scheme, outline, or plan before it is necessary. The aim of composing is not to tolerate or produce chaos for its own sake but to learn to put up with it while you discover the best ways out of it. That can be less difficult than generating chaos in the first place because, for one thing, the mind doesn't like chaos; ordering is its natural activity. A method should help you take full advantage of that need we all have to name, oppose, define, describe, analyze: that is, to compose.

You can think of ordering, or organizing, as a dialectic of chaos and form. Explanations of how compositions get made – whether they are of clay or marble, words or gestures, tones or lines – try to account for the origins and beginnings by finding some way of representing the dialectic. Paul Klee, for example, admits that a time comes when "I squeeze myself into the narrow confines of linear representation," but he waits until he has "a chaos to start with." Translated into more general terms, Klee's description lets us see that a chaos both affords the materials and encourages the ordering process. Could Charlotte have squeezed herself into a paragraph which says that "You don't have to be brilliant to see that these ads try to make you want to change yourself and spend money," if she had not had a disorderly page full of quotations, names, prices, images, pictures, and concepts like health, beauty, style, elegance, wealth, adventure, and love? Not even a fairly minor point, such as the claim that *Vogue* must be aimed at older women, could have been "ordered up" without that chaos of film stars, fur coat ads, articles on IRAs and "how to be fit at forty." A dialogue between a young woman and *Vogue* magazine has clearly been established, and it becomes even more subtle and interesting when Charlotte generalizes about the slickness of the magazine, only to challenge her own ordering by asking why it also includes essays on AIDS and the environment. What seems like a tension brought on by chaos is in fact order in the making.

Further, no one who composes can make meaning until he or she has a sense of alternative meanings. Those alternatives are defined by limits and those limits are generative; they help us in both our thinking and our writing. Just as Klee must work within the "confines" of space and line, so must a writer name, oppose, define, classify, and so forth. These are indeed limitations, but they are also essential to creation, to composing. They are *forms,* and in a dialogue, a dialectical relationship, with your *chaos,* they can be immensely productive.

Peter, whose assignment was to explain *in vitro* fertilization and suggest its implications for both the world today and its future, began with a list of interesting details, examples, facts, images, and opinions. Included were several necessary definitions, some newspaper stories about successful test-tube implantations in England and the United States, a quotation from the Pope on this matter, and a description of the process: "Egg cells are acquired from the female by a laparoscopy, or suction through an incision in the ovary, and then joined in a petri dish with sperm from a male donor. The dish is then placed in an incubator until the 'creation' divides into 8 to 16 cells." On the left-hand side of his dialectical notebook, Peter, a Catholic, wrote:

- man-made means of procreation are non-sacramental
- abortion rates up to 1.5 million a year in U.S.
- When do ends justify means?
- unitive vs. procreative aspects of conjugal sex
- strong evidence that test-tube babies have already encouraged some to argue for a new eugenics where parents can pick their kids' genes
- the test-tube babies are planted in the womb and all but one embryo is later destroyed
- "A noble purpose does not mean the necessary technology will be benign. Some manipulations of life must, over time, subvert our sense of mystery and so our reverence for life." (George F. Will, *Washington Post,* January 28, 1982)

After class discussion of this chaos, Peter added some new material: a long history of the adoption problem in this country (even excellent prospective parents now have a 5-7 year wait, for example); the danger and inadequacy of fertility drugs now available; the weaknesses of artificial insemination programs; the "surrogate motherhood" phenomenon; and some remarks from Drs. Steptoe and Edwards, who performed the first successful *in vitro* fertilization, and from Lesley and Gilbert Brown, the happy parents of Louisa. He had also discovered that more than 90% of these experiments are failures, and thus that there are many more unhappy couples than might be imagined. One of his paragraphs read this way:

Every time an attempt at *in vitro* fertilization is made, the dollars spent not only increase, but the hopes of the couple rise as well. When this hope is crushed by an unsuccessful pregnancy, more often than not, great emotional pain is experienced. They have invested so much time, money, and energy only to find out it was not worth the suffering they experienced. Merle Bombardieri, a member of Fertility Counselling Associates in Belmont, Massachusetts, states: "People can remain in a state of chronic depression they may not even realize" (*Newsweek,* November 30, 1987). This battle with failure, though, is usually taken up again by the couple in the hopes of success. For many, every time is their last and only hope of getting a child of their own.

We have spoken several times of how aspect, context, perspective, and point of view determine the way we make sense of the world. Peter is here attempting to take as many perspectives as he can on his subject and is thus gaining more and more depth as he develops the context in which he discusses it. The final draft of his essay reflected the dialectical process fully, as he tried to balance Dr. Steptoe with George Will, the Pope with Lesley Brown, the gains with the losses, the emotions with the logic, and so forth. He began with the strong opinion that *in vitro* fertilization is morally wrong and ended by agreeing with George Will that it has a "noble purpose" accomplished by a form of "manipulation" that carries with it the potential for great suffering. His last sentence: "The ends seem to justify the means only if, against poor odds, your prayers are answered."

The more you have on your list – the more chaotic your chaos – the more likely you are to represent both your subject and yourself accurately. The richer, the more varied, the more extensive your chaos, the more certain you are to see the form, the pattern, inherent in your subject, even if it's just a potato. With something extremely complex, like test-tube babies, of course, the pattern is more difficult to discern or to create for yourself, but, again, it's the dialectic between chaos and form that gets you where you want to be. Just as Peter strengthened his own judgment by reading and evaluating the opposing views, Charlotte added depth to her work by opposing the ads of *Vogue* to the contents of its articles. Neither of these compositions would have worked so well without those pages of random details, examples, quotations, opinions, questions, images, and expressions of feelings.

If you return to the branching system, you can grasp this important point: from a certain perspective and at a distance, the tree makes a pattern, the river delta makes a pattern; if you come close and have a good look, there will be more than a pattern of lines. A good composition has a pattern that any reader can discern, but it also takes into account mudcracks, marinas, and waves; the coves, the rivulets – and the alligators.

Chaos doesn't come in sentence form: if you stop to compose a careful sentence, attending to grammar and diction – getting the right words in the right place – you might also stop your thinking. When you're generating chaos, it's important to stay close to the words and phrases that come to mind. Stay with them and *write them down as they come.* Then, as you review this chaos of details and generalities, facts and images, you'll be ready to compose sentences. And it's at this point that composing sentences helps to compose thought. That's the dialectic in action: getting your thoughts together as you get your words together in sentence form. The way out of chaos is making statements about your oppositions. A statement predicates, i.e., it says something about something. You make statements by composing sentences about agent, action, manner, and purpose. Unless all of those sentences are to take the form of simple assertions, *This-is-that,* you will need a repertory of syntactical structures – sentence patterns. The reason for having sentence patterns on hand is not to have "variety" but to provide yourself with linguistic forms that can help find conceptual and expressive forms. A repertory of sentence patterns provides you with ways of putting meanings together. Here are a few for you to experiment with:

1. A structure for relating one observation to another. Note that the semicolon acts as a hinge; the sentence pivots at this point.

_____ ; _____ .

- *Trees branch out; so do river deltas.*

2. A structure to relate condition and result, cause and effect.

If _____ , then _____ .

- *If chaos is thought of as a source,* then *it is less frightening to the writer.*

3. A structure for listing and renaming. (The items can be listed as single words or as phrases, as particulars or as specifics.)

_____ , _____ , _____ : _____ .

- *Naming, opposing, defining: these three acts of mind continue throughout the composing process.*
- *The uses of chaos, the tolerance of ambiguity, the ways of dialectic: a writer must learn how to manage the complex relationship of language and thought.*

4. HDWDWW? Specification and Substantiation

Most of the writing you do in course work is not in response to things – objects, landscapes, figures, etc. – but to ideas. Nevertheless, since you don't become somebody else when you sit down to write, it makes sense to claim that what you do when you interpret an idea or a passage of writing is not fundamentally different from what you do when you interpret an object. Writing involves the same acts of mind as does making sense of the world: you construct the same way you construe. When you figure out what you're looking at, you name and compare, classify and rename: you do the same things when you write. Thinking is a matter of seeing relationships – relationships of parts to wholes, of items in a sequence, of causes and effects; composition is a matter of seeing and naming relationships, of putting the relationships together, ordering them.

A composition is a bundle of parts: you get the parts by generating a chaos of names and you bundle them as you identify and rename the relationships among them. Listing is the simplest way to bundle the parts, but when your purposes are more complex than a list can serve, then you need to know other ways of bundling, other ways of organizing chaos. If you're going to explain, describe, define, narrate, argue, or promulge – which is Walt Whitman's word for *promulgate* – then you will need to know just what and how much to say about what. Specifying is the way of classifying, of characterizing what goes in which group; as you specify, you give substance to the general. You can't decide how to go about that by asking, "What do I mean?" That question must itself be converted to more specific questions. Rick, for example, has already convinced himself that many details and concrete images are needed to sell his CDs, while Charlotte has determined that the *Wall Street Journal* will require little space in her paper, since women rarely appear there and, when they do, they project a sharp, plain image of professionalism and intelligence. A method of composing should offer means of establishing context so that you can develop criteria for judging what specification is needed.

The two most serviceable means of generating critical questions that can help you order chaos are very simple and infinitely adaptable: one is asking, *How does who do what and why?* which we will abbreviate from now on as HDWDWW? The other is one you know about: drawing a line lengthwise down the page in order to generate oppositions. Both are means of starting the process of naming and defining and of keeping it going. Answering HDWDWW? will give you names for *agent* and *action, manner* and *purpose;* if names are not in your chaos for substantiating the terms of the question, then you will know that you need to generate them. You can see how HDWDWW? works to guide the process of ordering chaos if you consider the problem of explaining a snowshoe. If you had nothing to guide you but "What is a snowshoe?" you might have a hard time getting started, but generating a chaos and then asking HDWDWW? gives the snowshoe a setting, makes it part of an activity and thus helps you develop a context so you can substantiate, specify, and define. Let's try it.

(*Note: HDWDWW?* is not an acronym, like CATE [California Association of Teachers of English] or HOG [Harley Owners Group]. An acronym is made up of the initial letters of other words and can be pronounced as a word itself, but unless you're a Welsh-speaker, I don't think you could say *HDWDWW* as a word. My intention is that you translate HDWDWW? every time you come across it: *How Does Who* [or *What*] *Do* [or effect, function as, act towards, etc.] *What* and *Why?* There could be two more Ws, but even a Welshman would have a hard time with HDWDWWWW?)

First, a little chaos, generated in response to SNOWSHOE:

SNOW: wet, deep, pretty, cold, white, fluffy
SHOE: foot, protection, Massachusetts, support, boots and slippers, warmth, protection
SNOWSHOE: An old trapper
        L.L. Bean
        Old-fashioned rug beater
        Bear paw
        Rats gnaw rawhide
        Lacquer
        Leather straps
        Sloan's Liniment
        Sport
        Practical

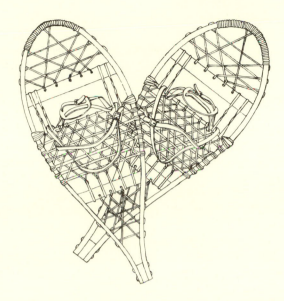

Note how space, time, and causality are represented: there are words that derive from seeing the snowshoe in *spatial* terms: *old-fashioned rug beater* and *bear paw* give us shape. There is a *temporal* (seasonal) term in the name itself. Several names in this chaos have to do with what snowshoes *cause* (aching muscles); others suggest *effects* or what snowshoes bring about or make happen or allow to happen (*sport* and *practical*). HDWDWW? orders this chaos by guiding us in asking these questions:

                WHO   DO

1. How does *the old trapper use* snowshoes?

                WHO

2. How does *L. L. Bean,* a manufacturer of sporting goods

                DO

   and hunting equipment, construct a snowshoe?

Naming an agent (a *doer*) lets us transform *DO* to *use* and *construct.* We can now ask questions about snowshoes as *something used for something* and as *something made out of something* – and we can then answer those questions.

                      USE

3. Why does the old trapper *wear* his snowshoes?
   Whenever the snow is deep enough so that walking is

               DO WHAT   WHY
   difficult, the old trapper wears snowshoes that support him on top of the snow.

4. How do snowshoes support the wearer?
   <small>HOW</small>
   By distributing the weight over a larger area than a regular shoe would cover.

If you combine those two answers, you get this sentence:

Whenever the snow is deep enough so that walking is difficult, the old trapper wears snowshoes, which support him on top of the snow by distributing his weight.

For the purposes of explanation, you don't need the old trapper, picturesque as he may be, so you can generalize:

Snowshoes are useful in deep snow, since they allow you to walk without sinking by distributing your weight over a larger area.

Snowshoes, which are like expanded shoe soles, enable the wearer to walk on the surface of deep snow without sinking.

Your explanation can continue with descriptions you can develop from a question about construction:

5. How are snowshoes made?
   Snowshoes are made of rawhide strips woven into a network in a frame.

   Snowshoes are made by weaving rawhide strips in a diagonal pattern secured by a frame.

   Snowshoes are constructed of rawhide strips woven into a diagonal, open-work pattern anchored to an oblong frame. They have leather straps so they can be tied to moccasins, boots, or shoes.

Rick started his paper on compact discs by imagining what a customer might want to know. Here's some of the chaos he worked from:

How are discs made?
Some key terms to work in somewhere in paper:
pre-master tape
glass mold

laser beam
injection-molding machine
reflective coating; vacuum-deposition method (explain)
aluminum, silver, gold
acrylic resin applied by spin-coating (explain)
ultraviolet light
silkscreening and ink process
quality-testing methods
analogies: high-tech audio pizza, jewel-box, farmer
whistling

molded, heavy-duty plastic in layers; plastic is reflective, has a diameter of 120mm and a thickness of 1.2mm ("Operating Instructions, Pioneer Electronics"); layers: plastic substance, reflective coating, sealing layer (like a pizza's crust, sauce, and cheese); aluminum or gold ions used for covers; digital codes installed in pits along surface; each pit contains "a little bundle of sound," referred to as a decibel or DB; DB levels adjusted to make sound more or less intense; the sound encoded in pits is transmitted to the ear by laser (a single, usually refracted beam of light, which is split into 3 parts). Quote: "The laser light is shown into the pits and reflected by the gold or aluminum ions back to a collection station. The deeper the pits, the less light reflected and thus the less light collected." Put DB chart on left margin.

Who buys them?

Music lovers want CDs, especially young people who like heavy-metal and rock music and need to hear all the instruments and intonations. People who listen to classical music, especially orchestras, want CDs, and people who enjoy music on speakers all over their homes like the feeling CDs give you of "being wrapped in sound."

Do CDs really beat out stereos? How do they?

First, basic records are just compressed vinyl with grooves that are easily damaged. Frequent play guarantees that parts of the record and the needle will wear down and even break off because friction is what makes the record work and friction is eventually destructive. Each playing of a stereo recording reduces the quality of its sound. "In the compact disc, however, nothing but light ever penetrates to the level where the music is stored." Because of protective layers, no human fingers ever touch the actual recording and it is impossible to scratch it (though you can easily scratch the top protective layer, causing no damage to the music itself). More important: lasts much longer, is much less expensive in the long run, and the sound is much more subtle/full/intense. CDs cover a range of 0-96 DBs, stereos only 0-70 DBs. CDs incorporate almost as much as the ear can hear. Very important to the serious listener: the S/N ratio (sound to noise) is much higher in the CD: CD sound is crisp, undistorted.

What makes CDs a good buy?

Besides the obvious advantage of durability and sound value, CDs are economical. They store much more information on them, maybe as much as 100%. "The CD is the densest storage medium available to man." Also work on only one side and are thus more convenient to use.

Why buy now?

Stiff competition lowering prices.
More and more is available on CD.
No need to keep buying obsolete LPs.

Note that Rick begins with more than just "What is a CD?" a question that cannot be answered easily. Generating a chaos and then asking HDWDWW? gives the CD a setting, makes it part of an activity, and thus helps him develop a context so he can substantiate, specify, and define. If you have a paper assignment or a topic you're supposed to develop, you can put HDWDWW? to work right away. Here's an assisted invitation to practice the procedure we've been demonstrating. (This exercise can be done in small groups.)

෴ Write a paragraph on the subject of expressways (or superhighways, freeways). Proceed as follows:

1. Generate a chaos of names by considering spatial, temporal, and causal aspects of an expressway from different points of view. If your chaos is skimpy, close your eyes and imagine an expressway at any time of day or night; at different times. Write down

words and phrases which come to mind as you consider your imagined representation of an expressway.

2. Ask HDWDWW? in order to add to your chaos, giving substance to the terms. Name various *who's* and *what's* and *actions.*

3. Make a statement explaining either agent, action, manner, or purpose. Decide how specific you want your terms to be; practice using different terms. *(The old trapper* or *the hunter-sportsman* or *the wearer? Parsnips* or *vegetables* or *soup makings? Ash tree in winter* or *tree* or *branching system?)*

4. Continue making statements until you have substantiated all the terms of HDWDWW? Do any of the sentences cluster? Can you arrange these clusters? Do you have a paragraph?

Learning to ask *How does who (or what) do what and why?* can help you put your observation skills to work in academic assignments. It will improve your glossing and it can help you get a handle on assignments in which you are asked to carry on a discussion. *Discuss* is a favorite word with teachers, and what they generally mean by it is something like this: "*Look* at this idea or problem or issue or structure carefully; *look again to see how* it relates to others you have studied; *consider* the implications of this particular case, how what you could say of it applies more generally to other such cases."

Suppose you've been asked to *discuss* a certain building which is in the neoclassical style, the kind of architecture frequently found in American statehouses and courthouses. You could begin by doing a contour drawing – or, if you know how, a scale drawing. Or you could simply trace the photograph you're working from. Can you *name* all the structural elements of the building? Do you know what their function is? Can you explain how they do what they do and why? Drawing and labeling your drawing will help you move beyond *How does it look?* to *How is it put together?* The more questions you can ask about *how* and *why,* the more specification you will be developing, the more substance you will be finding.

Discussion requires that you specify and substantiate, but it also requires that you relate kinds of causes to kinds of effects. Asking HDWDWW? is only the start, but it can help to generate chaos and also to provide ways out of chaos by helping you discover new relationships: that's what your instructor wants to read about when he or she says "Discuss."

In relating the terms of HDWDWW? you'll be making statements. Here are some more "workhorse" sentences you can put to use. The examples given of each structure were composed by a nursing student who was organizing a chaos about the question of why she chose this profession.

1. A structure for breaking an explanation down into several parts.

> To _____ , he/she _____ , which _____ , _____ , _____ .

- To satisfy her own needs, Florence Nightingale became a nurse, which allowed her to experience adventure, tend to others, and feel personally accomplished in a man's world.

2. A structure for conveying parallel points or reasons in a series.

> _____ did _____ in order to _____ , _____ , _____ , and _____ .

- Clara Barton founded the Red Cross in order to establish a means of delivering supplies to battlefields, insure that those who most needed tending got treated first, create a method for accounting for missing soldiers, and form a serivce that would bring relief to civilians when natural disasters occurred.

3. A structure for dividing a large topic into smaller, manageable units, with distinctions between the units.

> There are different kinds of _____ , from _____ , to _____ , through _____ , and even....

- There are different kinds of nursing, from the highly skilled work required in intensive care, to the geriatric care given in nursing homes, through the special kind of work required by emergency wards, schools, athletic teams, and, today, even hotels and cruise ships.

4. A structure for interpretation and analysis.

> In _____ , _____ makes it evident that _____ , _____ , and _____ .

- In his statement that young men want mistresses, middle-aged men companions, and old men nurses, Sir Francis Bacon makes it evident that nurturing is a female role in men's eyes, that even being a wife or companion is a kind of nursing, and that men like it that way.

5. A structure for explaining a concept by showing what it is not.

   _____ does _____ , not by _____ , and the result is _____ , not _____ .

- A nurse does the job by being detached and professional at all times, not by being "compassionate" or "feminine," and the result is that nursing in America is an established, respected profession, not just a job for women who yearn to nurture the less fortunate among them.

6. A structure for organized opposing, followed by a gloss.

   Rather than _____ , _____ , _____ , a _____ should _____ , _____ , _____ : _____ .

- Rather than thinking of a nurse as a woman, placing her in a special category as a "nurturer," and expecting her to work very hard for little pay, we should see that nurses are often men, always trained in a degree program, and thoroughly professional: times have changed, and patients should be glad about that.

Getting started on a composition requires knowing how and when to be specific, deciding how general the names can or should be for the purpose and how particularized they might be; and these decisions must be based on an accurate assessment of your audience. Your grocery list can be in code because you're the user, and you can particularize or generalize to suit your needs and purposes. But when you write for a larger audience (or even for yourself at another time), your composition will have to be on its own, so to speak, since you can't staple yourself to the cover sheet or the folder. You have to be sure that when particularization is called for, you'll know how to get down to brass tacks, and that when the subject needs to be defined in "larger" terms, you'll know how to develop the appropriate generalizations. Rick knows that explaining a CD is done for a purpose (that is, selling it) and Charlotte knows that one doesn't compare or contrast advertising styles in a vacuum, to no purpose, and that she must interest her reader in the subject by drawing larger conclusions about the importance of her project. In fact, everything in your chaos, and all the terms that we associate with composition (particulars, cause and effect, generalizations, etc.) imply the presence of a reader who has needs that you, the writer, will meet.

And who decides what is needed by the reader? You do: the composer does. Those decisions are what keep the composing process going. Of course, your decisions can be wrong: the most difficult thing for any writer to realize is that what's written on the page may not represent what's in his or her head. You may have written in a code without being aware of it, without properly translating. In conversation, you have feedback that lets you know: "Huh?" "Whaddaya mean?" "How's that?" "Hey, back up a minute." When you're writing what you have instead of audience feedback is your own inner dialogue, which you can train yourself to hear critically. Rick didn't imagine that any readers would be unfamiliar with shorthand terms like DB, CD, and S/N, or that even a familiar word like "clarity," used in his special context, required some definitions. His first draft was certainly in code. Think of yourself as a teacher and remember the frustration you felt when bad teachers assumed knowledge that you lacked: the computer teacher referring to DOS, floppies and booting, merging, widows and orphans, as if everyone but you was in tune; or the history teacher interpreting the *hegira* or some other obscure event as though knowledge of it were common. When you decide how much to specify and substantiate, criticize yourself as you criticize your ineffective teachers. And listen in.

5. Opposing and Defining: Dialectical Animals

We have been insisting that thinking is a matter of seeing relationships and have been using the term *opposition* to name all forms of relatedness, the ways that things are related to one another. When you write, you represent the relationships you see by means of oppositions. Oppositions can be *opposites,* but for our purposes, an opposition is anything you can set over against something else; anything you can bring into relationship with something else—word/word, thing/thing, member/class, particular/general, name/context, and so on. Oppositions are forms that find forms; oppositions are means of making meaning. In the exercises so far, you have set verbs over against nouns; one word over against those which have clustered around it; and the most general term with the names it has gathered. Your law-ruled paper lets you work with oppositions. Because it lets you see relationships, it can help you get started in the ordering process, developing contexts so that you can specify and substantiate with confidence.

In composing, opposing is the way you get from naming to defining. A definition establishes an opposition of a class and the specifics which describe members of the class. The oppositional character of definition is explained in terms of body and soul by Andrew Marvell, a writer of the seventeenth century:

> Definition always consists, as being a dialectical animal, of a body which is the genus, and a difference, which is the soul of the thing defined.

A definition must do two things: it names the class and it specifies so that one member of the class can be differentiated from another. Here's the structure of a definition:

The Volvo is a Swedish automobile.
Classification: genus: "body" = *automobile*
Specification: differentia: "soul" = *Swedish*

To say that a chair is an article of furniture classifies, but it doesn't define. To define, you need another limit: A chair is an article of furniture to be sat upon. That satisfies because it gives us both the body ("article of furniture") and soul ("to be sat upon").

It's useful to remember that the root of de*fin*ition derives from the Latin word for *boundary*. In defining both words and concepts, you indicate where the boundaries are and what meanings are possible within those limits. Setting the limits is up to you – up to a point. Defining words and concepts is not something you can do all on your own, or if you do, the judgment will be that you are mad.

When Humpty Dumpty explains to Alice that there's only one day a year when you can get a birthday present but 364 when you can get unbirthday presents, he says, "There's glory for you!"

> "I don't know what you mean by 'glory'," Alice said. Humpty Dumpty smiled contemptuously. "Of course you

don't – till I tell you. I meant, 'There's a nice knock-down argument for you'!"

"But 'glory' doesn't mean 'a nice knock-down argument'," Alice objected.

"When *I* use a word," Humpty Dumpty said, in rather a scornful tone, "it means just what I choose it to mean – neither more nor less."

"The question is," said Alice, "whether you *can* make words mean so many things."

"The question is," said Humpty Dumpty, "which is to be master – that's all."

The author of *Alice in Wonderland* and *Through the Looking Glass,* its sequel, Lewis Caroll (Charles Dodgson was his real name), was a mathematician who delighted in the puzzles and paradoxes of the language of signs employed in algebra and other branches of math. In this exchange, he is probably having fun with the notion of declaring "Let $x = 500....$" But what the mathematicians do deliberately, all of us do unconsciously every time we say a single word: A presupposition of every utterance is the comparable notion, "Let the following little squeaks and breathy rumbles represent certain syntactical structures according to the conventions of one language or another." Those linguistic conventions act as constraints when we establish criteria for classifying and specifying in order to define.

Once we're out of Wonderland, the dictionary is, in a sense, "the master": it gives us the conventions in generally accepted forms. But, of course, that's only the beginning. Dictionaries don't grow naturally; they are composed and the definitions that lexicographers list are as open to question as any set of facts is. A lexical definition, at best, gives you only the conventional range of meaning; it can't locate any particular meaning within the range without developing a context. The king of dictionaries, the Oxford English Dictionary, does just that: it cites sentences in which the word being defined occurs, sentences from over 1,000 years of English usage. (The OED is in twelve volumes, each over 1,200 pages.) The only way to understand the meaning of a particular word in a particular sentence is to supplement the lexical definition with a contextual definition.

The main reason for learning something about the formal character of definition is to understand how classifying and specifying provide limits that can help you discover and develop "what you want to say." Remembering that classification and specification operate dialectically can help you resist that temptation to depend on *thing* or to grab at the first word that offers itself as a substitute, without regard for the specifications that are to follow.

A radio is a thing you use to communicate with.

This provides neither class nor specifications. But when you substitute a less general term for *thing,* that class name should match what it is you want to specify. Here, for instance, is an illogical definition:

A radio is a commodity that receives and transmits signals.

The fact that radios can be bought and sold (a *commodity* is such an item) is not an appropriate classification, given the specifications that follow. If you want to specify in terms of function and structure (*how? why?*), then you need a class name that is appropriate to those names:

A radio is a device that receives and transmits signals.

On the other hand, if you wanted to classify the radio as a commodity, then you would need to specify accordingly:

A radio is a commodity that was considered essential in American households of the 1930s.

Sometimes class names and specifications are deliberately mismatched as a means of emphasizing a freshly perceived/conceived relationship. By defining a *chair* as a *machine for sitting in,* the architect-designer LeCorbusier called attention to the fact that sitting can be described as a mechanical operation to which a chair should be mechanically adapted. He thus formed a new concept of a chair and set about designing one to those specifications. You can be deliberately illogical, but you should know that you're doing so.

Another reason for studying the form of lexical (or "dictionary") definition is that that form can find other forms for you. When students of composition fail to ask HDWDWW? they tend towards definitions which simply repeat the class name in other words, without generalizing or particularizing.

Being homeless means having no shelter at all of your own.

This error is what logicians call a tautology. (*Tautology* derives from the Greek for "the same saying.") Breaking out of a tautological circle is easy if you can create a dialectical animal: What kind of thing is it you're defining? What class could it be said to belong to? What is it like? What is not like it? What examples are there of the members of this class?

                ∿ Practice breaking out of the tautological circles below. Classify and specify in a single sentence using a *who* or a *which* clause.

- Warriors make war.
- Fences fence.
- When many people are out of work, unemployment results.
- Writers write.
- Lovers love.
- In a universe divested of illusions and lights, man feels an alien, a stranger.

Definition is simple enough when you're working from *parsnips* to *vegetables, Volvos* to *automobiles, Blackburnians* to *warblers:* to know what a parsnip is means that you also know that it's a vegetable. The trouble for the student of composition (and occasionally for practiced writers as well: ask them!) arises not so much from trying to name the particular example and the class to which it self-evidently belongs, but in knowing how and when to generalize or to particularize.

Learning to use the form of a dictionary definition can help you name the class so that in referring to your subject you won't be limited to renaming with the same word. "The enzyme is secreted.... The enzyme reacts.... The enzyme is important.... The enzyme causes.... The enzyme's sources....": this kind of line-up can be avoided if you know how to particularize, renaming in more particular terms, or when to generalize, renaming in more general terms.

                ∿ A dictionary definition of *bead* reads like this: "*bead* n. small ball pierced for threading with others..." In the paragraph below, a concept of bead is formed. Remembering *produce-vegetable-root-vegetable-parsnip*, see if you can identify four degrees of generality in this description. They may not be explicitly named as classes, but they are implied in the descriptions and comment. Take as the most general class "objects serving practical purposes" and rank three other subclasses in descending order.

Another attribute of the bead is its usefulness as a counting device which can be carried on the person and manipulated where needed. In Chinese stores the world over one can still see in use the box with wire-strung beads which the shopkeeper deftly moves with his fingers in order to compute the price accurately and visibly. The abacus is also widely used in Russia even today. It was for this practical reason that beads became acceptable to that powerful patron, the Church, in the form of rosaries. During the Middle Ages, when the wearing of jewelry as mere playful adornment was frowned upon by the clergy as being frivolous and vain, the bead found a sanctified acceptance, and from this usage we have in fact derived the very word for our subject: for our English word "bead" has come down through the years from the same source as the German word *beten* meaning "to pray," and literally means "prayer" or, as in older English texts, "bede." The rosary, however, was adopted by the Catholic Church rather late in its history (366) and apparently was first mentioned by St. Augustine. The intention in its use was of course that no prayer should be omitted. It was, therefore, truly a counting device, probably incorporated in church ritual in acceptance of an ancient religious pattern, for throughout Asia and the Orient beads have been used as a way of "telling prayers." Marco Polo relates how, between Malabar and Zeilan "where they fish for pearls," "the king has a silken thread around his neck with 104 faire pearles as beads to number his prayers, of which he must daily say so many to his idols."

Joan Mowat Erikson, *The Universal Bead*

ᕦ Below is a list of words, each with three quite different uses (indicated at the right), but also with something in common. Identify what that is and make it the genus/class/body of a definition. Then the differentia/specific/soul will be that which changes. You'll be asking "What KIND of 'thing' is a recipe?" and "What does an object or an act or an idea have to have to do in order to be a 'recipe'?"

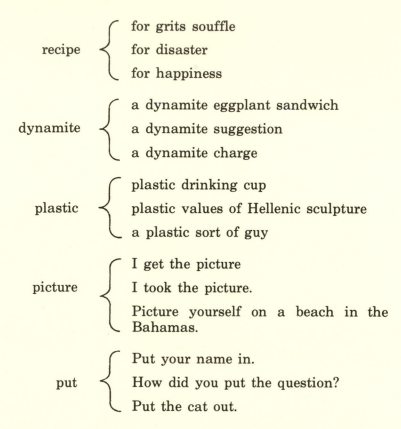

recipe
- for grits souffle
- for disaster
- for happiness

dynamite
- a dynamite eggplant sandwich
- a dynamite suggestion
- a dynamite charge

plastic
- plastic drinking cup
- plastic values of Hellenic sculpture
- a plastic sort of guy

picture
- I get the picture
- I took the picture.
- Picture yourself on a beach in the Bahamas.

put
- Put your name in.
- How did you put the question?
- Put the cat out.

Like every other aspect of the composing process, opposing goes on all the time. Seeing something *with respect to, in terms of, in relation to* something else involves oppositions, the forms of relatedness. Many students have had luck with the "Checklist of Oppositions." Try it on your own writing project, especially if you're stuck, and refer to it for use in the exercises that follow.

A Checklist of Oppositions

1. Is A *the same as* B?
2. Does A *belong to the same class* as B?
3. Is A *beyond, behind, next to, inside, ahead of, before,* etc. B?
4. Is A *the cause of* or *the effect of* B?
5. Is A *a repetition of* or *a duplication of* B?
6. Is A *an example of* B?
7. Is A *comparable in some respects to* B?
8. Is A *a part of* B? Is A *made up of* B?

9. Is A *derived from* B?
10. Is A *the opposite of (antithesis, antonym)* B?
11. Does A *complete* B?
12. Does A *depend on* B?
13. Is A *necessary to the function of* B?
14. Is A *a symptom of* B?

ꝏ Let the Checklist assist you in the following exercises.

1. If A is a trout fly, how many of these oppositions would be useful in describing it? What B's would you choose? Write out a few sentences of description.
2. If A is a front door, how would you explain its relationship to B, a back door? Which oppositions in the Checklist would be useful for this explanation? Write out your oppositions (use your dialectical notebook) and then compose them as a description of a front door.
3. Look up a description of pneumonia in a general encyclopedia and then in a medical dictionary. Taking pneumonia as A, are the B's the same in each case? Why or why not?
4. Using the Checklist as a guide to your questioning, see if you can explain the relationship between the two items in each of the pairs listed below. Write a sentence or two about each; you can incorporate the italicized phrases from the Checklist.

a. intelligence/common sense
b. gun/bullet
c. barn/house
d. ping/pong
e. elephants/blueberries
f. cellar/attic
g. streams/ponds
h. recognition/memory
i. interpretations/war
j. health/sickness
k. oars/paddles
l. time/eternity

Here are two paragraphs written in response to the invitation to think about how to explain relatedness.

Rick's Paragraph

Let A be the CD and B the LP

CDs are not the same as LPs, but actually way "ahead of" them in technical ability and effectiveness. CDs are definitely an effect or result of LPs though, because the faults of LPs drove serious music lovers to demand a better product. Though CDs do maintain all the good qualities of LPs and are "comparable" in some ways, they are not the same kind of thing at all. CDs are in some ways "derived from" LPs but in no ways "made up" of them. In sound, economy, and durability they are truly the "antithesis." CDs may be the "completion" of the sound revolution that started with victrolas and seemed to end with LPs (until CDs were developed, anyway). CDs do not depend on LPs but go so far beyond them that the "sky's the limit." CDs and LPs have the same function, yes, but they have nothing in common anymore.

Kate's Paragraph

Let A be Optimism and B be Pessimism

Optimism and pessimism are not, but also they are, the same ways of thinking. Some would put optimists or pessimists above or below the other, but many, like me, would put optimism before pessimism. I am sure that O causes P and that P is an effect of O. A person may have experiences that cause her to turn into an optimist, but sooner or later has similar experiences that sour her into a P person. These experiences are approached like an O but, when they are over, the person is a P. So A is an example of B and B of A(!), which means that they are "comparable" and that you can be one or the other at any time. Optimism and pessimism seem to be opposites, therefore but are really "made up" of each other, with P being derived from too much O. I am a pessimist about airplane travel, only because my last two plane trips took more than twelve hours, and because of my many previous successes, I was especially sour. I think, though, that pessimism is healthy – it "completes" optimism and depends on it. How can you ever be a pessimist if you have never been an optimist? Optimism is necessary if you want to function as a pessimist. Expect the worst and you know you have a chance to be happy!

∿ Making or identifying oppo-
sitions enables you to classify. In each of the paired
words below, use the opposition to guide you in naming
the class to which both things or ideas or activities
belong. Ask HDWDWW? to generate the words you
need in order to classify.

clarinet/trumpet   chanting/dancing
harpsichord/piano   oil drum/thermos bottle
men/mice   Thanksgiving/Christmas
swimming/flying   development/change
deserts/islands   first violins/second violins
caves/mountains   introduction/finale

Here are two paragraphs for you to de-compose in order to
see how naming/opposing/defining work together. In the first,
George Orwell is describing the Loyalists – those loyal to the
Republic – in the Spanish Civil War. In the second, Elspeth
Huxley develops a concept of some importance in economic
history.

∿ Gloss each paragraph. Draw
up for each a lexicon; identify the principal oppositions;
write out definitions of the concepts which have been
developed.

The essential point of the militia system was social
equality between officers and men. Everyone from generals
to privates drew the same pay, ate the same food, wore the
same clothes, and mingled on terms of complete equality. If
you wanted to slap the general commanding the division on
the back and ask him for a cigarette, you could do so, and no
one thought it curious. In theory, at any rate, each militia
was a democracy and not a hierarchy. It was understood
that orders had to be obeyed, but it was also understood that
when you gave an order you gave it as comrade to comrade
and not as superior to inferior. There were officers and
N.C.O's, but there was no military rank in the ordinary
sense; no titles, no badges, no heel-clicking and saluting.
They had attempted to produce within the militias a sort of
temporary working model of the classless society. Of course
there was not perfect equality, but there was a nearer
approach to it than I had ever seen or than I would have
thought conceivable in time of war.

George Orwell, *Homage to Catalonia*

It is hard for minds moulded by European conceptions to grasp the fact that land itself has no intrinsic value. Every acre in England has its established and often exorbitant price. But the price is not paid for the land itself, for the particles of silica and the humus. You pay money for two things – for the advantages of living closely packed among your fellows and for the labor of men long since dead who owned the land before you. The most valuable land is that in the heart of great cities. The further away you go the cheaper it becomes. Its price is mainly determined not by fertility or rainfall but by its nearness to markets and amenities.

Elspeth Huxley, Lord Delamere

Oppositions can also help you organize the terminology of a subject. You can't any more write about Third World countries by talking about how "they" face "problems" than you can properly describe the repair of a bicycle over the phone with such terms as "what's-it" and "thingamagig." The organization of a terminology according to what it names is a *taxonomy*, a schematization of class and subclass names. *Taxonomics* is especially important in the natural sciences where a tremendous amount of information must be classified; indeed, until the middle of the last century with the development of different methods and fundamentally different questions, taxonomics constituted science. Studying biology or botany meant learning how to categorize various specimens – examples of the membership of a certain subclass. Here's what the taxonomy of the horse looks like:

Kingdom:	Animalia
Phylum:	Chordata
Class:	Mammalia
Order:	Ungulata
Family:	Equidae
Genus:	*Equus*
Species:	*Equus caballus*
Breed:	Percheron

℞ Work out a "taxonomy" for a canoe or your favorite car.

The role of a taxonomy in the natural sciences is to offer a set of limits that guide choices as you follow a procedure that will lead to identification and definition; it provides a schema that makes it possible to organize data; it is an organizational form that helps you find particular forms. Two examples of taxonomic form are the botanical key and the flow chart used in a chemistry lab. Both are organized on the principle of *binary opposition*. The choices are made between two and only two alternatives: the stem is *either* round *or* triangular; the filtrate is treated with *either* a sodium chloride solution *or* a silver nitrate solution.

Here's an exercise in binary sorting and gathering.

❧ Generate a chaos of 20 animal names. Then form two sets into which *all* animals in your chaos can be fitted. You may have to resort to empty sets, e.g., *Tails/No Tails.* (Ginny decided on *Salads/Not-Salads:* tuna and turkey in *Salads;* lions and tigers in *Not-Salads.*) A good way to get started is to ask who needs to know.

Taxonomics by itself wouldn't be of much use; you also need to know how to use the terms, both to discover and to remember, to invent and develop. Taxonomics without field work – getting the facts – is unreliable; field work without taxonomics would be meaningless, since there would be no way of establishing or defining relationships, even if you could see them. Creativity in any art or science, craft or trade, is best defined as a capacity to respond to the ordinary in such a way as to be alert to the extraordinary: to identify the usual means knowing very well what to expect rather than being anxious to categorize dogmatically. Being tentative about taxonomy is the same thing as being sensible about any kind of limits – neither fearing nor rejecting them, but learning their uses.

It's instructive to consider the way a novice birdwatcher uses the limits provided by ornithological taxonomy, in contrast to the procedure of an experienced birder. The double page in a field guide showing "Warblers in Their Winter Plumage" is very depressing to the novice: 27 little heads in profile, all apparently alike but each with a different label. But this fact of seeming identity is exactly what delights the experienced birder with a life list of 400 birds. The novice may stare hypnotically at the warblers, memorizing the differentiating marks that can be discerned upon close inspection. But once the birder is in the field, how are such details to be remembered? The novice believes that she has just sighted an extremely rare bird because memorization of length of tail, colors of wing linings, presence of eye stripe, etc. has proceeded without regard for song and flight characteristics and with no attention paid to habitat. The experienced birder knows not to expect a Manx Shearwater on the Mississippi River or a Mallard on the open sea. On the other hand, she has the taxonomy in mind so that if a bird appears bearing certain very precise markings and behaving in a very distinctive manner, it can be identified, regardless of the fact that it has no business being where it apparently is. The novice sees the commonplace as the marvelous, but the experienced birder sees the marvelous among the commonplace.

      ꕔ Birdwatching involves the active mind at work naming and defining. The same is true for playing or watching a sport or game. Write a couple of paragraphs about the relationship of knowing the rules to enjoying the game, either as spectator or as player.

Recapitulation

To summarize the important points about getting started, we give you a list of our own:

1. This method allows you to keep things tentative so that you don't jump to conclusions or generalize too quickly.
2. This method encourages you to explore relationships in order to discover what you mean, or may find you mean.
3. Naming and opposing are your means of making those meanings. As soon as names begin to cluster, chaos is being shaped.
4. That clustering is itself a kind of classification; it's like gathering fruit and vegetables and laying them out under a sign that says "produce." It allows you to *produce* (using another pronunciation and another sense of the term), because, like a painter, you may now use your materials to draw a circle or a line around the items on the list that will make up your composition.
5. Drawing those lines, mentally, or physically with your pen, is a way of making a clear statement that those items go together, are bundled, for some reason or other.
6. That reason — or those reasons — have to do with your purposes in composing. From naming to defining by way of

opposing – relating – is a good way of thinking about the composing process, if you remember that defining leads, dialectically, to further naming, further purposing, further opposing. You let what you say discover what you mean.

7. What you mean is determined by the naming and defining you do as you make sense of your materials, and as you, inevitably, rename and redefine them from different perspectives, aspects, contexts, and points of view.

8. This method of composing will help you keep the dialectic alive and moving forward. You can take a general idea and bring it down to earth with lots of naming – examples, quotations, dictionary and other definitions, narratives, demonstrations, etc. – just as you can convert a generalized figure – a design – to a particular object by looking at it in a certain way, by incorporating the mudcracks, marinas, and waves.

9. A final motto (a long one):

Composing always involves both generalizing and exemplifying; both classifying and specifying. Deciding on the degree of generality is central to the composing process. The more details you develop, the more particular the form becomes; the fewer the details, the more general. That tradeoff is the dialectic in operation. It's not something you decide ahead of time; these are decisions you make in the course of writing.

KOREN

"Young man, at table you either particularize or generalize, but not both."

IV

FORMING CONCEPTS

1. Generalizing and Interpreting

Language can express ("Ouch!") and indicate ("There it is."), but its chief function is to give form to feelings and ideas, which it does by representing them, by re-presenting them. The form of language finds the form of thought and feeling; those forms then find further language. By re-presenting our thoughts and feelings, we make meaning.

Thinking is implicit in the very act of naming. Every time you name something *A,* you are simultaneously seeing its relationship to something else; you are differentiating and classifying. If it is *A,* it is therefore not *Not-A;* if it is *A,* then it must be recognized as a *kind* of thing. The most important fact about language is that we identify and classify at the same time. Naming means identifying, which is inconceivable without classifying. You tell what something *is* by seeing what it's *like,* what it goes with. Naming involves, simultaneously, the identification of a thing and the recognition of the *kind* of thing it is. As soon as we say, "This is a tree," we imply, "This is the kind of thing a tree is." A *kind* is a *class.* This is the reason for saying that naming both creates chaos and discovers the way out of chaos. As you figure out how one thing is related to another, how one name is related to another, seeing how things and words can be grouped, you are necessarily comparing and differentiating, deciding in which respects they are similar and in which they are dissimilar.

You don't have to learn to do this: you're born knowing how; it's the way your mind works. But as a student of composition, you have to learn how to put those natural facilities to work in organizing names into sentences and sentences into paragraphs. Here, again, you don't have to invent the means because the structure of language itself is what allows you to get from name to name. It's the discursive character of language – its tendency to "run along," which is what *discursive* means, gathering words to words, attaching groups to groups – which allows you to make meanings and thus to order chaos. When it comes to writing, you compose statements that represent your thinking; in the process, you are making meanings. Both the way you think and the way language works make that possible: language is a form that finds thought, and thought is a form that finds language. That is the dialectic of composing.

The composing process of naming, opposing, defining involves you in *forming concepts*. A concept is a supername. Logicians define a class as "the field of a concept's application." You can think of a concept as the name of a class. Forming concepts is a dialectical operation: concepts don't just "have" meanings; they are our means of making meaning. Forming concepts is not something you do before you write. ("How are you coming with your paper, Abner?" "Oh fine. I've thought it all out and tomorrow I'm going to put in the words.") A concept is like a hand that gathers; it is also the handful. Here's how it works:

- What's that?
- A boomerang.
- What's it for?
- Fun. It's for fun. You throw it and it comes back.
- Well, how does it work?
- It's like a foil. It's a wind foil.
- Like an airplane wing, sort of?
- Yeh, except it's all wing. The curve, the way it's made, determines the flight path so that it doesn't just keep going; it curves back.
- I'll bet you can't throw it around in your backyard.
- No way. This old football field is the only place. On the beach, it might hit somebody.
- You could hit me!

The inventors of the boomerang were the Australian aborigines. If HDWDWW? were directed toward an Australian bushman, the answer might be in narrative form, a telling rather than a definition. Or it might be wordless: a demonstration would serve. From a different perspective, HDWDWW? would generate different answers, but the appearance of the boomerang, its shape and construction, would obviously not be changed by one description or another.

But now consider what happens if *boomerang* is taken to refer not to the thing but to what it does. Not just boomerangs boomerang. As a verb, *boomerang* refers not to shape but to the kind of action in which something is thrown out, only to come back at the thrower in a surprising and generally sinister way. Remarks and good deeds and a solution to a problem can be classified as things that boomerang. Boomeranging gives a name to the action of going-out-and-coming-back-towards-you-on-its-own; and it gathers up examples of that action. Boomeranging is a concept because it provides the limits that guide you in classifying and exemplifying, the criteria by which you can judge how something resembles something else.

Here's a philosopher's explanation of how we form a concept:

> Consider...how many motions follow the general pattern called "oscillation." The swing of a pendulum, the swaying of a skyscraper, the vibration of a violin string over which the bow is passing, the chatter of our teeth on a cold day – all these are examples of the type-form called "oscillation." Now, if we were to define this type-form, we would omit all reference to skyscrapers and fiddle-strings and teeth, and describe it, probably, as "rhythmic motion to and fro," or in some such terms that would connote only the *sort of motion* we are talking about and not the *sort of thing that moves.* Probably each of us has learned the meaning of oscillation through a different medium; but whether we gathered our first idea of it from the shaking of Grandpa's palsied hands – or from the quiver of a tuning fork – or from the vibration of a parked automobile with the motor running – however our *mental pictures* may differ from each other, they have one thing in common: they are all derived from some rhythmic motion to and fro. The things exemplifying this *type* of motion are not necessarily alike in other respects; the swaying skyscraper and the vibrating violin-string are certainly not alike in appearance, origin or purpose. But their motions have the common property of going rhythmically to and fro. This property is the *logical form* of their motions, and so we may call all these motions diverse instances of the same form.
>
> When we consider the common form of various things, or various events, and call it by a name that does not suggest any particular thing or event, or commit us to any

mental picture – for instance, when we consider this common form of various movements, and call it by a name such as "oscillation" – we are consciously, deliberately abstracting the form from all things which have it. Such an abstracted form is called a *concept*. From our concrete experiences we form the *concept of oscillation*.

Susanne K. Langer, *Introduction to Symbolic Logic*

The organized comparing by which you discover "the common form of various things" is called *generalization*. When you use the abstracted form to identify further examples of the concept, this is called *interpretation*. You can go "up" from individual events, objects, activities to the idea that they could be said to represent – or you can go "down" from the abstracted form to the particular instances. Forming concepts involves moving in both directions. You can't form a concept until you know how it might apply, nor can you gather up examples and instances unless you know what they might be examples of. The composing process is dialectical: how can you know what you think until you hear what you say? How can you know what things belong together until you have an idea of what they have in common? How could you know what might be the common characteristics unless you had an idea of their commonality? Forming concepts is a circle all right, but not a vicious circle; it's a methodical circle:

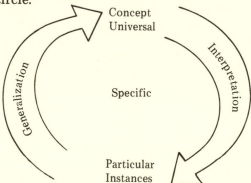

Concept
Universal

Interpretation

Specific

Generalization

Particular
Instances

Here's how generalizing and interpreting work together to form the concept of *city:* When you note that everywhere you go in a certain kind of place there are streets, you are generalizing, since any one street might look very different from the others. In generalizing, you note what is similar in a number of streets – forms that you recognize as being *different* from, say, open spaces. You note a general character as represented in particular streets. Then if you note that in other places there are also many streets, you can conclude that places-with-many-streets form a class that has the conventional name of *city*. As you discover that there are several such characteristics notable in every city you visit, that there are several general statements that hold true for the class of places named *city*, then by this organized comparing you are forming the concept of *city*.

Now then, suppose you have limited the field of application of the concept *city* by listing ten characteristics and that you begin to study the cities of China and India: what if only five of your general statements hold true for these new examples? By generalizing, you have formed a class, but in using this class-concept (the concept is the name of the class) to guide your investigation of other possible members of the class, you see that membership "rules" don't apply. You have two choices: either you deny membership to the new samples or you change the rules to allow entry. You could decide that in order to be classified as a city, a place need have only five specified characteristics, thus changing the criteria for membership in that class; or you could keep the specifications and decide that the conglomerations you've been studying aren't eligible for membership in the class "city." Forming concepts requires not just one such adjustment of class-name and specifications, but a continuing operation of naming and defining, renaming and redefining.

You form a concept by generalizing from particular examples and by interpreting those examples and others in the light of the class-concept you have formed. This process of forming should be kept dialectical because if you decide too quickly or too absolutely what belongs in the class, you lose the chance to discover ways in which the class itself could be changed in order to accumulate further interesting and important examples. It isn't a tick-tock, tick-tock operation. Each time you examine another instance and decide about where it goes or if it goes, you are evaluating both the class-concept and the particular object, event, thing, or word you are trying to place.

This dynamic character of concept formation means that you can't expect the dictionary to do much more than establish the outer limits. If you're writing a paper on revolution or urban renewal or on the allegation that women have been subjugated by religion, the dictionary can't offer much help in deciding what contexts are appropriate or what happens when one word is juxtaposed with another. The dictionary could tell you what the word *subjugate* means, but the concept of *subjugation* has to be critically analyzed in context: Who is using the word? About what? With what purposes? Using which examples? And so forth. "Webster tells us..." is an opening that can't help you know what to develop next, and it certainly doesn't engage your reader in the kind of dialogue that makes your composition interesting or persuasive. A dictionary definition can help you determine the presuppositions; it can encourage you to look at the history of the word in considering the range of its meanings; the listed antonyms can help you decide what it is you are not talking about so that you can build the opposite case. A dictionary definition indicates the range of meaning, but it's only by a process of organized comparing that you can explore that range. You can't make meanings unless you form concepts, and that involves you in generalizing and interpreting; in gathering examples and seeing how they are related to one another and to the class to which you are tentatively assigning them; in moving from the conceptual term to the field of its application and back again.

　Defining the term *aircraft* is something the dictionary does by setting the limits of what the word can mean, but seeing how the limits apply – interpreting those meanings – is something else. It requires that sorting and gathering that we've been calling concept formation. Watch how it works with *aircraft*. With that term you can gather up a Piper Cub, a Boeing 747, a DC-10, and a Messerschmitt. You can then use *aircraft* to help you find other examples of a somewhat different kind: balloons and zeppelins form a subclass of the class *aircraft: wingless aircraft*. But then there is the problem of how to classify something that has wings but no motor: would gliders go with balloons and zeppelins or with the 747 and the bomber? It depends on you; that is to say, it depends on how you are limiting the subclass, whether it is to include only things that fly, with or without a motor, and do not have wings, or if it is to include things that can have motors and which may or may not be winged.

　In classifying and in developing subclasses, it's the criteria of the one doing the classifying that determine how the items are to be sorted and grouped and gathered. There are constraints, of course. If you decided to classify as aircraft flying things that have wings and feathers and feet and that utter loud squawks, you would either be setting up as a cartoonist – a plane can be made to resemble a sea gull – or you would have to be considered as an inhabitant of Wonderland where meanings are determined solely by individual decision: the usually accepted criteria for defining aircraft include the fact of the object being man-made, mechanical, and nonnatural. You could include a herring gull with the 747 and the balloon, if you broadened the field to include *flying objects*. But you might be surprised to discover, then, that that class could include rolling pins, baseballs, UFO's, and Superman, as well as herons and plovers. Your choice would then be either to modify *flying objects* by adding an adjective and thus restricting the limits of the application of the concept or to abandon *flying objects* as too wide-ranging.

This schema represents the stage we've reached:

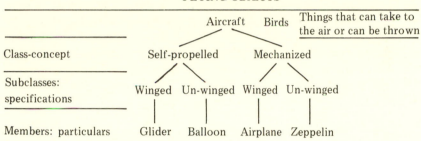

FLYING OBJECTS

	Aircraft	Birds	Things that can take to the air or can be thrown
Class-concept	Self-propelled	Mechanized	
Subclasses: specifications	Winged Un-winged	Winged Un-winged	
Members: particulars	Glider Balloon	Airplane Zeppelin	

Checking particulars by specifications and specifications by classifications reveals some illogical relationships here. First of all, gliders and balloons are correctly differentiated – one has wings, the other doesn't – but gathering them both under "self-propelled" creates a difficulty, since a balloon, although it doesn't have a motor, does have either hot air or gas and therefore is not "self-propelled" in the same way as a glider, which does not depend on anything but air currents. Gathering both glider and balloon under "self-propelled" makes it possible to see that the subclass is not well-defined. There are also difficulties with the classes: some birds are flightless, and "things that can take to the air or be thrown" includes so much that it can't be considered the same kind of class as Aircraft and Birds; indeed, it is simply another way of saying "flying objects." It doesn't limit "flying objects," and if it doesn't set limits, it can neither classify nor define. We can extend definitions to accommodate what we think we want to classify (the phrase used is "by extension"), but unless there is a limit, a definition can't function.

Aircraft is not the kind of concept that will give you trouble in writing papers, but if you can learn to listen in on the inner dialogue in progress when you are figuring out how such a simple word is defined, you'll be learning something about the operations involved when you're defining classes, which is what we've been calling concept formation. Sometimes a word phrase will look fairly simple; take *antiballistic missile.* You can look up *ballistic* and *missile* and by reading *anti-* as *against,* can develop a sound definition of an antiballistic missile as a defensive weapon used to defend against offensive missiles. But when you come to explain the antiballistic missile, you'll need to go farther in exploring this concept of a defensive weapon. You'll discover that if a government decides to build a great many antiballistic missiles (ABM's) or to deploy defense systems in space, such acts can be interpreted as development of offensive strength because they could signal a change from the *strategy of deterrence* – neither side will use thermonuclear weapons because each would suffer *unacceptable casualites* – to a strategy in which one side might plan on a *first strike capability* with an ABM defense system to protect against *the enemy's retaliatory response.* Each of these italicized phrases names a concept that has a complex field of application. After further analysis, you could well conclude that, in strategic terms, an ABM can be interpreted as an *offensive* weapon.

Here's how Charlotte uses a formal classification scheme at this point in her composition.

Women in Advertising

Class concepts:
> women as professionals (*Wall Street Journal*)
> women as wives, mothers, homemakers (daytime television).
> women as socialites and beauties (*Vogue*)

Subclasses: specifications

> Professional women:
>> skilled
>> professional
>> advanced degrees
>> good business people
>> cool under pressure
>> up-to-date and in-charge

> Wives, Mothers, Homemakers:
>> motivated to do housework

skilled with children
good shoppers and budgeters
excellent spouses
good cooks
good nurses (except when they are sick themselves)

Socialites and Beauties:
stunning to look at
exquisite makeup and hair
expensive, unusual clothes
slim bodies
middle-aged
fairly wealthy
interested in improving themselves

Members: Particulars

Ads for professional women
Computers (Macintosh, IBM, Apple, Teledyne,
Mitsubishi)
PR and Consulting Firms (Johnson and Higgins)
Banks (Manufacturers Hanover, Chase Man-
hattan)
Industry (Phillips Petroleum)

Ads for wives, mothers, homemakers
Food (Pillsbury Instant Chocolate Chip Cookies,
Applause by Kraft, On-Cor Lasagna, NutraSweet,
Dubuque Ham, Ore-Ida Microwave Fries)

Cleaning products (Dial germicidal soap; Bounty
paper towels; Bounce fabric softener)

Medicine (NyQuil, Midol, Excedrin)

Ads for socialites and beauties
Cosmetics with famous beauties (Linda Evans
and Ultress Colourant, Liza Minnelli and Revlon,
Elizabeth Taylor and Act II, Catherine Deneuve
and Deneuve).

Fur coats: Revillon, Grosvenor, Adolfo, Collection
Internationale, Fendi.

Particulars about particulars

> *Wall Street Journal's* ads treat women as equals
> and show them in ads with men as if they belonged
> there, with men, beside computers or behind desks.
> Women in these ads are executives, consultants,
> trained pros.
>
> Daytime television advertising pictures women as
> very competent in their private lives. They know
> all the latest products in every area and can solve
> any problem at home, including sickness, dirti-
> ness, dandruff, boredom with food, busy schedules,
> and, of course, stains and mildew.
>
> *Vogue* ads seem to say that we should be "all we
> can be" and they tell us that the key may be hair,
> or it may be "hosiery," or it may be jewelry or a
> fur coat. The main things, definitely, are makeup
> and clothes. "The foreigner the better." 75 out of
> 90 ads are for products named things like
> "Lancome," "Cache," and "Dior."

ᖇ The following words name
complex ideas: *people, defense, welfare, liberty, posterity.* The dictionary will define these words by giving
you the kind (*kind* is another word for *class*) of idea the
word names and the range of meanings it has by
examples of how the word is used. A dictionary definition classifies and specifies the meaning of a word.

When you form a concept, you do the same thing
with ideas as the dictionary does with words: you
develop an idea of how an idea works by showing what
kind of idea it is and how many different varieties/
cases/instances/specific examples there can be of this
idea. You formed the concept of a branching system in
studying Fig. 2, the "bare tree in winter" which was
also a "river delta," etc.

1. Look up the words listed above in a dictionary. Using your
   dialectical notebook, comment on the definitions. Ask
   HDWDWW? and note your own ideas about these ideas.
2. Read the Preamble of the Constitution of the United
   States, which follows:

   > We, the people of the United States, in order
   > to form a more perfect union, establish

justice, insure domestic tranquility, provide
for the common defense, promote the general
welfare, and secure the blessings of liberty to
ourselves and our posterity, do ordain and
establish this Constitution for the United
States of America.

3. Take note of the words you have defined and comment on
how they are used in the Preamble.
4. Choose one of the words and, drawing on all the defining
you've done, form the concept which it names.

ᖇ If you've been using your
dialectical notebook in a lecture course, review what
you have so far in the way of definitions. Have any of
these defined terms emerged as concepts in the course?
If, for instance, *evidence* has been defined, can you
form the concept of evidence by generalizing and
interpreting on the basis of your notes?

ᖇ Here's a famous definition.
Work out a schema to represent the generalizations
and specifications.

Let us define a plot. We have defined a story as a narrative
of events arranged in their time-sequence. A plot is also a
narrative of events, the emphasis falling on causality. "The
king died and then the queen died" is a story. "The king
died, and then the queen died of grief" is a plot. The time-
sequence is preserved, but the sense of causality over-
shadows it. Or again: "The queen died, no one knew why,
until it was discovered that it was through grief at the death
of the king." This is a plot with a mystery in it, a form
capable of high development. It suspends the time-sequence,
it moves as far away from the story as its limitations will
allow. Consider the death of the queen. If it is in a story, we
say "and then?" If it is in a plot we ask "why?" That is the
fundamental difference between these two aspects of the
novel. A plot cannot be told to a gasping audience of cave
men or to a tyrannical sultan or to their modern descendant,
the movie public. They can only be kept awake by "and
then – and then – "; they can only supply curiosity. But a
plot demands intelligence and memory also.

E.M. Forster, *Aspects of the Novel*

Any person, place, or thing, is like some other person, place, or thing, no matter how "unique" he, she, or it may appear. Any thing can be seen as an example of an idea, a principle, an attitude, judgment, or a state of affairs. You can look at an empty refrigerator, a crowded expressway, a television commercial, a milkweed pod, or a compact disk and say "Well! It just goes to show...." Or you can take any conceptual term – the name for any complex idea – and find or create a particular representation of it. What a writer must learn is to be a creative and critical thinker: he or she will have to know how to keep the generalizing and interpreting in a lively dialectic. If you simply keep generalizing, the reader will be unable to say what you're talking about, and if you give him strings of examples, the response is likely to be "so what?"

When you read/construe, you do the same things as when you write/construct: you are forming and thinking. Here's what's involved:

naming/opposing/defining
asking and answering HDWDWW?
generalizing and interpreting
classifying, specifying, particularizing
paraphrasing and identifying the opposite case.

       ✍ Here's an assisted invitation to form the concept of a place. As you read/construe the following passages in which the West of Ireland appears, you'll be asking what *kind* of place the West of Ireland is and you'll simultaneously be using that recognition to sharpen your sense of this particular place; as you write/construct, you'll be naming, re-naming, characterizing the kind of place the West of Ireland is. Write two paragraphs in which you form that concept. (This exercise works well in small groups.)

1. V. S. Pritchett, in this first passage, manages just about everything a writer ever does: he describes and generalizes, interprets and defines, setting forth a point of view that he then supports with facts and explains with his own interpretations. He names and develops oppositions, expressing personal opinions and general truths. By the end, he has established limits so that he can continue his interpretations and generalizations. In short, he has formed a concept.

In these western solitudes, where the sky puts on an even wilder show than it does over the Irish Sea, where the long twilight is like an evening in the theatre, the people have several kinds of foreignness, for Ireland is more Irish, less Cromwellian,* less genteel. People still talk of Cork men, Galway men, Limerick men, with a certain note of tribal mockery and touchiness in their voices. "Cork men hang together," says a Galway man in the voice of one preparing a cattle raid.† Another foreignness is an almost morbid quickness of mind: they listen to half your sentence, guess the rest and cap it, getting their blow in first. I call it morbid because of its mixed source in the desire to ingratiate and to flatter with an apparent sympathy and yet to be sure to win and give nothing of themselves. Unlike the English, the Irish do not wear their heart upon their sleeves. They prefer comedy: it hides the self from vulgar definition. And there is the final foreignness of having known what it is to be foreign in another country. Most of them have. Tragically, inevitably, Ireland has always been the country of good-byes. That is what nearly all the ballads are about, the ballads you hear at Howth, at Bray, in Galway, in some of the Dublin pubs. Perhaps the real foreignness of Ireland in the modern world is nothing to do with race, history or climate, but is created by its emptiness, the only emptiness in Europe, a spaciousness tragically made by all those goodbyes, but which we, in the crowded corner of Europe, look at with envy and with covetousness. There is a discreet immigration from abroad but whether the outsiders can ever join the secret society is another matter.

2. John Millington Synge, whose play "The Playboy of the Western World" was driven off the stage in Dublin and elsewhere at the turn of the century because it dealt with Irish life in a way considered scandalous, wrote personal narratives of his travels in the West of Ireland among the peasants, whose imagination he

*In the seventeenth century, some of those who had supported the rebellion against the English monarchy were rewarded by Oliver Cromwell, the ruler of republican Britain, with estates in the east of Ireland. Their descendants are Protestant and, in many cases, are more "English" than "Irish" in their temperament and sympathy.

†Cattle raids are important subjects in Irish epic and folklore. Pritchett's observation suggests that whatever is represented in the character of those heroic thieves is still alive in the modern Irishman, at least in the West of Ireland.

admired and with whose struggles he sympathized. In this passage (from "In West Kerry," 1907) he describes a scene and his experience at the time in the manner of a letter.

...I went on toward Dunquin, and lay for a long time on the side of a magnificently wild road under Croagh Martin, where I could see the Blasket Islands and the end of Dunmore Head, the most westerly point of Europe. It was a grey day with a curious silence on the sea and sky and no sign of life anywhere except the sail of one curagh – or niavogue, as they are called here – and that was sailing from the islands. Now and then a cart passed me filled with old people and children, who saluted me in Irish; then I turned back myself. I got on a long road running through a bog, with a smooth mountain on one side and the sea on the other, and Brandon in front of me, partly covered with clouds. As far as I could see there were little groups of people on their way to the chapel in Ballyferriter, the men in homespun and the women wearing blue cloaks, or, more often, black shawls twisted over their heads. This procession along the olive bogs, between the mountains and the sea, on this grey day of autumn seemed to wring me with the pang of emotion one meets everywhere in Ireland – an emotion that is partly local and patriotic, and partly a share of the desolation that is mixed everywhere with the supreme beauty of the world.

3. Thomas H. Mason has no claim to fame; he was an optician from Dublin, an antiquarian and a photographer of birds, who loved islands and wrote about his travels in an unpretentious little book called *The Islands of Ireland* (1936). Here he tells a story he heard on Clare Island, off the coast of County Clare in the West of Ireland.

There are no police on the island, but before the Free State regime they occupied Granuaile's Castle, often having to keep their prisoners for a considerable time until it was possible to make the crossing to the mainland, for there was no magistrate on the island. The social center is the kitchen of the hotel where, in the evening, one will always find some men sitting on forms [benches] placed against the walls. I heard many stories of the agitation before the island was "taken over" by the Land Commission. During the "Land

War" the entire population gathered together one evening with all the horses and donkeys on the island; they spent the night singing and dancing and turned the animals loose among the crops raised by the bailiff on a "seized" farm. Needless to say, the crops were ruined; the police were powerless, but when the excitement had somewhat died down a few of the supposed ringleaders were arrested and brought for trial to the mainland.

The country Irishman is a very astute witness in the courts and often scores at the expense of the lawyers. On this occasion the principal prisoner was asked on his oath had he not got his horse with him on the night in question. His reply, "On my oath, I never had a horse," was greeted with cheers and laughter by the islanders who thronged the court. They saw the point which the Crown Prosecutor failed to perceive: the prisoner had no horse, but he certainly had a mare. He was acquitted.

He boasts that he has done more for his country than any of the politicians, because he was arrested later for throwing stones at the bailiff's son and spent a month in jail. He is now an old man clad in homespuns, with a white beard and of venerable appearance. Although almost eighty years of age he is out before daybreak working on his farm, and his one great regret is that he paid his land annuities [taxes] when others on the island had already ceased to do so.

ᖇᖇ Consider a part of the country you know well and, by generalizing and interpreting, develop a concept of this region, large or small. Remember: you will be asking yourself what *kind* of place it is and answering that question by comparing it with comparable places and differentiating it from others, perhaps by developing an opposite case. ("If there's anything South Dakota is *not,* it's. . . .") Then compose a paragraph or two in one or another of the following modes: (a) a personal letter or a passage from such a letter; (b) a guidebook description; (c) an editorial. (Editorials are differentiated from features and news stories by explicitly setting forth opinion on public matters, urging one course of action or another, or thinking out loud about ideas, what's happening, etc. In an editorial you could, for instance, consider a region from a ecological point of view.)

༚ What kind of place is your neighborhood? Form the concept of the place where you now live or have recently lived. You might collect these descriptions as a brochure for new residents. Or you could prepare a short feature for radio broadcast. (This exercise can be carried on in small groups.)

One of the chief means of forming a concept is to state the opposite case. When you name something *A,* you imply that it is not *Not-A,* and in the process you more clearly differentiate *A,* thus establishing limits that will help you in interpreting, deciding just what is to be classified as *A.* Like all other kinds of opposition, "the opposite case" helps you discover what you want to say; it helps you form the concept you intend to explain or discuss. Saying what something is *not* is one way of determining what it *is.*

Here's how a master explainer uses the opposite case to characterize and define the language of epic poetry.

The language...must be *familiar* in the sense of being expected. But in Epic, which is the highest species of oral court poetry, it must not be *familiar* in the sense of being colloquial or commonplace. The desire for simplicity is a late and sophisticated one. We moderns may like dances which are hardly distinguishable from walking and poetry which sounds as if it might be uttered *ex tempore.* Our ancestors did not. They liked a dance which *was* a dance, and fine clothes which no one could mistake for working clothes, and feasts that no one could mistake for ordinary dinners, and poetry that unblushingly proclaimed itself to be poetry. What is the point of having a poet, inspired by the Muse, if he tells stories just as you or I would have told them? It will be seen that these two demands, taken together, absolutely necessitate a Poetic Diction; that is, a language which is familiar because it is used in every part of every poem, but unfamiliar because it is not used outside poetry. A parallel, from a different sphere, would be turkey and plum pudding on Christmas day; no one is surprised at the menu, but every one recognizes that it is not *ordinary* fare. Another parallel would be the language of a liturgy. Regular church-goers are not surprised by the service— indeed, they know a great deal of it by rote, but it is a language apart. Epic diction, Christmas fare, and the liturgy, are all examples of ritual – that is, of something set deliberately apart from daily usage, but wholly familiar within its own sphere.

C. S. Lewis, *A Preface to "Paradise Lost"*

In a critical reading of C. S. Lewis's explanation of the character of epic diction, you can see that he *classifies:* he tells us that epic diction has a kind of familiarity that he explains by *stating the opposite case.* He then *interprets* this concept by *exemplifying,* by presenting *particular* examples of activities that are like the language of epic poetry and thus can be grouped as members of the same class. He thus *establishes the field of the concept's application.* Lewis ends the paragraph by renaming this class of the familiar-which-is-expectable-but-not-common-place; he has *formed the concept* of ritual which dialectically has enabled him to explain epic diction.

Forming concepts is the way you see/explain relationships; as you form concepts, you are making meanings, and that is the purpose of language and the purpose of composition. Everything Lewis does in forming the concept of ritual in order to explain epic diction – I have italicized above the acts of mind involved – could be described in much more complex logical language, but no such analysis could help you learn from reading him how to compose your own definitions. For that to happen, you have to think about his thinking and thus learn ways of thinking about your own thinking.

꩜ Here is how Astrid used the opposite case to guide her description of a building. Read her paragraph (and reread Lewis's) and then compose your own paragraph(s) describing a ballpark, public building, supervisor, or personal friend, using the opposite case.

The Boston Public Library is a classically designed, symmetrically balanced edifice intended to be a lasting monument to wisdom and learning. It has a magnificent setting and facade facing Copley Square. One walks between the two symbolic Greek statues to the center entrance flanked by a series of identical round-headed windows. From the small main lobby, a grand divided staircase leads to the second floor and the main reading room, a spacious hall with a high vaulted ceiling supported by heavy pilasters. The decorations, both inside and out, are many and ornate:

the well-known wrought-iron gates and lamps at the entrance and the murals, decorated ceilings, and imported marble and tile used on the floors and staircase.

On the other hand, one is less impressed with the University of Massachusetts library as an individual edifice because it was designed to be a functional part of the whole university. This functional use of space is what sets modern architecture apart from the classical style. The building has no obvious facade or entrance. In fact it can only be entered from the underground garage or the glass catwalk that connects the university buildings. The use of steel beams presents the opportunity for cantilevered construction. This means that portions of the building can project or jut out over the perpendicular supports, using space that otherwise would not be available. The lines are simple, severe and clean; in effect, the building speaks for itself; any exterior decoration would detract from, not add to, its functional appearance. Inside, the poured concrete walls and severe geometrical shapes are softened by the use of carpeting, bright paint, and soft, inviting couches. This modern style is conclusively demanded by its use as a multimedia center.

◆ Form a concept by means of which you can explain *academic grading.* You can compare academic grading to other kinds of grading and then to other kinds of academic activity. Developing the opposite case can help you form the class, the field of application of the concept. Use Lewis's paragraph as a model for organizing your statements.

◆ Form the concept of *maturity* by describing examples of mature behavior, mature decisions, mature attitudes – or any examples of acts and manners you can think of. You can discover such examples by answering HDWDWW? Compose statements in which you interpret and generalize until you have established the concept's field of application.

◆ Form the concept of *the country.* When you come to the opposite case, develop three: *city, suburbs, wilderness.* Which one best helps you to establish the field of application of the concept of the country? Organize your statements in order to explain the character of the country.

〇〉 In Koren's cartoon (page 110),
Mama issues a reprimand. Compose a comeback for
the poor kid.

In learning to write you're learning to exercise choice by
recognizing and using limits that are, of course, forms that find
forms. But limits are not laid down in Heaven: they are subject to
change according to the composer's needs. Limits are recognized,
but they are also modified and adapted, discarded and reestab-
lished. That process — which is essential to the forming of concepts — is carried on by means of stating and restating. Paraphrasing — restating — is the best way of converting "What do I
mean?" to a critical question: "If I say it this way, how does that
make it different from what it is when I say it that way?" By
paraphrasing, you draw out the implications of your statement.
An implication is "wound into" or "bound up with" what is said.
When you paraphrase, you "spell out" what you mean. Sometimes you discover that an implication is unintended: what you
wrote didn't say what you meant. And sometimes you may
discover that what you meant didn't get written *or* implied.

You don't need to say "class" in order to classify, any more
than you have to say "Webster tells us..." in order to develop a
definition. But it's important for the writer to understand what's
going on in the process of making statments in order to be able to
control the making of meanings. When you know the kind of
thing you mean but are not interested in naming it, you simply
say "He's sort of lazy." That is an informal idiom for "He is the
sort of person who is lazy." The important thing to remember is
that every time you make a statement, you are classifying,
whether or not you announce that you are doing so, whether or
not you have named the class.

Recognizing the classification a statment makes is as
essential to critical reading as it is to the critical review of your
own writing: you are your own first reader. You can learn to
locate and make more emphatic the classifications in your own
statements by practicing recognizing them when you read. Begin
with this passage from Aleksandr Solzhenitsyn's *The Gulag
Archipelago:*

In 1949 some friends and I came upon a news item in the
magazine *Priroda* [*Nature*] of the Academy of Sciences. It
reported in fine print that in the course of excavations on
the Kolyma River a subterranean ice lens, actually a frozen
stream, had been discovered — and in it were found frozen

specimens of prehistoric fauna some tens of thousands of years old. Whether fish or lizard these were preserved in so fresh a state that those present immediately broke open the ice and devoured them on the spot.

As for us, we understood instantly. We could picture the entire scene down to the smallest detail: how those present broke the ice with tense haste; how, flouting the lofty interests of ichthyology and elbowing each other to be first, they tore off pieces of the prehistoric flesh and dragged it over to the bonfire to thaw it and bolt it down.

We understood instantly because we ourselves were the same kind of people as *those present* at the event. We, too, were from that powerful tribe of "zeks" [prison camp inmates], unique on the face of the earth, the only kind of people who could devour prehistoric lizard *with pleasure.*

❧ Does Solzhenitsyn classify implicitly or explicitly? Write a few sentences explaining the classification. Then check your reading against these attempts to answer that question:

1. Solzhenitsyn feels that because of his internment in a prison camp he is capable of a complete understanding of how persons coming upon a valuable and extraordinary find are able to act as savages and eat the same without showing and sharing with the rest of the world.
2. A rare find is an experience most people find exciting and the excitement generated is infectious.
3. Solzhenitsyn is demonstrating the similarities between inmates at a prison camp and desperate men on a nearly suicidal expedition.
4. The author and his friends are relating the article to an experience they had at a prison camp. They had once been so hungry they knew what the feeling was like. The prehistoric fauna could be the old ways and by devouring it they could get rid of these old laws.
5. The members of the excavation were starving in the freezing environment of the Kolyma River. Upon finding fish and lizards preserved in the ice, they scrambled savagely to eat it. Forced to for survival, blinded against all else, we are all creatures subject to the cages of reality, capable of stretching our capacities back to that of uncivilized man.

Which students misread Solzhenitsyn's account because they disregarded the class-announcer, "the same kind of"?

As you compose statements, what you want to say and why you want to say it determine how you name the classifications you're developing in the process of forming concepts. The names you give the classes – a class is the field of a concept's application – represent the way you see the relationships, your judgment of them. Solzhenitsyn could have said that zeks are *people who are starving to death in labor camps*. Naming the class that way would not change the reference; the people are the same as *those who could devour prehistoric lizards with pleasure*. What Solzhenitsyn's naming does is to express his feelings and to represent his judgment of the state of affairs. The way a writer names the classes is one of his or her chief means of expressing judgment, of implying evaluation; the naming of classes is an essential phase in the making of meaning.

Suppose you are to make a statement about a *marsh*. If you are seeking the legal right to drain the marsh in order to build a shopping center, it will be to your advantage to classify the marsh as a valueless, worthless, entirely useless tract of land for which you have discovered redeeming purposes. In your statements, it will be useful to name the marsh a *swamp,* which obviously belongs to the class of things named *useless ground.* Since *swamp* brings to mind yellow fever, rattlesnakes, cold feet, desperadoes, scum, stinky water, etc., that term furthers your purposes by establishing a context in which your scheme for a parking lot will be easy to classify as a "worthwhile project." If, on the other hand, you're a birdwatcher or a citizen interested in land use, it will suit your legal or moral purposes to refer to the marsh as *wetlands*. A marsh is a marsh is a marsh: it can be defined as a member of that class of topographical areas that are subject to periodic flooding, have a very high water table, are perpetually wet, etc., but how you name the marsh – how you "call" it – will be determined by how you want it to be interpreted; your choice of a name for *marsh* will help to determine the opinions of your audience or readers. The name you give the marsh doesn't change the marsh itself, but it powerfully controls the concept of marsh that you want your audience to form.

Concept	Speaker	Interest (from speaker's viewpoint)	Class-name
Completely worthless land in current condition	Businessman	Progress	Swamp
Area vitally important to the ecological system	Birdwatcher	Conservation	Wetlands

ᘯ Using the schema above, develop two different class-names for the following:

- A cross-town expressway
- An oral contraceptive developed under the auspices of the United Nations
- A public university admitting all high school graduates

ᘯ Compose a 100-word statement to be printed on a flyer in support of or in opposition to one of the above.

You don't have to introduce a statement with a phrase like "In my judgment..." in order to pass judgment any more than you have to announce that you are classifying: naming classes entails evaluation. For that reason, when it's to the advantage of the speaker/writer not to reveal just what his evaluation is, class-names are often opaque or neutral. One of the chief uses of jargon is to provide all-purpose class-names: *area, problem, problem-area, situation, parameters, trouble, matter, decision-making process, system.* With a little help from such noises as "in my judgment," "really," "in terms of," you can handle almost any question:

Well, that's a very important problem area. How we handle that situation, just what parameters we work with, should be, in my judgment, a matter for an open decision-making process. The American people deserve nothing less.

ᔆ Suppose you're a paid employee of a political candidate and that it's your job to get out a flyer, trying to name classes – of situations, comments, facts of his or her record, etc. – in ways that would appeal to voters and to rename those that probably aren't plusses for him. You can invent everything, but if there's a campaign in progress, you can develop a chaos by watching television reports and interviews, and by reading the newspapers, editorials as well as news stories. Then draw up the plusses and minuses and start to work.

ᔆ In Zimbabwe, use of the word "native" is considered by the black people to be profoundly offensive; in the United States, most "Indians" now prefer to be called "Native Americans." Look up "native" and discuss the ambiguities of its use.

ᔆ Read the following passage by the German writer Peter Handke. Consider his analysis of the class-name "poverty" and then do the same sort of analysis, choosing two words that refer to the same situation or event but that name different concepts, e.g., *barber/hair stylist; invasion/cross-border operation; terrorists/rebels; death squads/freedom fighters*. Explain how these words would be used and by whom.

The word "poverty" was a fine, somehow noble word. It evoked an image out of old schoolbooks: poor but clean. Cleanliness made the poor socially acceptable. Social progress meant teaching people to be clean; once the indigent had been cleaned up, "poverty" became a title of honor. Even in the eyes of the poor, the squalor of destitution applied only to the filthy riffraff of foreign countries.

"The tenant's visiting card is his windowpane." And so the have-nots obediently bought soap with the money provided for that purpose by the progressive authorities. As paupers, they had shocked the official mind with repulsive, but for that reason palpable, images; now, as a reclaimed and cleansed "poorer class," their life became so unimaginably abstract that they could be forgotten. Squalid misery can be described in concrete terms; poverty can only be intimated in symbols.

Peter Handke, *A Sorrow Beyond Dreams*

2. Details, Examples, Facts, Images

In naming the classes that emerge as you form concepts, you choose one word rather than another – *swamp* rather than *wetlands* – and thus express your opinion of the facts. In the same way, the kinds of examples you choose, the number of details you develop, will also help to determine what you want to get across. Composition requires a careful balancing of generalization and particularization. Too many particular examples without generalization will result in obscurity: nobody will be sure of what you're talking about. On the other hand, too many generalizations without examples of what you mean will make it difficult for your readers or your audience to understand the implications of or "to relate to" your view of the subject.

Suppose that you describe in very careful, highly particularized detail one teacher or supervisor you've known. You can list details of dress and manner, appearance and behavior; you can set down examples of how this person sees the world and so forth until we have a very clear picture – of one teacher or supervisor. If you wanted to define a typical teacher, even in so limited a context as your school, these details might stand in the way of any generalizing your reader could attempt. To typify – to provide a "profile" – you'd have to choose details that would be representative of more than just one teacher's habits and attitudes. Particularization and classification – describing the individual and characterizing the type – are both essential to almost any kind of writing.

That will seem obvious to anyone lucky enough to have avoided two directives that are great favorites with English teachers – almost as sacred as, "What is the author trying to say?" They are the admonitions "Show, don't tell!" and "Don't generalize!" Both are nonsensical. *Showing* – and there is no more problematic term in the language * – is a way of *telling*. What is generally meant by "Show, don't tell" is something like this: "Don't go on and on writing statements that are all conceptual: don't depend on dictionary definitions; show your reader the examples from which you have generalized." But "Show, don't tell" does not make any of that clear and indeed is sometimes meant to warn students away from concepts alto-

---

*Richards lists the main meanings as follows: "to look at (obsolete); to put in view, to let be seen; to make see, to point out; to be, or give, signs of; to prove, to make certain by argument..." See *How to Read a Page* (Boston: Beacon, 1959), pp. 139-141 for his analysis of this word whose "trickiness derives from our own lack of competence and candor in certain situations."

gether. "Don't generalize" is equally absurd, since if you don't generalize, you'll have to be contented with pointing. If you couldn't generalize, you couldn't think, since generalizing is necessary to the forming of concepts. The point is that you have to learn how to generalize critically, with an understanding of the role of supporting detail and the need for a balance of classification and exemplification. Hidden in these misleading directives – "Show, don't tell" and "Don't generalize" – is the notion that since concepts aren't "real" (they don't take up space, they can't be measured), they should be avoided by everyone except philosophers and critics, who are unaccountably attracted to them. Collecting examples without generalizing carefully to show what it is they exemplify characterizes the writing of students who have been taught that the "life" of writing is in the detail. But, of course, detail is meaningless unless it's a "telling" detail – and you can't tell without having something to tell.

In composing, you have to decide continually how much detail you need in order to explain your argument, what kind of examples can best support your argument or what kind of particular detail can tell your story. As you get more and more general, you give up the freedom to dwell on the particulars; the more your conceptual terms can gather, the less precisely they will characterize any one instance. Conversely, the more you concentrate on what's "in front of you," the less able you'll be to make those particular "particulars" representative. When you're close to certain experiences, it's hard to believe that anyone else has ever been through anything quite like it; if you're not involved in certain experiences, no matter how "dramatic," they can seem commonplace.

              ℘ Describe an automobile accident from the following points of view (the same accident):

- Victim or someone at fault
- Relative of victim or someone allegedly at fault
- Traffic policeman
- Newspaper reporter
- Statistician for insurance company

The way you compose is up to you, but the context of the situation should guide you in deciding whether to "talk it out" or "write it up," and thus to choose the kind of detail you need.

∾ The balance of particulariza-
tion and generalization in short stories is especially
important because there's no space to develop individual character through many incidents, as there would
be in a novel. Description, in the "classical" short
story, gives you a particular individual who is a type, a
person who is not only himself/herself but representative of a kind of person.

In the following descriptions,
see if you can give a name to the type represented by
the character. Then write your own description of an
individual person who could also represent the type.
You can present the character in a certain setting, as
in the second selection, or you can have the character
speak for herself (himself), as in the third selection.

Little Chandler's thoughts ever since lunch-time had been
of his meeting with Gallaher, of Gallaher's invitation and of
the great city of London where Gallaher lived. He was
called Little Chandler because, though he was but slightly
under the average stature, he gave the idea of being a little
man. His hands were white and small, his frame was
fragile, his voice was quiet and his manners were refined.
He took the greatest care of his fair silken hair and mous-
tache and used perfume discreetly on his handkerchief. The
halfmoons of his nails were perfect and when he smiled you
caught a glimpse of a row of childish white teeth.

James Joyce, "A Little Cloud"

While they were in the lake, for the dip or five-o'clock
swimming period in the afternoon, he stood against a tree
with his arms folded, jacked up one-legged, sitting on his
heel, as absolutely tolerant as an old fellow waiting for the
store to open, being held up by the wall. Waiting for the girls
to get out, he gazed upon some undisturbed part of the
water. He despised their predicaments, most of all their not
being able to swim. Sometimes he would take aim and from
his right cheek shoot an imaginary gun at something far
out, where they never were. Then he resumed his pose. He
had been roped into this by his mother.

Eudora Welty, "Moon Lake"

You would certainly be glad to meet me. I was the lady who
appreciated youth. Yes, all that happy time, I was not like

some. It did not go by me like a flitting dream. Tuesdays and Wednesdays was as gay as Saturday nights. Have I suffered since? No sir, we've had as good times as this country gives: cars, renting in Jersey summers, TV the minute it first came out, everything grand for the kitchen. I have no complaints worth troubling the manager about. Still, it is like a long hopeless homesickness my missing those young days. To me, they're like my own place that I have gone away from forever, and I have lived all the time since among great pleasures but in a foreign town. Well, O.K. Farewell, certain years.

Grace Paley, "Distance"

In many different kinds of writing – not just police reports – the purpose is to establish that a state of affairs is thus and so, to show that such and such is the case. This kind of writing requires "on the spot" investigation, interviewing, various sorts of measurement such as polls and statistical studies; in short, it involves "getting the facts." But as you know, if you've ever tried to report on controversial issues, "getting the facts" may be impossible and even if you manage to establish what the facts of the case are, you still have to interpret them.

At the heart of any controversial issue there is the question of what the facts "really" are. People on opposing sides of the abortion issue, for instance, will never agree about what the facts are, much less about how they are to be interpreted. The doctor who defines viability on the basis of one set of facts will judge a fetus differently – he may even call it a "baby" – from another who proceeds from different facts. The person who speaks of a "baby" has judged the facts one way or has selected one set of facts, disregarding another; the person who speaks of "the products of conception" has made a different judgment by leaving out of account certain facts or by proceeding from different assumptions about their significance. Getting the facts of the matter or of the case is not a skill like learning to use a linoleum cutter, because a fact is not a thing. Writers, like doctors, lawyers, housewives, and detectives, have to know how to "handle" the facts, but that doesn't mean that facts are thingy: "handling the facts" is a way of describing the process of seeing relationships, making sense of experience and interpreting how the world goes.

The word "fact" is not hard to define, but it is difficult to explain what you mean by it when you use it. If you declare that a fact is "something known to be true," you land right away in a philosophical swamp, since the meanings of *known to be,* and *true* are all problematic: *knowledge, being,* and *truth* are all concepts, and they can't be explained with dictionary defintions. The history of ideas concerns changes in such concepts, including the concept of *fact* itself. What one era takes as fact is likely to be what the next sees as highly questionable. What you take as a fact will depend on your experience, your memory, your own power of reason – the capacity to figure out relationships – as well as on your willingness to accept the judgment of others. But how you feel about an experience, the meaning it has for you,will depend on much more than just you. Attitudes, opinions, prejudices are formed and controlled not just by our personal lives – by our sensory and physiognomic knowing, our own private experience – but by the time and place we live in, by our culture.

One of the pleasures of reading travel literature (and anthropology) is to be reminded of this fact. Here is Freya Stark, arguably the best travel writer of our time, with such a reminder. One of her guides as she explored Persia sixty years ago was one Shah Riza, a maker of quilts, "but he looks like a philosopher, which, in his way, he is. His philosophy is one of passive resistance to the slings and arrows of fortune as they hurtle round him."

Thieves were around after dates, which hung in moonlit clusters on the palm trees, and Mahmud would wake at the slightest noise and go prowling round. But as a matter of fact there was little enough chance of sleep for anyone, for the moon went into eclipse, and a beating of tins from every roof, a wailing of women and frenzy of dogs, an occasional high yelp of jackal made chaos of the night. I sat up at last and tried to explain the solar system to Shah Riza, who was smoking meditatively, squatting on his hams.

"They say," said I noncommittally, as befitted so unlikely a theory, "that it is the shadow of our world which hides the moon."

Even the Philosopher's mild abstraction was roused. "That," said he, "is quite impossible. Anyone can see from here that it is an insect which eats the moon. It is alive. It has a spirit. It means war and trouble coming. But it is only a sign, and Allah will not allow it to go too far."

As if in answer to his words, the moon, a red and sullen ember, began to reappear: the blackness of sky dissolved again slowly into luminous spaces: the rattle of tins subsided: and leaving the matter of the solar system unsettled, we were able to sleep.

Freya Stark, *The Valleys of the Assassins*

If we never accepted the authority of tradition or science or witnesses or the community whose principles we affirm as our own, if we never took anyone else's word for anything, we would spend our days formulating and verifying such facts as that fire burns, that the last bus does indeed leave at 9:03 P.M., and that it is unlawful to spit in the subway. On the other hand, uncritical acceptance of authority can lead to an abdication of personal responsibility, which is dangerous psychologically and politically. All of us, especially bureaucrats, take advantage of uncritical attitudes about what is fact and what is a matter for conjecture. One of the chief things we do with language is to lie – to try to convert factual matters to conceptual problems and to make concepts and problematic terms seem matters of fact.

Trying to isolate matters of fact from concepts is a good way to discover the concepts themselves. Concepts aren't objects; they are ideas that you bring into being by naming. You can ask, "What concept would this fact support?" or you can ask, "What are some facts that could fill out this concept?" Try it.

        ∾ Concerning each of the following concepts, write out a statement of fact. As a working definition of fact, you can think of an aspect of a state of affairs or of a situation that you could point to, measure, or name, without being readily disputed.

- national security
- the right to life
- women's liberation
- mass transportation
- the nuclear family

        ∾ For each of the following statements of fact, name two concepts towards a definition of which they might be relevant. In other words, for which concepts could these statements be "for instances"?

- Twenty dogs and cats per week were treated at the Spay and Neuter Clinic in Boston in 1975.
- The membership of the Glassworkers Union as of July 1976 was 35,000.
- The composition of the five-cent coin continues to be 75% copper, 25% nickel, while the one-cent coins are 95% copper and 5% zinc.

- Mean annual snowfall for Boston, Massachusetts, based on records through 1972, is 42.8 inches.
- Retired and disabled workers and their families and survivors of deceased workers received 70.8 billion dollars in social security cash benefits in the 12 months ending June 1976.
- Surveys have determined that nonpoint sources (runoff from farm chemicals, mines, urban areas) account for 50% of water pollution.
- The Gulf Intracoastal Waterway, 1,137 miles long, extends from Apalachee Bay, Florida, to the Mexican border.

The terms *subjective* and *objective* should be avoided in discussing the roles of facts in composition, since depending on them encourages us in the notion that facts are "out there" where "it" is happening and that concepts are all "relative," merely personal, merely verbal. Insofar as they are formulated, talked about, named, written about, facts too are "verbal." We live in a world built by language; there is no "reality" that can be known or conceived without the mediation of our senses and the forms of thought and feeling the human mind provides. To be "meaningful" – bearers of meaning – facts must be seen in context, related to other facts, seen as being in support of one concept or another. We build up such relationships by means of language, which is not a veil between us and some ultimate reality but our chief means of making meaning and thereby conceiving reality.

       ℘ Read the following philosophical discussions of the concept of fact. Then suppose you are a judge who must instruct the jury that they are to attend to "the facts." Drawing on the philosophers' discussion, prepare a brief explanation of what is meant by "the facts."

1. The notion of a mere fact is the triumph of the abstractive intellect. It has entered into the explicit thought of no baby and of no animal. Babies and animals are concerned with their wants as projected against the general environment. That is to say, they are immersed in their interest respecting details embedded in externality. There is the merest trace of the abstraction of the detail. A single fact in isolation is the primary myth required for finite thought, that is to say, for thought unable to embrace

totality. This mythological character arises because there is no such fact. Connectedness is of the essence of all things, of all types. It is of the essence of types, that they be connected. Abstraction from connectedness involves the omission of an essential factor in the fact considered. No fact is merely itself. The penetration of literature and art at their height arises from our dumb sense that we have passed beyond mythology; namely beyond the myth of isolation. It follows that in every consideration of a single fact there is the suppressed presupposition of the environmental coordination requisite for its existence.

Alfred North Whitehead, *Modes of Thought*

2. "Facts" are the basic formulations of any system of apperception. They are not arbitrary logical constructions, neither are they "absolute" and stark in their own form — indeed, by pure sense-experience or intuition, if there could be such a thing, facts would not even be apparent. Definite experience is possible only where impression is met with understanding. But understanding does not consist merely of appropriate reaction to a given, preformed universe; understanding is *systematic* interpretation, the discovery of syntactical meanings in the world. It is the recognition of truth-forms, of symbolic relationships, of which there may be many — even as it grows more and more general, and we come nearer and nearer to the ideal of philosophy, the appreciation of all-connecting orders in the world.

Susanne K. Langer, *The Practice of Philosophy*

3. The conception of history as dealing with facts and nothing but facts may seem harmless enough, but what is a fact? According to the positivistic theory of knowledge, a fact is something immediately given in perception. When it is said that science consists first in ascertaining facts and then in discovering laws, the facts, here, are facts directly observed by the scientist, for example, the fact that this guinea-pig, after receiving an injection of this culture, develops tetanus. If anyone doubts the fact he can repeat the experiment with another guinea-pig, which will do just as well; and consequently, for the scientist the question whether facts really are what they are said to be is never a vital question, because he can always reproduce the facts under his own eyes. In science, then, the facts are empirical facts, facts perceived as they occur.

In history, the word "fact" bears a very different meaning. The fact that in the second century the legions began to be recruited wholly outside Italy is not immediately given. It is arrived at inferentially by a process of interpreting data according to a complicated system of rules and assumptions. A theory of historical knowledge would discover what these rules and assumptions are, and would ask how far they are necessary and legitimate. All this was entirely neglected by the positivistic historians, who thus never asked themselves the difficult question: How is historical knowledge possible? How and under what conditions can the historian know facts which, being now gone beyond recall or repetition, cannot be for him objects of perception? They were precluded from asking this question by their false analogy between scientific facts and historical facts. Owing to this false analogy, they thought such a question could need no answer. But owing to the same false analogy, they were all the time misconceiving the nature of historical research.

R. G. Collingwood, *The Idea of History*

A detail or a fact or an example can be brought to life if it is given a form that we can *imagine,* bring to the mind's eye. Such a form is called an *image* and though it generally is visual – a form that could be seen – an image can also be auditory or kinetic, a form that brings to mind something heard or perceived as being in motion. Some kinds of poetry depend on imagery for their very being, though other kinds may have little or none. A poetic image pictures not just a particular thing; it also *re*presents a conception of that thing and the poet's feelings about it. Using imagery is one way to realize a concept – to make it real – by giving it a shape. You can't visualize *freedom,* but you can imagine something that can represent it.

An image must have a context in order to be meaningful, just as a word or an object or anything else we respond to must have a setting, and the meaning changes or shifts as the context changes. An Afro-American storyteller who calls himself Brother Blue accompanies his songs and tales with the clinking and clanking of a chain meant to symbolize the continuing struggle of his people for liberation. A chain in the dark corner of a garage shelf is just a chain; a tire chain shaken with a certain intent, which can be interpreted by an audience, becomes an image.

Visualizing images that can represent concepts is a skill of fundamental importance to anyone who has to explain, argue, persuade – all of us. Even scientists, some would claim, are dependent on imagery, once they forsake mathematical formulations. For any writer, exploring the relationships between images and concepts can be useful in getting the dialectic started and in forming a concept. The relationship of an *image* to what it represents or expresses is as complex as the relationship of a name and an idea, a word and a thing. (The word *image* has collected as many meanings as the word *form*. It derives from the Latin *imago*, which means *conception, thought, idea,* as well as *likeness. Image* is cognate with *imitation.*) You can think of an image as a visual name. The commonest error in thinking comes from confusing the image with what it represents, but that error is not avoided by staying away from imagery.

Sometimes, in a certain mood or situation, we will see something – an object or a happening – which strikes us as meaningful, though of what we may not be sure. Once we name what that importance is, the object becomes an image, a means of representing the feeling. Here is Virginia Woolf setting down in her diary an experience of seeing something which is important and trying to name the feelings which it elicited. The time is shortly after the beginning of World War II.

Thursday 30 May, 1940
Walking today (Nessa's birthday) by Kingfisher pool saw my first hospital train – laden, not funereal, but weighty, as if not to shake bones. Something what is the word I want: grieving & tender & heavy laden & private – bringing our wounded back carefully through the green fields at which I suppose some looked. Not that I could see them. And the faculty for seeing in imagination always leaves me so suffused with something partly visual partly emotional, I can't though its very pervasive, catch it when I come home – the slowness, cadaverousness, grief of the long heavy train, taking its burden through the fields. Very quietly it slid into the cutting at Lewes. Instantly wild duck flights of aeroplanes came over head; manoeuvered; took up positions & passed over Caburn. Percy has seen Westmacot[t]'s man, home on leave, very thin, drawn & aged; says it's a hell: was at Arras: all had to fight. And the same stories as the papers about the brutality to refugees.

        ❧ *Image* has the following lexical definitions: 1) an imitation or likeness; statue, form, aspect, likeness, semblance; 2) copy or counterpart; 3) conception or idea; 4) optical counterpart of an object produced by a lens.

Decide which meaning is appropriate for each of the following instances:

1. This camera gives you a really sharp image.
2. "Here's your catalog from *Sharper Image*."
3. He has destroyed my self-image.
4. He's the spittin' image of his grandfather.
5. She wears hiking boots for the sake of her image.
6. *Lear* is full of images of the horror of life.
7. "I suddenly realized that I could use examples in my history paper to explain what was happening over those three hundred years the way poets use images."

Like all other forms, an image is a way of seeing relationships. *Imagine* a person, a place, a landscape, an animal, or a thing – singly or in combination – that could represent a concept; that *image* will, at the same time, represent an attitude towards the concept. Imagery is part of the adman's repertory ("Come to Marlboro Country!"), but, as we have noted, it is also central in many kinds of poetry. Symbolic gardens, caves, islands, cities, deserts, valleys abound in epic, narrative, and lyric poems and also in some kinds of novels. Here is an account of how a real place became an image for the poet W. B. Yeats. The poem he mentions follows immediately after this passage from *Autobiographies*.

I was in my Galway house during the first months of civil war, the railway bridges blown up and the roads blocked with stones and trees. For the first week there were no newspapers, no reliable news, we did not know who had won nor who had lost, and even after newspapers came one never knew what was happening on the other side of the hill or of the line of trees. Ford cars passed the house from time to time with coffins standing on end between the seats, and sometimes at night we heard an explosion, and once by day saw the smoke made by the burning of a great neighboring house. Men must have lived so through many tumultuous centuries. One felt an overmastering desire not to grow unhappy or embittered, not to lose all sense of the beauty of nature. A stare (our West of Ireland name for a starling) had built in a hole beside my window and I made these verses out of the feeling of the moment – "The Stare's Nest by My Window."

"The Stare's Nest by My Window"

The bees build in the crevices
Of loosening masonry, and there
The mother birds bring grub and flies.
My wall is loosening; honey-bees,
Come build in the empty house of the stare.

We are closed in, and the key is turned
On our uncertainty; somewhere
A man is killed, or a house burned,
Yet no clear fact to be discerned:
Come build in the empty house of the stare.

A barricade of stone or of wood;
Some fourteen days of civil war;
Last night they trundled down the road
That dead young soldier in his blood:
Come build in the empty house of the stare.

We had fed the heart on fantasies,*
The heart's grown brutal from the fare;
More substance in our enmities
Than in our love; O honey-bees,
Come build in the empty house of the stare.
> W. B. Yeats, from "Meditations in Time of Civil War"

        ✍ What characteristics of the honey bee make it an appropriate image by means of which the poet expresses a "sense of the beauty of nature"? What are the images that give substance to the concept of civil war, a time of troubles?

Students, like poets, lawyers, biographers, historians, and popular explainers, can use images to help give form to feelings and ideas. John Wain demonstrates in a passage from his biography of Samuel Johnson how images do that. He has been discussing life in eighteenth-century England.

So on we could go, contrasting and comparing, trying to decide which of the two Englands would be preferable to live in, safe in the knowledge that the issue can never be decided. To me personally, to think of the quality of life in

---

*Yeats here refers to the fact that the Irish uprising against English rule had started with romantic expectations, nourished by dreams of past glory and encouraged by the literary celebration of a Celtic tradition, which included fabulous and heroic exploits. The reality was a bloody defeat.

the eighteenth century is inevitably, sooner or later, to think of Josiah Wedgwood's leg. Wedgwood, another Midlander who was to trade and commerce in many ways what Johnson was to literature, was troubled in his younger days by some kind of circulatory complaint in one leg. If he happened to knock it against anything, it swelled up and put him in bed for a few days; and since he was constantly making journeys up and down England in the course of building up his business, he found the waste of time irritating and had the leg amputated.

Most of us, I fancy, would accept the fate of being a mediocrity in business rather than consent to have a leg amputated without anaesthetic. Wedgwood's decision symbolizes many features of eighteenth-century England – the toughness, the realism, the determination to be up and doing, whatever the price that had to be paid. In a thinly populated country such giant individualities stand out clearly. Wedgwood knew that if he did not succeed in the pottery industry, he could not simply subside into comfortable obscurity as the tenth vice-president in some large faceless corporation, with his name on the door and a carpet on the floor. He had to get out there and do what it was in him to do, or he would be nothing. In such a spirit, also, did Samuel Johnson live his life....

A great photographer, like Cartier-Bresson, creates images which, in capturing "the decisive moment," bespeak more than the actual scene or face they depict. For this reason, a good collection of photographs can provide excellent practice for the student of composition. But even a commonplace photograph can become an image if you bring to it certain questions; you can train yourself to read almost any photograph as an image – and that is precisely what advertisers expect you to do. And if you compare the pictures of a public figure chosen by one newspaper with those appearing in another, you can often describe the political viewpoint of either, before reading the editorial pages.

ᘉ Faye had a paper assigned for a political science course with no helpful constraints: "Write 5,000 words on a modern city." She decided to write on Bogotá because she had a huge and very detailed photograph of the city. She "read" the photograph, translating what she saw into images representing the concepts she'd learned in the course. You can try this with almost any assigned paper.

Or you can invent your own image and then interpret it. Here's the way Julia began her paper on how we interpret our interpretations.

One afternoon last week I fell asleep listening to a piece of music called "The Unanswered Question." I dreamt I was asking for the answer, the big one, the one about life and destiny. I stood there waiting, and finally some voice moved through my throat, and I said to myself: "It's not that the answer couldn't be told straight out, but you're a person and you wouldn't be able to hear it if it was. It must be explained to you – you must explain it to yourself – in a series of tests." The "tests" appeared in front of me, large silver camping vehicles that looked like Winnebagos. They were all over the place. I couldn't look at more than one at a time, though I knew there were many.

As I stood there scrutinizing each big silver car, voices began rippling through the air. In real life my roommates had come home and were talking in the hallway: "You have a message – Maria called." "Oh thanks – and did you get the messages from Lisa and Mary?" In the dream the Winnebagos turned into Maria and Lisa and Mary, and there they stood, messages and messengers, talking amongst themselves. Their speech echoed what my roommates seemed to have been shouting up and down the hall to one another (including, "Is Julia home?"). Gradually the three figures wavered into shadows, as I wavered into waking. The phone rang, I sat up suddenly, and the dream darted away from me like guppies when a foot plunks itself down into the water.

I woke and began interpreting: my roommates are home, understanding is constructed in parts, and there's more to my three friends than I thought, ex-Winnebagos and part speakers of an answer that they are. The dream itself reminds me that we construct meanings and make interpretations through, with, from, in them: Winnebagos are made for living in, and also for traveling. I need some kind of a vehicle to "arrive at" or "come to" an understanding. Knowledge, in other words, is "gotten to" with language, mediated by language, whether it be my dream language or the English my roommates were speaking.

Here are some assisted invitations to exercise a capacity that is natural, innate: your capacity to construe and construct images.

﹏ Imagine and describe in single sentences the following:

- *Landscapes* to represent each of these: youth, maturity, old age
- *Persons* to represent each of these: faith, hope, charity
- *Animals* to represent each of these: cleverness, courage, timidity
- *Places* to represent each of these: fear, despair, authority
- *Weather or other natural phenomena* to represent each of these: mercy, justice, equality

﹏ Develop a context for an object that is valueless in itself but is of great significance to you. Or try to explain someone else's peculiar attraction to (for instance) a greasy, torn jacket, even though there are others hanging in the closet.

﹏ Convert one of the following objects to an image representing a concept. Then compose an editorial denouncing the concept so represented, beginning with a description of the object.

- *The National Enquirer*
- station wagons
- paperback novels
- saunas
- a clear, fresh river by a deserted factory
- designer jeans
- shopping malls

﹏ Look up the word *talisman* in a good dictionary. Describe a talismanic cermony in another time, far away. Or describe an everyday action (toasting a slice of bread) as if it were talismanic.

3. Waterfalls and Rails

Just as you must specify in order to compose a sound definition, so you have to have the specifications when you come to make any kind of decision, whether it's a matter of pricing a pair of shoes or choosing a college. A contractor must have the "specs" in order to give you an estimate of what it would cost to build a garage. But specifications aren't automatic and they don't come out of thin air: they're developed according to one or another *criterion* (derives from the Greek word for *test* or *standard*) or set of *criteria*. And where do criteria come from? What makes us decide according to which standards? These questions are what make courts of law necessary; if criteria were automatic or if we all agreed without question about the meanings of words, the dictionary could solve all problems.

Take the case of ice cream. In a sense, everybody (*everybody*?) knows what ice cream is and you might think that the only question would concern flavor. But once you consider manufacture, the problem of definition becomes more complex. Several years ago, dairymen were up in arms when it seemed that ice cream manufacturers were to be allowed to substitute imported casein for American-produced non-fat dry milk. They wanted the Food and Drug Administration to rule against this spurious "ice cream." This was an argument about *criteria*.

                       ℘ If you watch the newspapers for a few days, you'll probably find cases in which conceptual definitions are at issue. If you can identify a definition problem, see if you can write a headline which would make it clear.

Just because two objects or activities or states are named by the same word doesn't mean that they share a conceptual character. *Caning,* for instance, is the name for the use of a certain natural material in making chair bottoms. School children were once punished by being whipped with a bamboo cane; the punishment was called *caning*. The material is the same — though in different states — but it doesn't follow that the manufacture and the punishment belong to the same class. In this sense, there is no concept of *caning* that would include *caning* a chair and *caning* a boy.

                       ℘ Look up *rail* in a good dictionary. What do the King Rail, the Virginia Rail, a rail fence, and a railway track have in common?

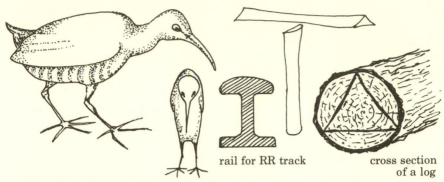

rail for RR track

cross section
of a log

Rallus elegans: "compressed laterally"

Identifying and naming the generic character which unifies (organizes, composes) a number of items, a mass of data, a chaos of specifications – this is at the heart of the composing process. For some people, classifying is harder than differentiating and naming; for others, classifying comes easier. Psychologists try to account for this difference in what they call "cognitive styles." Some people tolerate chaos better than others; some are much more comfortable with frameworks, graphs, grids, and maps. In order to make meaning, we have to generalize and interpret, but the way we proceed differs according to our temperament. It's helpful to a writer to be able to assume a style that's not necessarily the one he or she naturally or habitually chooses. The following exercise invites you to look again at *what* you do in forming a concept so that you can learn *how* to do so.

         What *kind* of "thing" is a waterfall? As resources for forming the concept of a waterfall, we offer six texts: a selection from a personal essay by a geologist, a guidebook description, three poems, and a print. You're invited to add a description or an account of your own.

These texts provide the specifications for defining a waterfall: your job is to generalize by interpreting these specifications. What characteristics can be named/opposed/defined in order for a classification to emerge? You should, of course, generate a chaos, ask HDWDWW?, gloss, draw up a lexicon, develop oppositions, practice making statements in various syntactical patterns. Aim, then, for an essay of three substantial paragraphs in which you form the concept of a waterfall.

1.

This darksome burn, horseback brown,
His rollrock highroad roaring down,
In coop and in comb the fleece of his foam
Flutes and low to the lake falls home.

A windpuff-bonnet of fawn-froth
Turns and twindles over the broth
Of a pool so pitchblack, fell-frowning,
It rounds and rounds Despair to drowning.

Degged with dew, dappled with dew
Are the groins of the braes that the brook treads through,
Wiry heathpacks, flitches of fern,
And the beadbonny ash that sits over the burn.

What would the world be, once bereft
Of wet and of wildness? Let them be left,
O let them be left, wildness and wet;
Long live the weeds and the wilderness yet.

Gerard Manley Hopkins, "Inversnaid"

2.

From Rowardennan the steamer takes 20 minutes to reach Tarbet, prettily situated on the W. bank, and commanding the best view of Ben Lomond. A coach plies hence every morning to (24M.) Inverary, via (2¼m.) Arrochar and (14M.) Cairndow. – Our steamboat journey ends at Inversnaid, one of the finest points on Loch Lomond, affording splendid views of the mountains above Arrochar. Just before reaching the pier we pass a pretty waterfall.... At Inversnaid the steamer is met by a coach to take the passengers across the ridge between Loch Lomond and Loch Katrine, a distance of 5½M. Those who prefer it have plenty of time to walk (1½ hrs.), but the ascent from this side is long and somewhat fatiguing... The finest scenery is at the E. end, where steep cliffs alternate with beautiful woods, in which bright green foliage of the birch is predominant...

Baedeker's *Great Britain* (1894)

3.

TAKI NO OTO WA
The sound of the waterfall

TAETE IHSASHIRU
has for a long time

NARINNUREDO
ceased
NA KASO NAGERETE
Yet with its name
NAO KIKOE KERE
we can hear it still.
From *Shohaka Taki Meguri (Famous Waterfalls of Various Provinces)*

4.

Katsushika Hokusai, "Woodcutter Gazing at Waterfall"
Stanford University Museum of Art 9263
Ikeda Collection

5.

Human beings are, it seems, irresistibly attracted to those places where nature has not become passive but is still full of force and the possibility of movement. One of the most visited of such places is Rocky Valley, near Tintagel, where the stream falls in a number of cascades, each hollowing a round basin at its foot.

I once had an experience there which, though it seemed slight enough, has remained in my mind with a brightness and tenacity that suggest some sort of special significance. I remember how I walked through the sadly colored countryside where the whitewashed cottages were roofed with huge sheets of local flagstone. I went past the headland that cloudy memories have associated with King Arthur, and where, certainly, Celtic monks meditated on God as the Atlantic spray blew across their cabins. Scrambling down the steep sides of Rocky Valley, I saw a dipper and followed its flight until I found I was looking down into one of the deepest of the rock basins. My inner eye can still project the spectacle with the clarity of a colored lantern slide. The white plume of cascade fell from a height into a basin shadowy below but full of sun in its upper parts; a light spume blowing off the spray held a miniature rainbow that bridged the shadows of the lower basin. In a narrow fissure, wet with spume, was the dipper's nest with its neat domed roof and an opening at the side which seemed too small to allow the passage of the sleek body of the bird. Immediately below the nest, imprisoned in the smaller basin made by the fissure, a large and brilliantly colored rubber ball rose and fell and spun around with the seething of the water. Through the opening of the nest I could see the dipper's eye fixed upon me, and the roaring of the fall seemed to enclose me in this small, intense and perfectly incongruous world. Twenty years before I had held a ball of that kind in my hands and looked with love at its bright red and green paint; millions of years from now the river will have leveled Rocky Valley, will have grown tame and shed its rainbows. These are chance comments; the image can be interpreted at will.

Jacquetta Hawkes, *A Land*

6.
With what deep murmurs through times silent stealth
Doth thy transparent, cool and watry wealth
      Here flowing fall,
      And chide and call,
As if his liquid, loose Retinue staid
Lingring, and were of this steep place afraid,
      The common pass
      Where, clear as glass,
      All must descend
      Not to an end:
But quickned by this deep and rocky grave,
Rise to a longer course more bright and brave.

      Dear stream! dear bank, where often I
      Have sate, and pleas'd my pensive eye,
      Why, since each drop of thy quick[1] store

1. *quick:* living

Runs thither, whence it flow'd before,
Should poor souls fear a shade or night,
Who came (sure) from a sea of light?
Or since those drops are all sent back
So sure to thee, that none doth lack,
Why should frail flesh doubt any more
That what God takes, he'll not restore?

O useful Element and clear!
My sacred wash and cleanser here,
My first consigner unto those
Fountains of life, where the Lamb goes!
What sublime truths, and wholesome themes,
Lodge in thy mystical, deep streams!
Such as dull man can never finde
Unless that Spirit lead his minde,[2]
Which first upon thy face did move,
And hatch'd all with his quickning love.
As this loud brooks incessant fall
In streaming rings restagnates all,
Which reach by course the bank, and then
Are no more seen, just so pass men.
O my invisible state,
My glorious liberty, still late!
Thou art the Channel my soul seeks,
Not this with Cataracts and Creeks.

Henry Vaughan, "The Waterfall"

Working out the criteria by which you can arrive at a legally sound defensible definition (*ice cream*); discovering whether a single word in different contexts names a class or one or another specification (*rail, caning*); interpreting a number of specific examples in order to arrive at a generalization (*waterfalls*): all these exercises involve you in naming/opposing/defining. When there's no clear sense of what the questions should be – the questions which would enable you to develop criteria – some people speak of *problem-posing;* if you know what you have to do, the usual term is *problem-solving.*

❧ Following is a discussion of problem-solving by a chemical engineer who is also a manager and an inventor. Read it, gloss it, and com-

2. See *Genesis* 1.2.

ment on the relationship of problem-solving to conceptual definition and on the relationship of both to the composing process. Then compose two paragraphs in which you offer advice about writing to 1) engineering students; 2) nurses in training; 3) pre-law students; 4) pre-med students; 5) any group you wish to identify. (This exercise is appropriate for small group work.)

Mr. Murphy and his friends and relatives are often the whipping boys for things that go wrong unexpectedly. When the unexpected, almost always negative, event occurs in our innovative project, we take solace in Murphy's Law and its many derivations. We are victimized once again. But is it Murphy who is really out of step, or are we the ones living in a fantasy world? Maybe he has a firm grasp of reality, while the innovator struggles with an idealized view that consistently lets him down.

Why is this so? Perhaps it's because whenever we try to take a step into unknown territory – that is, whenever we try to innovate – we encounter not only things that are unknown, but also things that are at first unknowable. Our sense of how well we are doing – how much progress we are making into the unknown – is based initially on the best yardstick we have at the time. If we are reasonably smart, we refine this yardstick as more facts come to light. But often, new knowledge of the science, the product, or the market brings about a major dislocation in our sense of progress. The upheaval can be temporary or terminal. The participants feel victimized – Murphy has struck again! And we struggle to get back to where we thought we were.

But we are not really victims, and we cannot lay the blame at Murphy's door. The blame, if any, lies in our failure to recognize the nature of the innovative process of highs and lows, of setbacks and apparent reversals. Participants in innovation projects need to be aware that unexpected problems await them down the road. Unfortunately, many of them are not. And this naiveté is reinforced by today's managerial climate – by a discrepancy between the way the creative process is idealized and the way it actually is. We are the victims not of unexpected setbacks, but of a desire to portray technical development as logical and systematic. We teach the high points and omit the lows. We write our reports as if setbacks were exceptions to the norm. We do not report that "the unknown, but expected, problems forecast at project initiation turned out to be..." Such a statement about the likelihood of unspecified problems in a project plan would be unacceptable in most industrial organizations. In short, we fail to "tell it like it is." The result: the entire project is undermined because it costs more and lasts longer than we had planned, and the output is never as clear-cut or satisfying as we had expected.

A not atypical example of the last minute "stab in the back" from Murphy occurred in a project aimed at developing an improved cold hair wave. Laboratory tests proved the effectiveness of the chemical approach, "half-head" comparisons in the experimental salon were favorable, less odor masking was necessary than in current products, and the formulations were kinder to the hair and skin. Naturally, enthusiasm and excitement prevailed – a new breakthrough in a long-mature area of technology!

Then we learned of a problem that was unforeseen and, I claim, unforeseeable. The product worked well in preliminary tests by a few consumers. But when the hair was wetted several days after the waving, the subjects noticed an unfortunate "wet dog" odor. In spite of frantic work, no complete solution to the problem was found, and negotiations between technical and marketing for some reasonable compromise were the next step.

As a second example, with a different twist, the engineering department of a work glove manufacturer in search of a more economical fabrication process came up with an adhesive seaming technique for part of a cotton glove. Wear tests conducted by the work force in the plant and in their homes indicated that the seaming technique would stand up to normal wear and tear, and the economics looked good. The glove satisfied the requirements for this class of product in every respect.

Success seemed near until the marketing manager got into the act. He looked at the glove and asked if the adhesive was gasoline-resistant. The engineer said it had been used in the presence of oils and greases and had survived. The marketing manager went out to their truck maintenance garage, dipped the glove in gasoline, tugged at the seam, and it failed. The engineers pleaded with him, saying that no one would dip a glove in gasoline. "Perhaps not," said that marketing manager, "but if I were a salesman for our competition, that's exactly what I would do." Disaster struck, and recoup began.

This pattern of events is painfully familiar to all those who have had much to do with innovative work, particularly those engaged in lab-based technology. The pattern is worth analyzing, not because it will enable us to plan and avoid the suspected, but unknown event, but rather because recognizing the pattern gives us a basis for realistic expectations and useful behavior. The apparent progress of a typical innovation project can be analyzed by examining its five stages.

A generalized version of the stages through which most innovative projects progress is shown in the graph. On the vertical axis we show apparent progress toward a goal — i.e., levels leading to successful completion. (Note that we speak of "apparent" progress; all progress is positive in the sense of uncovering new information.) What this curve attempts to show is the apparent progress measured by the yardstick available at any particular time as time and money are expended, represented by the horizontal axis.

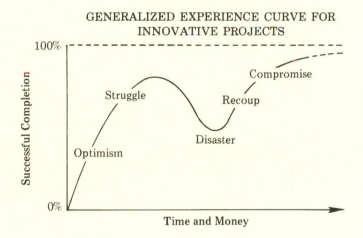

GENERALIZED EXPERIENCE CURVE FOR INNOVATIVE PROJECTS

- *Optimism*

  The first stage is one of optimism. A giant step has been made. Patent applications have been filed. Energy and enthusiasm for the project abound. The temptation to inform management is hard to resist. Those responsible for the initial "breakthrough" may exhibit a protective and proprietary attitude toward their "baby."

- *Struggle*

  The second stage is that of struggle. The goal is now being approached more slowly. Obstacles appear, but they yield to energetic work; the project is still on track. Participants feel that the deadline can still be reached within the time and money allocated. No cause for real worry.

- *Disaster*

  The third stage is disaster. Unforeseen (and, in fact, unforeseeable) aspects of the problem manifest themselves. The goal is farther away and more difficult to achieve than was first thought. Gloom and despondency prevail, and people become defensive. There may be scapegoating and second-guessing. Questions will be raised about the validity of the project and the competence of those undertaking it.

- *Recoup*

  The next stage is what one might call "recoup" — dogged perseverance becomes the operational mode. There is much worrying and loss of sleep; the project is opened up to all comers, and there is willingness to try any approach. Eventually, the team gets back to where they thought they were, although the goal is still ahead. The deadline will have been passed and the original budget spent, but the prize appears to be within reach, and confidence in the success of the project returns.

- *Compromise*

  In the final stage, which I have called compromise, participants recognize that progress toward the original goal is again slowing down. Indeed, there are doubts about whether it can ever be reached. Sometimes the goal itself will change; it may become more exacting as a result of more sophisticated marketing knowledge. During this period, therefore, we frequently find technology and marketing negotiating with respect to what might be *acceptable* versus what might be *ideal*.

  Derek E. Till, "Innovation Revisited"

    ꙮ Using the following as a model, compose a workplace dialogue of your own.

Down at "Sun 'n' Sand," the sportswear factory Maureen designs for, Jack, the owner, is in a panic.

Jack: Maureen! We don't have a line! I thought we had until the end of the month, but now New York says next week – and we don't *have* a line! All we've got is this bunch of garments!

Maureen: We're fine, Jack; we're in good shape. We've got all these garments and all we have to do now is pull the line together. Now look (shifting shirts and pants and coats around on the racks): we can put these here with those and that tells the print story. Now we've got the solids in hot pink, yellow, green, turquoise, and they can either go with the polka dot shirts (demonstrating how *that* looks) or by themselves, establishing the color theme – though we should add purple and orange so you get the impact of the whole color range.

Jack: But what about the bombays? They've always been our best items.

Maureen: They work right in here – see? It gives a good contrast to the polar fleece. There! Now you've got a line!

Jack: But where do these jumpsuits go? They don't fit in anywhere?"

Maureen: Right – they don't. Well, we'll just have to consider them an early start on the holiday line. But they *don't* belong in this one. Because they're part of a different story. Cynthia, what do you think?

Cynthia (who has been reading *Forming/Thinking/ Writing*): I think you've just formed a concept.

4. Forming

The paragraphs in this sequence are selected from the writings of artists and critics concerned with the creative process. Each one has something to say about how or why or what the artist composes. You are invited to form the concept of *forming,* drawing on these statements. There are no right answers nor is there any final truth hidden in these selections. They are intended as points of departure for your own thinking about works of art and about your own experience, if you've ever danced, painted, sculpted, designed a house, written a poem, composed a piece of music, or taken a picture. Here's some assistance:

1. If you ask HDWDWW? in reading each selection, you'll be developing a lexicon, a list of terms, which can then help in rereading each selection in the context that the other selections provide.
2. Critical reading means rereading – looking and looking again. You can take a phrase or a statement which you find obscure in one selection and try to translate it into the terms of another. Experiment with using the terms of one writer or artist to gloss what another one says.
3. Note the verbs which substantiate *forming* and then identify what is being formed, what the form is like, what its source is, etc. (Use the Checklist of Oppositions on pages 102-103.)
4. Note the images and analogies a writer uses to explain his or her idea of composing. Comparing such images can help to explain the difference in opinion you'll find about the process and function of artistic creation.

These artists and critics have written essays of various kinds, tracts, articles, lectures, letters and so forth, and although they appear as paragraphs, that is not how they were published. These are all passages from larger works. It is inappropriate to say, "In her excerpt, Barbara Hepworth explains..." or "Max Black says in his paragraph...." Instead you can name the form in which they are writing – letter, essay, etc. – or you can refer to the rhetorical form – *argument, analogy, description,* etc. The *excerpts* are ours; the *arguments* are theirs. For our present purposes, when you want to allude to these writers, it's best to say simply: "Ackerman explains that...," "Gertrude Stein says that...," "Paul Klee develops a metaphor which...," etc.

1. All the clues for [a theory of dance composition] come from life itself. Every movement made by a human being, and far back of that, in the animal kingdom too, has a design in space; a relationship to other objects in both time and space; an energy flow which we call dynamics; and a rhythm. Movements are made for a complete array of reasons involuntary or voluntary, physical, psychical, emotional or instinctive, which we will lump all together and call motivation. Without a motivation, no movement would be made at all. So, with a simple analysis of movement, in general, we are provided with the basis for dance, which is movement brought to the point of fine art. The four elements of dance are, therefore, design, dynamics, rhythm, and

motivation. These are the raw materials which make a dance, and so fundamental are they that, without a balanced infusion of each, the dance is likely to be weakened, and without any two of them it will be seriously impaired. To be sure, all four parts of movement will be there in some degree no matter what is done, but to use them skillfully so that all the mutations are understood and can be intelligently chosen to support the idea, takes quite a lot of study.

Doris Humphries, *The Art of Making Dances*

2. I don't feel any difference of intention or of mood when I paint (or carve) realistically and when I make abstract carvings. It all feels the same – the same happiness and pain, the same joy in a line, a form, a color – the same feeling of being lost in the pursuit of something. The same feeling at the end. The two ways of working flow into each other without effort... [the two methods of working] enhance each other by giving an absolute freedom – a freedom to complete the circle.... Working realistically replenishes one's *love* for life, humanity and the earth. Working abstractly seems to release one's personality and sharpen the perceptions, so that in the observation of life it is the wholeness or inner intention which moves one so profoundly: the components fall into place, the detail is significant of unity.

Barbara Hepworth, "Letter to Herbert Read," quoted in Herbert Read, *The Philosophy of Modern Art*

3. If a photograph is to communicate its subject in all its intensity, the relationship of form must be rigorously established. Photography implies the recognition of a rhythm in the world of real things. What the eye does is to find and focus on the particular subject within the mass of reality; what the camera does is simply to register upon film the decision made by the eye. We look at and perceive a photograph, as a painting, in its entirety and all in one glance. In a photograph, composition is the result of a simultaneous coalition, the organic co-ordination of elements seen by the eye. One does not add composition as though it were an afterthought superimposed on the basic subject material, since it is impossible to separate content from form. Composition must have its own inevitability about it.

In photography there is a new kind of plasticity, product of the instantaneous lines made by movements of the subject. We work in unison with movement as though it were a presentiment of the way in which life unfolds. But inside movement there is one moment at which the elements in motion are in balance. Photography must seize upon this moment and hold immobile the equilibrium of it.

The photographer's eye is perpetually evaluating. A photographer can bring coincidence of line simply by moving his head a fraction of a millimeter. He can modify perspectives by a slight bending of the knees. By placing the camera closer to or farther from the subject, he draws a detail – and it can be subordinated, or he can be tyrannized by it. But he composes a picture in very nearly the same amount of time it takes to click the shutter, at the speed of a reflex action.

Sometimes it happens that you stall, delay, wait for something to happen. Sometimes you have the feeling that here are all the makings of a picture – except for just one thing that seems to be missing. But what one thing? Perhaps someone suddenly walks into your range of view. You follow his progress through the view-finder. You wait and wait, and then finally press the button – and you depart with the feeling (though you don't know why) that you've really got something. Later, to substantiate this, you can take a print of this picture, trace on it the geometric figures which come up under analysis, and you'll observe that, if the shutter was released at the decisive moment, you have instinctively fixed a geometric pattern without which the photograph would have been both formless and lifeless.

Composition must be one of our constant preoccupations, but at the moment of shooting it can stem only from our intuition, for we are out to capture the fugitive moment, and all the interrelationships involved are on the move. In applying the Golden Rule,* the only pair of compasses at the photographer's disposal is his own pair of eyes. Any geometrical analysis, any reducing of the picture to a schema, can be done only (because of its very nature) after the photograph has been taken, developed and printed – and then it can be used only for a post-mortem examination of the picture. I hope we will never see the day when photo shops will sell little schema grills to clamp onto our viewfinders; and that the Golden Rule will never be found etched on our ground glass.

*The Golden Rule is a formula for proportions in designing sculptural, architectural, and other spatial forms. The ratios are 3:5:8. Thus, in the Golden Rectangle, the width is to the length as the length is to the sum of the two.

If you start cutting or cropping a good photograph, it means death to the geometrically correct interplay of proportions. Besides, it very rarely happens that a photograph which was feebly composed can be saved by the reconstruction of its composition under the darkroom's enlarger; the integrity of vision is no longer there. There is a lot of talk about camera angles; but the only valid angles in existence are the angles of the geometry of composition and not the ones fabricated by the photographer who falls flat on his stomach or performs other antics to procure his effects.

Henri Cartier-Bresson, *The Decisive Moment*

4. The composition is the thing seen by every one living in the living that they are doing, they are the composing of the composition that at the time they are living is the composition of the time in which they are living. It is that that makes living a thing they are doing. Nothing else is different, of that almost any one can be certain. The time when and the time of and the time in that composition is the natural phenomena of that composition and of that perhaps everyone can be certain.

No one thinks these things when they are making when they are creating what is the composition, naturally no one thinks, that is no one formulates until what is to be formulated has been made.

Composition is not there, it is going to be there and we are here...

Gertrude Stein, "Composition as Explanation"

5. It is known that this preoccupation with locale is frequent among the creative who find in their imagination richer sources of inspiration than in copying reality. It was in a Burgundian village that Debussy patiently studied the play of waves for La Mer and in his lodging in the Batignolles that he condensed, without having crossed the Pyrenees, the intoxicating perfumes for *Ibéria*. Two well-known anecdotes of Fauré and Ravel confirm this observation. To an admirer who begged him to reveal the divine countryside which had dictated the sublime harmonies of the *Nocturne No. 6 in D flat Major, Op. 63* to him, Fauré answered with a secret satisfaction, "the Simplon Tunnel." And Ravel, during a trip to Morocco, confessed, "If I were involved in composing Arab music, it would be much more Arabic than the real thing."

Emile Vuillermoz, *Gabriel Fauré*

6. A kind of urbanistic thinking prompted Palladio to draw together the discrete functions of the villa into a compact organism; he wrote in the Quattri Libri that a house is nothing other than a small city. Behind this metaphor there was a social theory of architectural history: man, according to Palladio, first lived and built alone, but later, seeing the benefits of commerce, he formed villages by bringing houses together. By analogy, a farm center would become more economical and natural as its functions were drawn together. Mere clustering, however, would not do. Palladio believed in a hierarchy of functions, and compared the dwelling to the human body, the noble and beautiful parts of which the Lord ordained to be exposed, and the ignoble but essential parts to be hidden from sight. The metaphor of the organism reminds us that every Palladian work is designed as if members are joined symmetrically to a central spine. Whether or not the villas were planned consciously to be built outward in symmetrical units from the spine – as against being raised all at once, storey by storey – this process proved to be eminently suitable to the uncertain economy of the time. The master's dwelling had to be habitable, but from there on Palladio's patrons added just what they could afford of the annexed loggias and towers.

James Ackerman, *Palladio*

7. The arch is nothing else than a force originated by two weaknesses, for the arch in buildings is composed of two segments of a circle, each of which being very weak in itself tends to fall; but as each opposes this tendency in the other, the two weaknesses combine to form one strength. As the arch is a composite force it remains in equilibrium because the thrust is equal from both sides; and if one of the segments weighs more than the other the stability is lost, because the greater pressure will outweigh the lesser. Next to giving the segments of the circle equal weight it is necessary to load them equally, or you will fall into the same defect as before. An arch breaks at the part which lies halfway from the center. The way to give stability to the arch is to fill the spandrils with good masonry up to the level of its summit.

Leonardo da Vinci

8. May I use a simile, a simile of the tree? The artist has studied this world of variety and has, we may suppose, unobtrusively found his way in it. His sense of direction in nature and life,

this branching and spreading array, I shall compare with the root of the tree. From the root the sap flows to the artist, flows through him, flows to his eye. Thus he stands as the trunk of the tree. Battered and stirred by the strength of the flow, he moulds his vision into his work. As, in full view of the world, the crown of the tree unfolds and spreads in time and in space, so with his work. Nobody would affirm that the tree grows its crown in the image of its root. Between above and below can be no mirrored reflection. It is obvious that different functions expanding in different elements produce vital divergences. But it is just the artist who at times is denied those departures from nature which his art demands. He has ever been charged with incompetence and deliberate distortion. And yet, standing at his appointed place, the trunk of the tree, he does nothing other than gather and pass on what comes to him from its depths. He neither serves nor rules – he transmits. His position is humble. And the beauty at the crown is not his own. He is merely a channel.

Paul Klee, *On Modern Art*

9. The poet, described in ideal perfection, brings the whole soul of man into activity, with the subordination of its faculties to each other according to their relative worth and dignity. He diffuses a tone and spirit of unity, that blends, and (as it were) *fuses,* each into each by that synthetic and magical power, to which I would exclusively appropriate the name of Imagination. This power, first put in action by the will and understanding, and retained under their irremissive, though gentle and unnoticed, control, *laxis effertur habenis* [swept along, unreined], reveals itself in the balance or reconcilement of opposite or discordant qualities: of sameness with difference; of the general with the concrete; the idea with the image; the individual with the representative; the sense of novelty and freshness with old and familiar objects; a more than usual state of emotion with more than usual order; judgment ever awake and steady self-possession with enthusiasm and feeling profound or vehement; and while it blends and harmonizes the natural and the artificial, still subordinates art to nature; the manner to the matter; and our admiration of the poet to our sympathy with the poetry.

Samuel Taylor Coleridge, *Biographia Literaria*

V

ARTICULATING RELATIONSHIPS

1. "Is A *Definable in Terms of B?*"

When you understand what's going on in reading or conversing, you're seeing the relationships of one statement to another; you follow what is being said or written. "I don't follow you" means "I don't understand." When you write, the principal question, once you learn to frame it, is: "How do I get from here to there?" The problem of sequence is not – alas – solved by figuring out which words follow which. Getting from here to there is not a matter of lining up words but of articulating meanings.

To be *articulate* means to speak so that every syllable is clear and, by extension, to demonstrate clearly the relationship of one idea to another. *Articulation* derives from the Latin word *(artus)* for *joint*: anatomists speak of the articulation of the skeleton, meaning the relationship of bone, tendon, ligament, and muscle that makes motor activity possible. Without articulation, the skeleton would be merely a clutter of bones; without articulation, there can be statements but no composition. Articulation implies understanding the terms in which the relationships are seen, named, known. You can learn a lot about what articulation involves by considering that little phrase *in terms of*. In describing anything, you identify characteristics in terms of categories determined by your interest and purpose. *To speak in terms of* is short for *to speak in the terms that the category provides for description and definition.*

The phrase *in terms of* is frequently misused: "What'll we have for supper?" "Oh, I've been thinking in terms of soup and sandwiches." Or: "The Antarctic has a very austere beauty and, of course, on the fringes, it has fantastic wildlife, in terms of penguins and so on." *In terms of* should be used when you mean the descriptive and defining words that are offered by a concept when you are naming the members of the class. (A class, you remember, is the field of a concept's application.) Here are some examples of correct use:

- This problem cannot be understood *in terms of* banking concepts alone; we need to develop a political understanding.
- *In terms of* cost accounting, it's a good budget.
- If you're considering education *in terms of* its economic benefits, you're in for a surprise.
- Consumer education is directed toward changing people's attitudes about purchasing so that they judge various products *in terms of* performance and value rather than *in terms of* appearance and benefits alleged in advertisements.

You can think of *in terms of* as a kind of signal that announces that such and such an instance or example or case is to be discussed as a member of a certain class: writing *in terms of* is a way of explicitly classifying. The "terms" are the names provided by the class, the concept, or the category; a *terminology* is the collection of such terms.

Any discipline requires the capacity to define *in terms of* certain categories — to be able to classify by differentiating according to criteria derived from those categories. Take the professions, for instance. The lawyer makes a case by arguing along certain lines, *in terms of* such categories as jurisdiction, legality, culpability, etc. Learning the law means learning how the categories work to guide you in arguing a case. The physician diagnoses diseases and malfunctions by reading symptoms *in terms of* normal expectations about the functioning of the human organism. The preacher proclaims the truth as it can be defined *in terms of* dogma, revelation, ecclesiastical law and history, the sacred texts, the lives of the saints and martyrs, etc.

Articulating relationships as we form and develop concepts depends on a capacity to see the form of one thing in another and to use the form of one to explain and define the other. Such a description is called an *analogy* and it re-presents the way we see relationships. The continuum of the composing process depends on the fact that we can see one thing — shape, event, concept — *in*

terms of another. Describing a malfunctioning kidney and describing a bankruptcy case require different terminologies, but to
emphasize a point the lawyer can use medical terminology just
as the physician can use legal terminology. The analogy can
clarify certain relationships and help to form the concept.

There are many varieties of analogy, many different names
for analogous relationships, some of which may be familiar to
you if you have studied poetry: *metaphor, simile, allegory,* for
instance. It won't surprise you to be told that in all its varieties,
analogy is a form that finds form: a form of comparison that
helps discover likenesses; a form of argument that helps you to
discover implications; a form of statement that helps find the
form of feeling and thought you intend to express and represent.
Analogy is the principal means of articulating relationships and
thus of forming concepts.

One way to sharpen your sense of what *in terms of* means
and to learn how to use analogies is to practice deliberately
seeing one thing in the terms that are generally used in describing another class of things. This transforming goes on all the
time as you make sense of the world. Transforming is a way of
seeing what-would-happen-if; it shakes up the categories of
understanding and makes you more aware of context.

 ꙮ At the time we were sending a
man to the moon, an article appeared entitled "Landing a Man Downtown." What was it about?

 ꙮ Thorstein Veblen invented a
phrase that exemplifies the inventive use of analogy:
he called industrialists *"captains* of industry," thus
suggesting the military-like character of capitalist
structures. Using that phrase as a pattern, rename the
following:

students: the _____ of _____
teachers: the _____ of _____
patriots: the _____ of _____

 ꙮ Try another pattern with these:

_____ are the mice of _____ .
_____ are the moths of _____ .
_____ are the dinosaurs of the _____ .

Analogy is a form which can help you make meaning because it requires that you focus on the grounds of a comparison: something is like something else *in certain respects:* that phrase is as useful as *in terms of.* In order to use analogy effectively, a writer must know how to assure that the logic of the analogy is sound. Here are two ways of making sure that you know the grounds of an analogy.

1. You can use a ratio form to represent these "certain respects." Veblen's famous analogy would look like this:

$$\frac{\text{captains}}{\text{army}} : \frac{\text{capitalists}}{\text{industry}} : \frac{\text{leaders}}{\text{hierarchically organized institutions}}$$

This is shorthand for "The relationship of *captains* to *army* is comparable to that of *capitalists* to *industry* . . . ." Once you have lined up the equivalence relationships this way, you can decide what else could belong. *Priests, students, clerks, managers:* can you tell which of these terms are logically of the same sort as *captains* and *capitalists,* those respects defined in the most general equivalence? As you think of others, you may need to adjust the most general terms; for instance, is *hierarchically* essential to what is meant?

2. Like *in terms of,* the phrase *in light of* is very useful. If you have a good idea of the idea you want to explain and you need an analogy to help articulate the relationship among possible examples, you can imagine a street light and the area it illuminates.

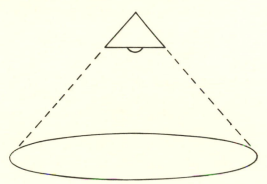

Think of the area illuminated by the street light as the field of the concept's application. Anything in that field is potentially an analog of everything else in it, but you must name your idea carefully. If you are going to try to compare certain countries *with respect to* their democratic government, that's going to be difficult: the light cast by that idea is too diffuse, too dim. *In the light* of such a general idea, you can't really see well enough to determine just what's in the field of the concept's application and what isn't.

Analogy is one of the chief means a writer has for articulating relationships – for assuring that the argument he or she is developing has "joints." But these joints won't be strong unless the writer remembers that in making a comparison it isn't enough to say that *something* is like *something else:* he or she must know in what respects X is like Y. If you're to define X *in terms of* Y, those terms must define a field of application to which both X and Y can be said to belong.

Now here are some invitations to look at what analogies do and thereby to see how to construct your own.

        Sue built a bunkhouse on her ranch in Texas. That is to say, she designed it, drew up the plans with all measurements indicated, had the lumberyard cut the lumber, borrowed the cattle trailer to load it, laid the concrete floor with the help of her son, who also worked with her doing the framing and roofing. "How did you do that?" asked her surprised husband when he got back from a trip. "Building a house isn't too hard," Sue answered, "if you know how to sew."

Work out the equivalences, beginning with

$$\frac{\text{floor plan}}{\text{dress pattern}} : \underline{\hspace{2cm}}$$

Remember that this is shorthand for : "The floor plan bears the same relationship to a dress pattern as...."
Then compose a sentence which explains Sue's analogy.

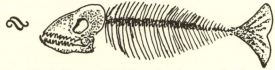

Why is this called a "fish frame"? What is the *analog*?
(Look up that word.) Fill out the ratios:

$$\frac{\text{fish}}{?} : \frac{?}{\text{frame}}$$

℘ Here's a poem by Ho Chi
Minh, the revolutionary who for over fifty years led the
Vietnamese people in their struggle for independence,
first from the French and later from the United States
and our surrogates. Work out the equivalencies in ratio
form and then compose a title for the poem. (Think of it
as a gloss.) Write a sentence or two explaining your
title. Begin with the equivalence itself, rather than
saying "I chose X as my title because...."

> The wheel of the law turns
> without pause.
>
> After the rain, good weather.
> In the wink of an eye
>
> The universe throws off
> its muddy clothes.
>
> For ten thousand miles
> the landscape
>
> spreads out like a beautiful brocade.
> Light breezes. Smiling flowers.
>
> High in the trees, amongst
> the sparkling leaves
>
> all the birds sing at once.
> Men and animals rise-up reborn.
>
> What could be more natural?
> After sorrow, comes happiness.
>
> Ho Chi Minh

〰 A story known to any literate Chinese tells how Wang Hsi-Chih learned the secrets of beautiful calligraphy by studying the graceful movements of geese. Name the idea(s) which illuminate the area where you would find both *calligraphy* and *graceful movement of geese.* (To what class could they both belong?)

〰 In the closing years of the eighteenth century, John Smeaton rebuilt the lighthouse at Eddystone on the Southern coast of Britain so that it withstood terrific gales for many decades. Here he explains the analogies from which he derived his design. Work out the ratios and then compose a poem celebrating Smeaton's feat, using Ho Chi Minh's as a model. (Or you could compose your poem in the ballad meter of "My father was the keeper of the Eddystone Light." That could be a group project for a forestry student, an engineering student, and a music major or poet.)

On this occasion, the natural figure of the waist or bole of a large spreading oak, presented itself to my imagination. Let us for a moment consider this tree: suppose at twelve or fifteen feet about its base, it branches out in every direction, and forms a large bushy top, as we often observe. This top, when full of leaves, is subject to a very great impulse from the agitation of violent winds; yet partly by its elasticity, and partly by the natural strength arising from its figure, it resists them all, even for ages, till the gradual decay of the material diminishes the coherence of the parts, and they suffer piecemeal by the violence; but it is very rare that we hear of such a tree being torn up by the roots. Let us now consider its particular figure. Connected with its roots, which lie hid below ground, it rises from the surface thereof with a large swelling base, which at the height of one diameter is generally reduced by an elegant curve, concave to the eye, to a diameter less by at least one-third, and sometimes to half of its original base. From thence its taper diminishing more slow, its sides by degrees come into a perpendicular, and for some height form a cylinder. After that a preparation of more circumference becomes necessary, for the strong insertion and establishment of the principal boughs, which produces a swelling of its diameter. Now we can hardly doubt but every section of the tree is nearly of an equal strength in proportion to what it has to resist; and were we to lop off its principal boughs, and expose it in that state to a rapid current of water, we should find it as much capable of resisting the action of the heavier fluid, when divested of the greatest part of its clothing, as it was that of the lighter when all its spreading ornaments were exposed to the fury of the wind: and hence we may derive an idea of what the proper shape of a column of the greatest stability ought to be, to resist the action of external violence, when the quantity of matter is given whereof it is to be composed.

It is farther observable, in the insertions of the boughs of trees into the bole, or of the branches into the boughs, (which is generally at an oblique angle) that those insertions are made by a swelling curve, of the same nature as that wherewith the tree rises out of the ground; and that the greatest rake or sweep of this curve, is that which fills up the obtuse angle; while the acute angle is filled up with a much quicker curve, or sweep of a less radius. I immediately rough-turned a piece of wood, with a small degree of tapering above; and leaving matter enough below, I fitted it to the oblique surface of a block of wood, somewhat resembling the sloping surface of the Eddystone Rock; and soon found, that by reconciling curves, I could adapt every part of the base upon the rock to the regularly turned tapering body, and so as to make a figure not ungraceful; and at the same time carrying the idea of great firmness and solidity.

I had occasionally observed in many places in the streets of London, that in fixing the curbs of the walking paths, the long pieces or stretchers were retained between two headers or bond pieces; whose heads being cut dovetail-wise, adapted themselves to and confined in the stretchers; which expedient, though chiefly intended to save iron and lead, nevertheless appeared to me capable of more firmness than any superficial fastening could be; as the tie was as good at the bottom as at the top, which was the very thing I wanted; and therefore if the tail of the header was made to have an adequate bond with the interior parts, the work would in itself be perfect.

John Smeaton, *A Narrative of the Building and a Description of the Construction of the Eddystone Lighthouse with Stone*

∾ Gloss the following paragraphs. Work out the ratios for Kubler's analogies. Compose a couple of paragraphs in which you form the concept of *historical evidence*.

Knowing the past is as astonishing a performance as knowing the stars. Astronomers look only at old light. There is no other light for them to look at. This old light of dead or distant stars was emitted long ago and it reaches us only in the present. Many historical events, like astronomical bodies, also *occur* long before they *appear,* such as secret treaties, aide-mémoires, or important works of art made for ruling personages. The physical substance of these documents often reaches qualified observers only centuries or millenia after the event. Hence astronomers and historians have this in common: both are concerned with appearances noted in the present but occurring in the past.

The analogies between stars and works of art can profitably be pursued. However fragmentary its condition, any work of art is actually a portion of arrested happening, or an emanation of past time. It is a graph of an activity now stilled, but a graph made visible like an astronomical body, by a light that originated with the activity. When an important work of art has utterly disappeared by demolition or dispersal, we still can detect its perturbations upon other bodies in the field of influence. By the same token, works of art resemble gravitational fields in their clustering by "schools." And if we admit that works of art can be arranged in a temporal series as connected expressions, their sequence will resemble an orbit in the infrequency, the regularity, and the necessity of the "motions" involved.

Like the astronomer, the historian is engaged upon the portrayal of time. The scales are different: historic time is very short, but the historian and the astronomer both transpose, reduce, compose, and color a facsimile which describes the shape of time. Historical time indeed may occupy a situation near the center of the proportional scale of the possible magnitudes of time, just as man himself is a physical magnitude midway between the sun and the atom at the proportional center of the solar system, both in grams of mass and in centimeters of diameter.

Both astronomers and historians collect ancient signals into compelling theories about distance and composition. The astronomer's position is the historian's date; his velocity is our sequence; orbits are like durations; perturbations are analogous to causality. The astronomer and the historian both deal with past events perceived in the present. Here the parallels diverge, for the astronomer's future events are physical and recurrent ones, while the historian's are human and unpredictable ones. The foregoing analogies are nevertheless useful in prompting us to look again at the nature of historical evidence, so that we may be sure of our ground when considering various ways of classing it.

George Kubler, *The Shape of Time*

೪ In the following, M.R. Montgomery argues that a can of beer is, in certain respects, like a wrist watch: which kind of watch? in which respects? How would you name the field of application in which both the wrist watch and the beer can can be located? Give this essay a title.

I haven't seen an advertisement for a digital watch in months. You go to the drugstore, you go to Tiffany's, they've got analog watches that say it's supper time when the little hand is on the seven and the big hand is on the 12. It doesn't matter if it's $20 or $2,800, it's got one little hand and one big hand, and sometimes a sweep-second hand, and that's the end of the digital watch revolution.

The world is full of analog measuring devices, which can be described, roughly, as continuous measurements, rather than discrete, or digital, points on a measurement from here to there and back again.

The old vegetable-store scales, where the hand sweeps around from zero to 20 pounds, oven thermometer settings on the continuous dial from off to 550 degrees, ordinary kitchen timers that you turn to set and start ticking, gasoline gauges that wiggle from "f" to "e." You probably don't know how much your tank holds, and you probably can't figure out how many miles you can go on a quarter of a tank. You don't need to, because you have this nice, acquired, analog understanding of the relationship between the needle and the fact that it's not a waste of time to stop for gas.

I think people always have lived in an analog world, and always will. We measure things continuously, not always accurately, but continuously and with reference to ourselves. That is why, when you do go home again, the old house isn't as big, and the elementary school isn't a brick fortress the size of Cheop's Tomb.

If we measured things digitally, with discrete little numbers, we'd know exactly how big the old house was, and we wouldn't be that confused about the quality of Mom's apple pie, which was eaten before we knew anything about cholesterol, tooth decay and middle-age spread. If her pie measured 11.7 on the digital pie scale, we'd know a 12 or 13.3 when we got one.

Middle-age spread, by the way, is the classic analog-measured condition. You never find out by standing on the digital-readout bathroom scale. A scale tells you how much you weigh, it doesn't tell you where you weigh. The belt, however, is a classic continuous, analog, measurement. Middle-age spread is when you use the second hole, not the third hole.

I suspect that the current problems in the personal computer business are reflections of our preference for analog measurements and analog displays. How would you write your mother a letter on a word processor? A letter to your mother is supposed to fill up at least one page, or fill up the message side of one postcard, if you're not feeling very prolix.

Mothers can tell when you're not trying, and one of the clues is when you don't fill up at least one whole side of something. But you can write bigger or smaller on the postcard, usually bigger if you are not very prolix or very imaginative. "Having wonderful time, wish you were here." can actually fill up the message space on a picture postcard if you write "WONDERFUL" in capital letters and under-line it. To put it simply, an analog message to your mother is long enough to get from here to there and not a comma wasted.

But on a word processor, you have to write enough stuff in letters that are all the same size to fill up an entire page, which is theoretically easy to do, as far as measuring it all, because any respectable word processor will count the number of words you have written. However, it can be very difficult to write all those words, especially when you are not only not prolix, but you are even antilix, which is something that can happen to the most dutiful of children.

Most people – and that includes people that work with computers and numbers all day long – are not necessarily interested in digital printouts and readouts, once they get home. What they usually want when they get home is a beer, or two beers, which is certainly not 12, or 24, ounces of a 4.1-percent alcohol solution. If that's all there was to a beer, we'd take it intravenously, and not watch the dew condense on the bottle in a perfectly understandable, analog, measurement of the heat and humidity of a July evening.

༄ The tar and gravel amalgam which is used to surface roads is called "macadam," after the Scots engineer who invented it, John McAdam. He developed a system of roadbuilding which greatly improved transportation in Britain. Here's an example of the way he went about it (as described at Culzean Castle in Ayrshire):

Tradition had it that no roadstone might be used that would not go in a man's mouth, so every road gang had one member with a huge jaw. McAdam was more precise: "The size of stone used on a road must be in due proportion to the space occupied by a wheel of ordinary dimensions on a smooth level surface. This point of contact will be found to be longitudinally about an inch, and every piece of stone put into a road which exceeds an inch in any of its dimensions is mischievous." (*System of Roadmaking,* 1821)

1. Does McAdam use an analog in his specifications? Explain.
2. What do you imagine M.R. Montgomery would have to say about this choice between digital and analog measurement? (See his essay, above.)
3. Would the man with the big jaw be the *ping* or the *pong* of his road gang? (See pages 39-40.)

It's useful to think of analogy as a *transformation:* one object or idea is at least temporarily transformed into another object or idea. To see *something* as *something else* is really the way we see anything at all. Do you remember Barfield's "meaningless man" and the argument that re-cognition is necessary to cognition? (pages 44-45) Both poets and scientists deal in transformations.

When Wordsworth explained what he and Coleridge intended in their revolutionary new kind of poetry, he said that his aim was to make the familiar *strange* and that Coleridge was attempting to make the strange *familiar*. This Romantic poetics is alive and well in science fiction writing. It is also common practice with inventors and other problem-solvers who deliberately try to see the familiar in fresh ways and to assimilate the strange by pretending that it's familiar by inventing a perspective from which it would be familiar.

∾ See if you can transform some of the objects in the list below, making the strange familiar and the familiar strange. You can transform most easily if you consider the object or idea from an unusual perspective. The technique of horror movies is to distort scale: picnic ants become monsters from the deep lagoon.

Make the familiar strange	Make the strange familiar
a tin can	the Finnish language
a traffic jam	a viola da gamba
the moon	the Himalayas
a mosquito	a cow's digestive system
an orange tree	a llama
Christmas	the Stone Age
a nuclear power plant	a radiation victim

∾ Explain the procedures for a chemical analysis of an unknown substance. How is transformation involved?

Thinking is seeing relationships; composing is the art of representing that "seeing." Composing is the art of naming, opposing, and defining in order to articulate relationships. Transformations are one of the chief means by which the thoughtful composer can put things in a new light and thus clarify relationships and form concepts. A whole range of techniques is available for effecting such transformations. Satire, for instance, often employs a distortion of scale to force us to see some aspects of reality more clearly. In *Gulliver's Travels* – to take the most famous example – Jonathan Swift tells how his hero is shipwrecked among the Lilliputians, in comparison to whom he is a giant, and how, then, on a subsequent voyage, he finds himself among giants. Gulliver is placed in the care of Glumdalclitch, a 40-foot tall nurse who carries him in a padded box at her waist.

I remember one morning when Glumdalclitch had set me in my box upon a window, as she usually did in fair days to give me air (for I durst not venture to let the box be hung on a nail out of the window, as we do with cages in England) after I had lifted up one of my sashes [windows], and sat down at my table to eat a piece of sweet cake for my breakfast, above twenty wasps allured by the smell, came flying into the room, humming louder than the drones of as many bagpipes. Some of them seized my cake, and carried it piecemeal away, others flew about my head and face, confounding me with noise, and putting me in the utmost terror of their stings. However I had the courage to rise and draw my hanger [sword] and attack them in the air. I dispatched four of them, but the rest got away, and I presently shut my window. These insects were as large as partridges: I took out their stings, found them an inch and a half long, and as sharp as needles. I carefully preserved them all, and having shown them with some other curiosities in several parts of Europe, upon my return to England I gave three of them to Gresham College, and kept the fourth myself.

Continual reference to the insects and small animals as gigantic monsters prepares us for the scene in which the King of Brobdingnag tells Gulliver, whom he holds in the palm of his hand, that from what Gulliver has told him of the customs and habits of his countrymen, he "cannot but conclude the bulk of your natives to be the most pernicious race of little odious vermin that nature ever suffered to crawl upon the surface of the earth."

Satire offers what Kenneth Burke, a learned and witty rhetorician, calls "perspective by incongruity." Things that don't belong together can, in juxtaposition, give us new insights, help us form concepts. Transforming is at the heart of Burke's theory of rhetoric, which he summarizes as follows: "Instead of viewing words as *names* for *things,* we should view them as abbreviated *titles* for *situations.*" HDWDWW? is a transformer that allows us to do just that—to convert names and things to titles and situations. And stories are very powerful transformers.

A *story* told to illustrate a concept is one of the oldest literary forms. (*Story* is cognate with *history;* they derive from the Greek *histor,* knowing.) Parables and fables, for instance, spell out the implications of statements about the way of the world, the nature of evil, pride, envy, love, etc., by telling stories that dramatize these concepts. Here's an example:

A farmer, being on the point of death, and wishing to show his sons the way to success in farming, called them to him and said, "My children, I am departing from this life, but all that I have to leave you will be found in the vineyard." The sons, supposing that he referred to some hidden treasure, as

soon as the old man was dead, set to work with their spades
and ploughs and every implement that was at hand and
turned the soil over and over again. They found indeed no
treasure; but the vines strengthened and improved by this
thorough tillage, yielded a finer vintage than they had ever
yielded before, and more than repaid the young husband-
men for all their trouble.

So truly is industry in itself a virtue.

Aesop, "The Farmer and His Sons"

      ✑ Just as you can transform
objects into events, you can transform statements into
stories. Try it with these adages: write a brief story
demonstrating the principle or dramatizing the saying
and use the adage either as the title or the final line.
You'll need to develop a context by composing a
question to which the adage could be considered an
answer. Determine presuppositions by asking HDWDWW?
Once you've worked out the logic of the analogy, the
story will virtually write itself, but you must be sure to
transform the terms of the saying: don't write a story
about a stone that rolls continually down a stream bed
to illustrate the first adage.

- A rolling stone gathers no moss.
- Make hay while the sun shines.
- Grub first; then morals.
- A bird in the hand is worth two in the bush.
- If you can't stand the heat, get out of the kitchen.

Parables – stories meant to represent a principle – are popular with preachers and television advertisers and others who are
not dependent on the written word as their medium of communication. One estimate is that half of the world's population can
neither read nor write; it follows that any political leader who
would like to reach them would have to be skilled in oral
communication. Propaganda, advertising, and homiletics (the
art of preaching) are analogous *in certain respects:* each can be
described *in terms of* the others; all three can be defined *in the
light of* a common purpose, namely, to convince and exhort,
especially (though not necessarily) those who can not read.

      ✑ Traditionally, a sermon offers
an interpretation of a Biblical text; tells a story which
illustrates a principle or draws an analogy which

explains the interpretation; concludes with a summary of the lesson and an exhortation – some version of "Go and do thou likewise." Using this homiletic form as your model, analyze the form of a television advertisement and/or a political speech or address.

❧ In the following, Bertholt Brecht has the Buddha tell some of his followers a parable which explains an earlier response. Then Brecht interprets both the response and the parable of the burning house. Work out the equivalences in ratio form, proceeding backwards from *non-submission, proposals of an earthly nature, human tormentors,* etc., identifying the phrases in both the Buddha stories which are analogous.

The Buddha's Parable of the Burning House

Gautama the Buddha taught
The doctrine of greed's wheel to which we are bound, and advised
That we shed all craving and thus
Undesiring enter the nothingness that he called Nirvana.
Then one day his pupils asked him:
'What is it like, this nothingness, Master?
　　Every one of us would
Shed all craving, as you advise, but tell us
Whether this nothingness which then we shall enter
Is perhaps like being at one with all creation,
When you lie in water, your body weightless, at noon,
Unthinking almost, lazily lie in the water, or drowse
Hardly knowing now that you straighten the blanket,
Going down fast – whether this nothingness, then,
Is a happy one of this kind, a pleasant nothingness, or
Whether this nothing of yours is mere nothing, cold,
　　senseless and void.'
Long the Buddha was silent, then said nonchalantly:
"There is no answer to your question."

But in the evening, when they had gone,
The Buddha still sat under the bread-fruit tree and to the others,
To those who had not asked, addressed this parable:
"Lately I saw a house. It was burning. The flame

Licked at its roof. I went up close and observed
That there were people still inside. I entered the doorway
    and called
Out to them that the roof was ablaze, so exhorting them
To leave at once. But those people
Seemed in no hurry. One of them,
While the heat was already scorching his eyebrows,
Asked me what it was like outside, whether it wasn't
    raining,
Whether the wind wasn't blowing, perhaps, whether
    there was
Another house for them, and more of this kind. Without
    answering
I went out again. These people here, I thought,
Must burn to death before they stop asking questions.
                      And truly, friends,
Whoever does not yet feel such heat in the floor
    that he'll gladly
Exchange it for any other, rather than stay, to that man
I have nothing to say." So Gautama the Buddha.

But we too, no longer concerned with the art of submission,
Rather with that of non-submission, and offering
Various proposals of an earthly nature, and
    beseeching men
To shake off their human tormentors, we too believe
    that to those
Who in face of the rising bomber squadrons of Capital go on
    asking too long
How we propose to do this, and how we envisage that,
And what will become of their savings and Sunday trousers
    after a revolution,
We have nothing much to say.

                                  Bertolt Brecht

2. The Logic of Explanation: Inferences

Analogy is an essential element of your repertory as a writer because it allows you to formulate and articulate the relationship of *likeness*. Analogy guides you in asking if something can be defined in terms of something else. Definition, as we've discussed it, is the way to form concepts – and the reason for forming concepts is explanation. When you explain, you're answering the question *why,* the last term of HDWDWW?

When you explain something, you are relating cause and effect. Those who have learned the art of explanation will be less likely to think of causes as single and of effects as inevitable. The commonest fault in logic – and, of course, in our daily thinking about thinking – is to conclude that because something is *followed* by something else, the second is *caused* by the first. The technical name for this error in logic is *post hoc ergo propter hoc:* "after that and therefore because of that." The error arises from looking for "real" causes – that is, whatever can be easily identified. When you bark your shins on a low table, you feel like kicking the table. (Parents are warned of the dangers of encouraging the child who has just fallen down to spank the bad old table.) The most primitive analysis is to look for what caused an effect in terms of material objects.

෬ Aristotle analyzed cause into four categories.* They can be schematized as follows in the case of a house:

Material cause	Stuff	The stones that compose it
Efficient cause	Agency	The mason who laid them
Formal cause	Structure	The blueprint he followed
Final cause	Purpose	The purpose for which the house was built

Using the schema, work out an Aristotelian analysis of the following: 1. the broken window of a commuter train; 2. a skiing accident; 3. a particular military engagement (check your daily paper); 4. the closing down of an industrial plant. In each case, which cause would be most likely to be disputed in a court of law?

*Category in the original Greek meant *to speak against the assembly.* To categorize came to mean not just an accusation but any assertion or predication. In logic, *category* refers to any class used in an inquiry or discussion. For our purposes, a philosophical definition is most useful: a category is a class that helps define choices.

When the facts of a case are not immediately accessible—and even when they apparently are—we must depend on our ability to reason, to draw *inferences* from the situation or whatever information we can gather. We can reason only because we have language to hold things in mind; we not only can look but we can look again. The trout can interpret, but it cannot reason because it cannot interpret its interpretations. As a writer, you learn to develop and deploy your capacity for drawing inferences, for figuring things out.

An inference is an interpretation developed by drawing out the implications of statements of fact. Since we make meaning by means of meanings, we must always be ready to interpret those means, as well as the ends which they make it possible to reach. An inference, like any interpretation, is indirect; it is mediated by our senses, by our remembrance, by our expectations and attitudes. No inference can ever be proved to be absolutely correct; consequently, we must learn to establish our claims so that they can be judged *probably* correct and therefore justified.

Logicians differentiate between necessary and probable inferences. A necessary inference, when stated, is a tautology. If you have a son and a daughter, it necessarily follows that you have children. If you have three quarters and a nickel in your pocket, it necessarily follows that you have change. This difference is important in logic and mathematics, but we live in a world of probabilities. If we gather the *ascertainable facts,* we can draw some probable conclusions. This procedure holds true for doctors, lawyers, merchants, and chiefs; it holds true in our personal, as well as our professional, lives: we come to conclusions by drawing inferences.

To say that our inferences are probable and not necessary is not the same as saying that they are all in error. The fact that we can know only indirectly does not mean that "everything is relevant," unless we mean by that that the criteria for judging the evidence and the procedures by which we draw inferences are themselves subject to critical review. Everything is relevant to certain criteria, relevant to our purposes which must, of course, be interpreted. The reason that we must think about our thinking is that we can never be sure that we're right. Since we might be wrong, it's a good idea to cultivate the habit of having on hand more than one good idea so that we can test them all.

༄ Suppose you find yourself sneezing and your eyes watering. Is it probable that you have a cold? That depends on the evidence, the context of situation, and the improbability of other explanations. What *alternative hypotheses* can you construct in this case? Why does a physician need your medical history?

                        ᘱ Here's an observation Henry David Thoreau once made: "Some circumstantial evidence is very strong, as when you find a trout in the milk." What is the inference to be drawn from this evidence? What fact does it seem to establish? Is it a necessary inference? (The context of situation is illuminated by the historical fact that before the advent of the milk bottle and milk delivery to home or store, milk was purchased in bulk. Or you went to the barn with your bucket.)

Presuppositions are necessary to all thought. (Review pages 62-75.) When you're trying to explain something, it's useful to dredge up these presuppositions so that you can examine them carefully. If presuppositions aren't identified, they can't be corrected and you'll probably pre-judge whatever is at issue. (A pre-judgment is a *prejudice*. You won't confuse spelling and pronunciation if you remember that this word means judging *pre,* beforehand.) Only if presuppositions are brought to light can fresh inferences be drawn. Scientific discoveries, inventions, new theories all come about because someone has asked a new question that allows relationships to be articulated in a new way. To deduce that your eyes are smarting because a nearby smoke-stack is belching forth "smoke" takes no great insight; developing a political context for watering eyes may be harder.

Here's a useful account which suggests the relationship of presuppositions and inference, written by a historian who is interested in detective fiction.

Because historians deal with the inexact, they have developed certain common-sense rules for evaluating evidence in terms of its reliability, its relevance, its signifi-cance, and its singularity. Inference is notoriously unreliable, as are eyewitnesses, memories of old men, judgments of mothers about first children, letters written for publication, and garbage collectors. At the moment, I drive a much battered 1954 Cadillac, full of wayward lurchings, unidentifiable rattles, and unpredictable ways upon the road. Recently I shifted a shovel, which I carry in the trunk as proof against New England snows, to a new position. No sooner had I closed the lid than a new and penetrating noise arose from the back of the car which clearly was a metal shovel bouncing about within a trunk. My inference was that this was so, and for a week I drove without investigating the noise. Then the gas tank fell off, proving my inference wrong....

[Notions of relevancy are applied outside the library and] the historian needs to be the most practical of men as well. One of my acquaintances worked with Marine intelligence during World War II. He was asked to help judge how many Japanese had dug in on one of the strategically crucial South Pacific islands, an island which the Marine Corps planned to make their own, whatever the losses, within a few days. No Japanese could be seen from aerial reconnaissance, since their camouflage was nearly perfect. The historian provided an accurate figure, however, for he noted from aerial photographs that particularly dark patches could be identified as latrines, and upon consulting a captured Japanese manual, he learned how many latrines were to be dug per unit of men. The rest was so simple a matter of calculation that even the historian could provide an answer without the aid of a computer.

Robin W. Winks, *The Historian as Detective*

❧ What were the presuppositions of the Marine Corps historian?

To explain is to account for. Identifying presuppositions is one place to begin the account; identifying a *motive* is another. Detectives speculate about motive as a way of generating hypotheses that could order a mass of "clues" that may turn out to be evidence for causal relationships. A clue is a fact looking for a context. Historians also form hypotheses to account for what "really" happened. Winks includes in his list of unreliable sources the accounts of old men, but here's one who sounds convincing:

What made the farmers fight in 1775? Judge Mellen Chamberlain in 1842, when he was 21, interviewed Captain Preston, a 91-year-old veteran of the Concord fight: "Did you take up arms against intolerable oppressions?" he asked.

"Oppressions?" replied the old man. "I didn't feel them."

"What, were you not oppressed by the Stamp Act?"

"I never saw one of those stamps. I certainly never paid a penny for one of them."

"Well, what then about the tea tax?"

"I never drank a drop of that stuff; the boys threw it all overboard."

"Then I suppose you had been reading Harrington or Sidney or Locke about the eternal principles of liberty?"

"Never heard of 'em. We read only the Bible, the catechism, Watts' Psalms and hymns, and the almanac."

"Well, then, what was the matter? And what did you mean in going to the fight?"

"Young man, what we meant in going for those Redcoats was this: *We always had governed ourselves, and we always meant to. They didn't mean we should.*"

S. E. Morison, *The Oxford History of the American People*

        🙟 Translate (paraphrase) each of the *meants* and *means* in the old man's reply.

        🙟 How would you answer someone who dismissed this dialogue as "poor evidence"?

        🙟 Conduct an interview with someone involved in the student protests against the Vietnam War, 1968-74. Working from your notes, record it in the form of the Chamberlain-Preston dialogue. (As a group project, this could involve establishing contexts by reading contemporary accounts of what was going on in Indochina. The reports of Senator Edward Kennedy's Subcommittee on Refugees are excellent sources. *The Pentagon Papers* is another.)

An explanation accounts for a state of affairs by relating an *effect* to a probable *cause*. To develop strong, sound inferences by means of which you can establish probable causes, the best procedure is to develop alternative hypotheses so that you can show what follows, given this or that set of assumptions. This logical procedure – which is technically known as *abduction* – is represented in the sentence form:

If _____ , then _____ ; otherwise, _____ .

The *if* part is the hypothetical supposition; the *then* part is the inference; the *otherwise* part is a signal that another hypothesis might be required if all the data is to be accounted for.

         ∾ Abduction can help you articulate relationships. If you review glosses and other comments in your dialectical notebook about one or another topic, you can practice abduction by continuing with the *then* after these *ifs*:

If $\left\{\begin{array}{l}\text{these are the facts, then} \ldots \\ \text{this is what happened, then} \ldots \\ \text{we think (hold, decide) that, then} \ldots \\ \text{we can describe these symptoms, then} \ldots \\ \text{we can marshall this evidence, then} \ldots\end{array}\right.$

         ∾ If you have studied computer science, explain the Boolean algorithm to someone who has not.

         ∾ Here is a recapitulation of our discussion of the logic of explanation. Complete it by continuing from *otherwise*.

If you can learn to identify and question presuppositions, to consider contexts when you analyze causal relations, *then* you will be working to assure that your assertions are reasonable; *otherwise*, ...

3. The Rhetoric of Explanation: Warrants

      In situations outside the composition classroom, your writing is most likely to take the form of *argument*, a term which suggests dispute or debate but which really refers to the art of making a topic or position clear by means of a dialectic between you and your audience. In your dialectical notebook, you've been continually working to make a topic clear to yourself. Once that has been achieved, however, a real-world task is at hand: making it clear and persuasive to others. When you argue well, you let the inner dialogue go public. You phrase your ideas, form your sentences, and organize your materials in terms of what you know about your audience and its needs, preferences, or expectations. Logic, by an old analogy, is a closed fist. It's tightly knit and indisputable as demonstrated truth. Rhetoric, in contrast, is an open palm — ready to perform whatever task is necessary in order to *persuade* the audience that what we are talking about is more likely than the alternatives. Very few situations in a writer's life will allow him or her to depend entirely on logical demonstration; almost always, rhetoric is required.

Of course, no argument gets anywhere without sufficient data, facts, details, examples, all developed from the chaos generated by research. When you have determined that your *evidence* is strong and ample, and when you have, by means of the dialectic, interpreted that material well-enough to make a *claim,* you're close to the point where your argument can begin. What's still missing, however, is the bridge between the data and the claim, the link that will make it clear to your audience that the evidence adduced really does support your claim. In most recent theories of argument, that bridge is called a *warrant.*

When a warrant for an arrest is issued, it means that the authorities have good reason to *believe* that the suspect has committed a crime. If you buy a product with a warranty, you have received a certificate of good *faith* from the manufacturer, who promises to repair or replace the item if it doesn't work properly for a specified time. It's the manufacturer's best *judgment* that the product will perform as warranted, and you assume it will. Similarly, a search warrant states that your right to privacy is being suspended temporarily and legally on the *grounds* that you may well be harboring evidence of a crime.

Shakespeare's characters use the statement "I warrant" to indicate conclusions based primarily on experienced observation, intuition, shared values or opinions, community standards, human feeling, instinct, sense of probability, and even hunches. All these forms of generalization fall into the category of "educated guesses"; now, as then, warrants enable you to proceed with legal, personal, or rhetorical agendas without fear of offending or losing your audience. Warrants of this kind are implicit in your argument; that is, you take certain values, feelings, or opinions for granted. You assume certain knowledge and opinions based on that knowledge. As writers, we have a much greater chance of establishing and making use of warrants than we do of getting readers to agree on facts or the meaning of facts. If you have established warrants with your audience, you have gained what's called rapport, a relationship based on affinities, or mutual beliefs and feelings, shared principles.

In *Much Ado About Nothing,* Shakespeare's classic tale about the importance of warranting, the "nothing" is "something." That is, the whole plot turns on what most people call evidence: what is seen, what is heard, what people say to each other (as opposed to what they want to say), what is written or printed, and precedent, or what has happened before. The plot consists entirely of actions generated by lies, misunderstood statements, half-overheard conversations, and silences – what is not said when it should be said. If you think about it, you may realize that much of what we call evidence consists of carefully selected and misinterpreted *facts,* half-heard or understood conversations, or that which is not reported ("Well, *I* never heard anything about it").

In *Much Ado,* a villain sets out to ruin the reputation of a young woman who is about to be married; in this way, he will spite her father and all the other noblemen who have treated him as an inferior. He manages to get most of those noblemen to come out very late on the night before the wedding and to watch the young lady's bedroom window until a "ruffian" with a ladder arrives and is "entertained" by her. At the wedding on the next day, the innocent young woman is denounced by her husband-to-be as a "rotten orange," rejected by her father, and abused by most of the wedding party, who quickly leave. Fortunately, the officiating priest "warrants" her innocence. He has no "evidence" at all, except against her. She was seen by highly reliable witnesses consorting with a disreputable man on the night before her wedding; she was in her nightgown and seemed quite friendly with the thug. Her denial – she has done no more "than that which maiden modesty doth warrant" – makes it look even worse for her: she doesn't have the confidence to argue back or the sense to lie. But the priest warrants her innocence, which means that he believes firmly in his generalization and believes also that others will join him in that belief, if they give him a chance to defend it.

What is the basis for that warrant? For one thing, *common sense* tells him that it's unlikely that such a young woman would be capable of breaking a solemn vow, especially on the night before her wedding; for another, simple values dictate that no young person deserves the kind of humiliation she has received and that virtue is a quality which an inexperienced person finds difficult to fake; further, the priest assumes her innocence until her guilt is established beyond a reasonable doubt. His hunch is right – she has been "framed" by the villain and a female accomplice who had dressed as the heroine and entertained the ruffian at her bedroom window. Thus, by means of warranting, a near-tragedy is turned back into a comedy.

A warrant is a *presupposition* held in common by you and your audience. It articulates the meaning of your evidence and gives form to the constructions – the claims – that you have grounded on that evidence. The priest in *Much Ado* establishes warrants with the heroine's family and friends by claiming that people accused of crimes or bad faith deserve time to prove their innocence and that common social and moral values must force us to believe the person innocent until she is proved guilty. His evidence is skimpy but persuasive: she has always been virtuous and decent; her vows of fidelity and love were apparently heartfelt; she blushed deeply and denied her guilt fervently when accused; she demanded proof; she fainted. Most of the people at the wedding construed this behavior as evidence of guilt, but the priest saw that it was the fashion of her clothes which caused others to believe that she was at that window. A good argument must now be "fashioned" that will proclaim her innocence. New and overriding assumptions must be established.

To warrant is to assume on the basis of many things which, by themselves, don't constitute admissible evidence in a hearing or a court of *law*. We're talking about personal experiences, values and standards, religious and moral perspectives, "human feeling" or compassion, instinct and intuition, probability, judgment, and opinion. If you attempt to apply such standards in a trial, the judge may rule on the opposing attorney's protest: "objection sustained."

And yet legal systems have always attempted to adapt to the human situation and to the complexities of contemporary life by taking account of community standards, values, opinions, and belief. The character of both defendants and witnesses, as established by many testimonies, can swing judges or juries in one direction or another. It has been argued that a courtroom trial is a miniature version of life itself, and that no issue raised there can be *fairly* considered without accounting for the variables that may be introduced.

In his poem, "Thirteen Ways of Looking at a Blackbird," Wallace Stevens gives us a concrete illustration of this point:

> I was of three minds,
>> Like a tree
>> In which there are three blackbirds.

Looking at three blackbirds, each of which is looking out from a tree from its own perspective, reminds him that the number of angles or slants that can be taken on anything – visible or abstract – is infinite. Each of the blackbirds has its own angle of vision, and the tree, perhaps, has its angle, and there's the poet, whose own "three minds" are like the tree's but also like the separate visions of the three birds.

If there are thirteen ways of looking at a blackbird, there are at least that many perspectives on any issue important enough to argue about. The best case can be made when you are of at least three minds: the judge, the jury, and the prosecutor; or the claimant, the disclaimer, and the compromiser; or the thesis, the antithesis, and the synthesis. You can play all three roles in any argument if you remember to establish warrants firmly as you go along. But let's make it a little more complicated.

∾ Take the roles of all three birds, the tree, and the poet on any of the following claims. What warrants must each role-player establish? How would that be accomplished?

1. Mastery of a foreign language is unnecessary for an American student.
2. Humanities and sciences are important, but the modern student should concentrate on technology and business.
3. An official's private life is nobody else's business.

In composing an argument, you keep the structure in mind at all times. In order to articulate relationships clearly, you substantiate your claims with specific data and you refer to the warrants – the bridges – implicitly or explicitly, as often as necessary. In the real rhetorical world, passion, prejudice, and personal needs come into play in all arenas, whether they be classrooms, courtrooms, business situations, or personal encounters. One who argues well takes all the perspectives and seeks warrants for each. Arguing is indeed articulating by means of the dialectic, bearing in mind what Stephen Toulmin calls "the perils of simplicity," or the dangers of generalizing too easily and quickly.

∾ What warrants are the following paragraphs from student essays attempting to establish?

1. Every week when I go to the grocery store with my little bit of money for food, I have to stand behind a whole bunch of fat, usually dirty, women with lots of kids. They all have handfuls of filthy food stamps and they count them out very, very slowly. Their carts are totally full of potato chips, TV dinners, ice cream, candy bars, cakes, soft drinks. They never have any fruits or vegetables. You can tell by looking at them that they never eat anything good for them. These people are definitely poor, but I can't see the point of the government paying for this kind of junk. The stamps should be for milk, good meat, vegetables and fruit, unsweetened cereal, and food like that. Bad nutrition kills your brain

cells. These people will never be smart enough to get off welfare.

2. My father and grandfather both went to war and sometimes they brag about it. Even though I don't want to go into a place in the Middle East or Central America and fight in deserts or jungles, I can see why things like that are necessary sometimes. Right now, men between 18 and 21 have a good chance of going to Libya, Israel, Afghanistan, Nicaragua, Iran, Iraq, Haiti, or the inner cities of New York, etc. And people wonder why we lose ourselves in rock music or something worse.

3. Jogging is the best way to keep in shape that I know. You can escape the crowds and all the little daily miseries by getting into your jogging suit and hitting the trail. When I jog, I run into another world of music (my headset) and action (my muscles), and I don't *think* or *worry* about anything. When I'm finished, I take a shower and face the world. If you want an easy way to inner peace, take up jogging.

෴ A group of top PBS reporters and correspondents got together for an hour-and-a-half panel discussion on January 1, 1988. Their topic, loosely labeled, was what most needs to be done in this country to ensure the next generation a decent life in the 21st century. Below is a list of those tasks nominated by the panelists as most crucial. If you wished to choose a career that would benefit society most, especially the new generations, which of these tasks would you aim to undertake? Establish a ranking system that allows you to compare the tasks and select the ones most important, according to your own criteria. This is an exercise for "thirteen ways of looking at a blackbird."

1. The U.S. must find new and better ways of cooperating with other nations with nuclear arsenals so as to control nuclear buildup.
2. The rich countries of this world, led by the United States, must engage in a massive effort to get the Third World out of debt and on its way to full financial recovery.
3. The United States should concentrate on the homeless and poverty-stricken within its own boundaries and strive to provide basic shelter and dignity for all its people.
4. The only way that this country will be in a position to

reach any of its major goals is to concentrate first on reducing the national debt by a significant percentage.

5. No problem can be understood, much less addressed, if the educational system in this country does not receive a complete overhaul from kindergarten through graduate school.

6. The most tragic long-term event in modern American history has been the collapse of the family structure and that cluster of values that it represented; that structure, in some new form, must be restored. The rest will follow.

7. The most tragic event, really, has been the dramatic increase in single mothers with families, 60% of whom live below the poverty line, and have been betrayed by both government and society; this problem must be addressed first.

8. The loss of the middle class in this country, aided by a tax structure that favors the rich, is – as it was in Greece and Rome – the first sign of the end of a civilization; history shows us what to do about it, but time is short.

9. Clearly, the AIDS epidemic is the one problem that *must* be solved before the 21st century.

10. The increase of violent crimes, especially in the cities, and the increase in their savagery and in the number of victims, is a sign that our society is in trouble.

11. The takeover of the American mind by the media is in one sense our biggest problem. Typically, if a problem is mentioned at all, we get three minutes of reporting, or two columns, even for the most complex and urgent issues. A good example is the massive decline of the Midwest and the farm belt states that never makes the news unless thousands of people drive trucks to Washington, DC or Willie Nelson gives a free concert.

12. The spread of dangerous and addictive drugs, especially among the young, seems most threatening and most in need of immediate attention.

13. The continuing unrest in the Middle East and Central America is the greatest threat to America's security in the coming years.

                          ❧ Throughout this discussion of the logic and rhetoric of explanation, certain terms have been italicized. Review the last two sections and copy out these words in your dialectical notebook. Construct definitions for each and then check them against what your dictionary tells you.

Four of them are used in the diagram below. This diagram allows you to draw an analogy between the construction of a wheel and the construction of an explanation and the way you argue it. From your list, you could probably invent further oppositions which could be spokes. What word/term/concept do you think belongs in the middle? Is this name in the list?

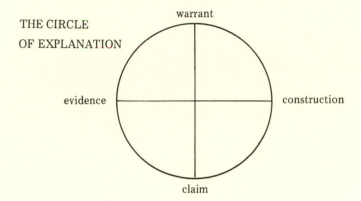

THE CIRCLE
OF EXPLANATION

warrant

evidence   construction

claim

A Procedural Guide to the Logic and Rhetoric of Explanation.

1. Generate chaos by doing research on your topic. Include personal experiences. Consider all the perspectives that an audience could take on the topic.
2. Carefully consider all your data and draw up a list of claims that you can make, based on your data. On the opposite side of the page list the counterclaims that could be made and the data on which they would be based. Try to rank your claims and the counterclaims in terms of their persuasive power. Determine which items in each category need special attention or explanation.
3. Make a list of the warrants you will have to establish with your audience. Include current opinion, shared values and assumptions, passions or feelings, and common knowledge. Distinguish clearly between what you know your audience thinks or feels and what, at the moment, is uncertain to you. On the opposite side of the page, make notes about warrants on which counterclaims might be based.

4. Make a list of all the items in your argument that will have to be explained in detail. Answer these questions: where do you need definitions? where will contrasts, analogies, and cause/effect relationships be helpful? are there places where naming the classes will be necessary? are there any warrants that can be established on the basis of social and moral values, precedent, character, compassion, common sense, instinct, or intuition?

5. Develop all your claims as sentences. Below each claim, state briefly the data on which the claim is based, and in parentheses next to each item of evidence name the warrant you think it establishes. Finally, state the opposite case for each claim and the data and warrants on which it may be based.

6. Group and classify your claims according to their relative persuasive power. Then explain in each case what you had to go on and how you got there.

4. "Do You Know Your Knowledge?"

Consciousness...mind, life, will, body, organ (as compared with machine), nature, spirit, sin, habit, sense, understanding, reason: here are fourteen words. Have you ever reflectively and quietly asked yourself the meaning of any one of these, and tasked yourself to return the answer in *distinct* terms, not applicable to any of the other words? Or have you contented yourself with the vague floating meaning that will just save you from absurdity in the use of the word, just as the clown's botany would do, who knew that potatoes were roots, and cabbages greens? Or, if you have the gift of wit, shelter yourself under Augustine's equivocation, "I know it perfectly well till I am asked." Know? Ay, as an oyster knows its life. *But do you know your knowledge?*
Samuel Taylor Coleridge, *Notebooks*

The paragraphs in this sequence concern topics and employ terms like those in Coleridge's list — conceptual terms. There are many difficult passages, but the experience of reading them carefully can help you practice discovering complex meanings without having them broken down into bits and neatly packaged for ready consumption. Critical reading can help you learn to talk back without settling for "I don't agree." There's a trade-off: the paragraphs are hard, but they are well-written and they repay careful study. Construing them will, we hope, encourage you to construct paragraphs of your own. The best way to learn something about critical writing – re-presenting analyses of what you read and think – is to keep at it *in the process of* critical reading. To know your knowledge is to search for meanings, to discover and articulate relationships – and that's what the composing process is.

As we've continually emphasized, anything and everything you learn about writing can be adapted to your reading: how you construct is how you construe. Any device, principle, or structure that can help you construe and/or construct is a *heuristic*. (Deriving from the Greek word for *find, heuristic* is both an adjective and a noun.) Heuristics are forms that find forms; they are ways of auditing the meanings you are construing and constructing.

To introduce this paragraph sequence, we will take the first group and slow down the process of forming the concept which emerges, identifying certain things you can do to carry out an audit of the meanings you are making. Read the three paragraphs through and then the heuristics which follow.

1a. To judge of the appearances that we receive of subjects we had need have a judicatory instrument: to verify this instrument, we should have demonstrations; and to prove demonstration, an instrument: thus we are ever turning around. Since the senses cannot determine our disputation, it must then be reason: And no reason can be established without another reason; then we are ever going back to infinity.

Montaigne, *Apology for Raimond Sebond* (trans. John Florio)

1b. A perpetual doubting and a perpetual questioning of the truth of what we have learned is not the temper of science. If Einstein was led to ask not "What is a clock?" but "How, over great distances and with great precision, do we synchronize clocks?" that is not an illustration of the scepticism of science; it exemplifies rather the critical reason creating a new synthesis from paradoxes, anomalies, and bewilderments, which experiments carried on with new precision and in a new context brought into being.

J. Robert Oppenheimer, *Science and the Common Understanding*

1c. Facts and assumptions are often regarded as opposites, and empirics agree that we should strive to have as many of the one and as few of the other as possible. But science is dull when it is all facts; that would give us vast tables of constants, such as melting points and gravitational intensities. These could be memorized, but they become science only when they have been integrated into a comprehensible fabric. Before this can happen a clearing must be made in the jungle of fact. This is the process of selection, which at first sight seems so scientifically immoral. The justification is simple. Nature is a complete series of cross-connections, with every phenomenon existing in the environment created by others. A full description of any phenomenon would therefore be enormously, even infinitely long. It is the recognition of the omnipresence of interconnections that has abolished the simple truth of our forefathers. Of necessity therefore we set up a canon of relevant facts, and the skill with which that is done controls the progress of science.

N. W. Pirie, "Selecting Facts and Avoiding Assumptions"

Read through all the steps below and when you've recovered, set yourself a certain amount of time – say forty-five minutes – and do not work past that time. Return for another forty-five minutes at a later time. In your dialectical notebook, make three columns, each headed with the name of one of the authors; the wide margin or the facing page is for response and for working with what you've developed on the right.

1. Begin by rereading all three paragraphs and glossing them. Those glosses can be the first entry in each column.
2. In the appropriate column, list the conceptual terms in the paragraph you find most accessible.
3. Reread the other two paragraphs, listing in the other columns any words or phrases which seem analogous to those you have selected from the easy paragraph. Write them across from the comparable terms recorded in Step 1.
4. On the left, compose a few sentences which articulate the relationships these matching terms seem to suggest – and of course the missing terms will be significant.
5. Copy out from each paragraph the sentence which best articulates the relationship of agent and purpose, question and answer, problem and procedure, or whatever relationship you can identify. Which sentence best answers HDWDWW?
6. For each paragraph, compose the first sentence of what you

imagine to be a succeeding paragraph. You'll be drawing inferences from the statements made in the selected paragraphs. Do your three sentences all seem to be heading in different directions? What conclusions do you draw about that?

7. Compose several sentences in which you explain which writers seem on the same wave length and why. What are the principal differences? A useful structure for this kind of statement is as follows:

_____'s " _____ ," like _____'s
"_____," defines (expresses, reveals, belies, etc.) his _____ .

You'll be practicing an extremely important skill, namely, "embedding quotations": you use certain language of the text you're studying as an element in your own statements.

8. Arrange your sentences so that your claim about the arguments being made by the three writers is intelligible. How can you tell if it's clear? By glossing your paragraph. If you can't, you need to return to Step 6 and compose further statements. Or perhaps simply rearranging the ones you've written will help you see where the gaps are. Write the first sentence of a succeeding paragraph.

Slowing down the process this way has a serious drawback: it could suggest that this is the way you always must proceed. These steps are meant only to suggest how interpretation and analysis are related to the process of composing statements. It may be more useful for you simply to remember that naming/opposing/defining are all going on when you read critically.

Anything that helps you know *that* you know, *what* you know, *how* you know is a heuristic. Heuristics help you ask "Do I know my knowledge?" Proceed, now, with the paragraphs that follow, always glossing after the first rereading, and using any heuristic that will help you interpret what is being said and to interpret your interpretations of what is meant.

2a. The function of a name is always limited to emphasizing a particular aspect of a thing, and it is precisely this restriction and limitation upon which the value of the name depends. It is not the function of a name to refer exhaustively to a concrete situation but merely to single out and dwell upon a certain aspect. The isolation of this aspect is not a negative but a positive act. For in the act of denomination we select out of the multiplicity and diffusion of our sense data certain fixed centers of perception. These centers are not the same as in logical or scientific thought. The terms of ordinary speech are not to be measured by the same standards as those in which we express scientific concepts. As compared with scientific terminology the words of common speech always exhibit a certain vagueness; almost without exception they are so indistinct and ill-defined as not to stand the test of logical analysis. But notwithstanding this unavoidable and inherent defect, our everyday terms and names are the milestones on the road which leads to scientific concepts; it is in these terms that we receive our first objective or theoretical view of the world. Such a view is not simply "given"; it is the result of a constructive intellectual effort which without the constant assistance of language could not attain its end.

Ernst Cassirer, *An Essay on Man*

2b. Without getting over one's head with the larger question of truth, one might still guess that it is extraordinarily rash of the positivist to limit truth to the logical approximation – to say that we cannot know what things are but only how they hang together. The copy theory gives no account of the *what* we are saying *how* about. As to the what: since we are not angels, it is true that we cannot know what it is intuitively and as it is in itself. The modern semioticist is scandalized by the metaphor, flesh is grass . . . . He is confusing an instrument of knowing with what is known. The word *flesh* is not this solid flesh, and this solid flesh is not grass. But unless we name it *flesh* we shall not know it at all, and unless we call flesh grass we shall not know how it is with flesh. The semioticist leaves unexplained the act of knowing. He imagines naively that I know what this is and then give it a label, whereas the truth is, as Cassirer has shown so impressively, that I cannot know anything at all unless I symbolize it. We can only *con*ceive being, sidle up to it by laying something else alongside. We approach the thing not directly but by pairing, by apposing symbol and thing. Is it not premature to say with the mythist that when the primitive calls the lightning serpentine, he conceives it as a snake and is logically wrong? Both truth and error may be served here, error insofar as the lightning is held to participate magically in snakeness, truth insofar as the conception of snake may allow the privately apprehended inscape of the lightning to be formulated. I would have a horror of finding myself allied with those who in the name of instrumentality or inner warmth or what not would so attentuate and corrupt truth that it meant nothing. But an analysis of the symbol relation reveals aspects of truth which go far beyond the notion of structural similarity which the symbolic logicians speak of. Two other traits of the thing are discovered and affirmed: one that it *is;* two that it is *something.*

Walker Percy, "Metaphor as Mistake"

2c. Human existence cannot be silent, nor can it be nourished by false words, but only by true words, with which men transform the world. To exist, humanly, is to *name* the world, to change it. Once named, the world in its turn reappears to the namers as a problem and requires of them a new *naming.* Men are not built in silence, but in word, in work, in action-reflection. But while to say the true word — which is work, which is praxis — is to transform the world, saying that word is not the privilege of some few men, but the right of every man. Consequently, no one can say a true word alone — nor can he say it *for* another, in a prescriptive act which robs others of their words. Dialogue is the encounter between men, mediated by the world, to name the world.

Paulo Freire, *Pedagogy of the Oppressed*

3a. Whenever an ancient cult image, the pattern on a brooch, a broken column or a painted potsherd asks to be interpreted, any historian worth his salt will try to make sense of it in such terms as his creative imagination suggests. But a critical mind will not rest with this vision. He will watch for further evidence to fit it into the image of the lost culture. Usually, of course, such further evidence is available in one form or another, and the historian's task is precisely to fit it all together into a context that "makes sense." And so intensely does his imagination become engaged that he begins to people the past with men who might have created those very brooches and done those very deeds of which the sources tell us. There is much to be admired in this effort of the imaginative historian to "wake the dead" and to unriddle the mute language of the monuments. But he should never conceal from himself that his method is circular. The physiognomic unity of past ages which he reads from their various manifestations is precisely the unity to which the rules of his game have committed him. It was he who unified the clues in order to make sense of them.

E. H. Gombrich, "Physiognomic Perception"

3b. There is no isolated event. Any event is connected with other events, those which brought it about and those which it brings about. Nor does connection of events in itself make a story, let alone history. To form a story, the *connection* of happenings must have some substratum, or focus, something to which it is related, something to whom it happens. This something, or somebody, to which, or whom, a connection of events relates, is what gives the plain connection of events an actual, specific *coherence,* what turns it into a story. But such specific coherence is not given of itself, it is given by a perceiving and comprehending mind. It is created as a *concept,* i.e., as a meaning. Thus, to make even a simple story, three factors are indispensable: connection of events, relatedness of this connection to something or somebody, which gives the events their specific coherence and creates the concept which means a meaning. What I propose to demonstrate in the following is that the questioning of and the questing after a meaning of history both beg the question. There is no story, there is no history without meaning.

Erich Kahler, The Meaning of History

3c. To control the interpretation of an individual work of art by a "history of style," which in turn can only be built up by interpreting individual works may look like a vicious circle. It is, indeed, a circle though not a vicious but a methodical one. Whether we deal with historical or natural phenomena, the individual observation assumes the character of a "fact" only when it can be related to other analogous observations in such a way that the whole series "makes sense." This "sense" is, therefore, fully capable of being applied, as a control, to the interpretation of a new individual observation within the same range of phenomena. If, however, this new individual observation definitely refuses to be interpreted according to the "sense" of the series, and if an error proves to be impossible, the "sense" of the series will have to be reformulated to include the new observation.

Erwin Panofsky, Studies in Iconology

3d. [Biologists] usually proceed in such a way that from certain facts gained by analysis we sketch a picture of the whole organism, which in turn, so long as we encounter discrepancies between this picture and factual experience, stimulates further questions and investigations. Upon the basis of new inquiries the picture of the whole is again modified, and the process of discovering new discrepancies and making new inquiries follows, and so on. By such empirical procedure in a dialectic manner, a progressively more adequate knowledge of the nature of the organism, of its "essence," is acquired, and an increasingly correct evaluation of the observed facts, and of whether or not they are essential to the organism is obtained.... As skepticism toward a naive copy-theory of knowledge grew, and as it was realized that "empirical" facts are not a simple expression of reality but are also produced through the method of investigation, it became more and more clear that it was the task of natural science to transcend the "empirical" facts and create images, "symbols," which are suited for gaining a coherent understanding of the "facts."

Kurt Goldstein, *Human Behavior*

4a. To early man, standing on his earth arched by the dome of its sky, it could never occur that life might be a side issue in the universe, and not its pervading rule. His panvitalism was a perspective truth which only a change of perspective could eventually displace. Unquestioned and convincing at the beginning stands the experience of the omnipresence of life. In such a world-view, the riddle confronting man is *death*: It is the contradiction to the one intelligible, self-explaining "natural" condition which is the general life. To the extent that life is accepted as the primary state of things, death looms as the disturbing mystery. Hence the *problem* of death is probably the first to deserve this name in the history of thought. Its emergence as an express problem signifies the awakening of the questioning mind long before a conceptual level of theory is attained. The natural recoil from death takes courage from the "logical" outrage which the fact of mortality inflicts on panvitalistic conviction. Primeval reflection thus grapples with the riddle of death, and in myth, cult, and religious belief endeavors to find a solution to it.

Hans Jonas, *The Phenomenon of Life*

4b. Probably the profoundest difference between human and animal needs is made by one piece of human awareness, one fact that is not present to animals, because it is never learned in any direct experience; that is our foreknowledge of death. The fact that we ourselves must die is not a simple and isolated fact. It is built on a wide survey of facts that discloses the structure of history as a succession of overlapping brief lives, the patterns of youth and age, growth and decline; and above all that, it is built on the logical insight that *one's own life is a case in point.* Only a creature that can think symbolically *about* life can conceive of its own death. Our knowledge of death is part of our knowledge of life.

Susanne K. Langer, *Philosophical Sketches*

4c. Death, too, is an enhancer. Through him, life gains its color, clinging precarious like some Alpine flower that digs its tenuous and tenacious roots in the rock face against the darkness of the drop below. The secret joy of peril comes from the veiled presence, without which most savor goes; and this is no morbid feeling, for the ecstasy belongs not to death in itself, but to *life,* suddenly enriched to know itself. So, after a summer dawn and climb til noon, among clefts and icy triangles or wind-scooped crannies, the mountaineer returning sets foot again on the short turf and flowers; and the breeze that cools him is the same breeze that sways the harebells; the blood that tramples in his ears and runs like chariots through his veins is the kind, swift, temporary stuff by which the smaller things of earth are fed; he is back in the community of his kind and descends, light-footed, among the pastures: but he remembers how in the high silences he has known himself on the edge of Silence and how its wing has brushed him. Once, looking down into a valley of the Lebanon, I have heard below me as it were the swish of silk and seen, within a pebble's drop, an eagle's wing outspread; and so we watch death's flight, in our sunlight.

Freya Stark, *Perseus in the Wind*

5a. ...What I know, what is certain, what I cannot deny, what I cannot reject—this is what counts. I can negate everything of that part of me that lives on vague nostalgias, except this desire for unity, this longing to solve, this need for clarity and cohesion. I can refute everything in this world surrounding me that offends or enraptures me, except this chaos, this sovereign chance and this divine equivalence which springs from anarchy. I don't know whether this world has a meaning that transcends it. But I know that I do not know that meaning and that it is impossible for me just now to know it. What can a meaning outside my condition mean to me? I can understand only in human terms. What I touch, what resists me – that is what I understand. And these two certainties – my appetite for the absolute and for unity and the impossibility of reducing this world to a rational and reasonable principle – I also know that I cannot reconcile them. What other truth can I admit without lying, without bringing in a hope I lack and which means nothing within the limits of my condition?

Albert Camus, *The Myth of Sisyphus*

5b. ...It is essential that we distinguish the viewpoint of the scientist from that of the acting person. The superior wisdom of the scientist may unfortunately blind him to the process of growth that is actually taking place. The scientist's frame of reference is like the frame of an omniscient being: to him all things have time, place and determined orbits. But this frame is definitely not the frame of the acting person. The situation is much like that of the watcher from the hilltop who sees a single oarsman on the river below. From his vantage point the watcher notes that around the bend of the river, unknown as yet to the oarsman, there are dangerous rapids. What is present to the watcher's eye still lies in the future for the oarsman. The superior being predicts that soon the boatman will be portaging his skiff – a fact now wholly unknown to the boatman who is unfamiliar with the river's course. He will confront the obstacle when it comes, decide on his course of action, and surmount the difficulty. In short, the actor is unable to view his deeds in a large space-time matrix as does an all-wise God, or the less wise demigods of science. From his point of view he is working within a frame of choice, not of destiny. As psychologists, we ought to know, and do know, that the way a man defines his situation constitutes for him its reality. Choice for him is a paramount fact; how matters appear to the watcher on the hill is irrelevant. It is because existentialism takes always the acting person's point of view that it insists so strongly upon the attribute of freedom in man's nature.

Gordon Allport, *Becoming*

5c. We have only to speak of an object to think we are being objective. But, because we chose it in the first place, the object reveals more about us than we do about it. What we consider to be our fundamental ideas concerning the world are often indications of the immaturity of our minds. Sometimes we stand in wonder before a chosen object; we build up hypotheses and reveries; in this way we form convictions which have all the appearance of true knowledge. But the initial source is impure: the first impression is not a fundamental truth. In point of fact, scientific objectivity is possible only if one has broken first with the immediate object, if one has refused to yield to the seduction of the initial choice, if one has checked and contradicted the thoughts which arise from one's first observation. Any objective examination, when duly verified, refutes the results of the first contact with the object. To start with, everything must be called into question: sensation, common sense, usage, however constant, even etymology, for words, which are made for singing and enchanting, rarely make contact with thought. Far from marvelling at the object, objective thought must treat it ironically. Without this malign vigilance we would never adopt a truly objective attitude.

Gaston Bachelard, *The Psychoanalysis of Fire*

5d. However, in choosing a subject and an object radically different from one another, anthropology runs a risk: that the knowledge obtained from the object does not attain its intrinsic properties but is limited to expressing the relative and always shifting position of the subject in relation to that object. It may very well be, indeed, that so-called ethnological knowledge is condemned to remain as bizarre and inadequate as that which an exotic visitor would have of our own society. The Kwakiutl Indian whom Boas sometimes invited to New York to serve him as an informant was quite indifferent to the panorama of skyscrapers and of streets ploughed and furrowed by cars. He reserved all his intellectual curiosity for the dwarfs, giants and bearded ladies who were exhibited in Times Square at the time, for automats, and for the brass balls decorating staircase banisters.... All these things challenged his own culture, and it was that culture alone which he was seeking to recognize in certain aspects of ours.

Claude Lévi-Strauss, *The Scope of Anthropology*

VI

GATHERING/SORTING/ GATHERING

1. Composing Sentences

When you compose, you give form to thought. The ways you do that – the *hows* of composing – can be studied in terms of concept formation as we've done in Chapters III and IV and in logical and rhetorical terms, as in Chapter V. The *what* resulting from the *how* is called *discourse*. Think of the course of a river and you have the essential fact about discourse: it has direction, it's going somewhere, it *flows*. Think of what is meant when we say that someone speaks *fluent* Spanish or is *fluent* in German, and you can remember that *fluency* means easy and ready expression.

For the student of composition, developing fluency is as important as learning the uses of chaos. Fluency is what makes prose enjoyable; it's the essential character of *style*. To be fluent doesn't mean that you write easily but that your writing reads *as if* you had not struggled. In other words, fluency is not a magical gift; most of us must work very hard to achieve the effect of effortlessness. If you've ever played a musical instrument, you'll recognize an analogy; it takes a great deal of practice before a piece sounds as if you're performing it without pain.

A professor of philosophy was once heard to say that he would be chagrined if his readers could understand him easily; that would be a sign, he thought, that he wasn't saying anything of real interest. He had a point: to go on and on about the self-evident is the chief characteristic of a bore. We all feel like saying

"Okay, okay, okay! So what?" But this philosopher failed to differentiate the difficulty we have in reading when the matter is difficult and the difficulty we experience when it's the style that's at fault. This second kind of difficulty is really a matter of sentences: one thing professors of philosophy may have in common with novice writers is an inability to hear their sentences. Both may lack an ear for language, which means more than an ability to appreciate pleasant turns of phrase or oratorical flourishes; it's an ability to judge the dialectical relationship of structure to idea, sound to sense. You can write grammatically correct sentences which are nevertheless stylistically faulty: they get off the track; they're dull and substanceless; they're directionless. There's no *fluency*.

Fluency is really a reflection of the way a good talker talks. Unfortunately, good talkers are not inevitably good writers; the voice sometimes evaporates the minute they set pen to paper or fingers to keyboard. But it's also true that sometimes people who have no gift of gab can nevertheless write in a supple, graceful, and articulate style. Accomplished stylists can write in two registers: they can be informal—conversational, personal—or they can, if they choose, write formally and impersonally. Furthermore, they can balance these different modes in a single piece of writing.

The greatest stylist of the century in English is probably Winston Churchill; in the century before, there are crowds of stylists, but Lincoln would surely be in the forefront. Every student of composition should find a writer she likes and read him continually. If you can memorize easily, do so: learning by heart a half dozen complex and beautiful sentences can do more for your own sense of language than hours spent with a handbook. The aim is to develop an ear for language. You could begin by memorizing the Gettysburg Address.

            Ꝺ Meanwhile, you can test your ear on these two sentences, both extraordinarily long. One is readable, holding your interest right to the end; the other is overloaded and directionless. Analyze the composition of each so that you can account for this difference. The first was written by George Kennan, U.S. Ambassador to the Soviet Union for many years; the second is from an anonymous grant application.

1. If you ask me as a historian to say whether a country in the state this country is in today, with no highly developed sense

of national purpose, with the overwhelming accent of life on personal comfort and amusement, with a dearth of public services and a surfeit of privately sold gadgetry, with a chaotic transportation system, with its great urban areas being gradually disintegrated by the headlong switch to motor transportation, with an educational system where quality has been extensively sacrificed to quantity, and with insufficient social discipline even to keep its major industries functioning without grievous interruptions; if you ask me whether such a country has, over the long run, good chances of competing with a purposeful, serious, and disciplined society such as that of the Soviet Union, I must say that the answer is "no."

2. The salient administrative challenge facing the museum over the past several years has been to maintain and enlarge its customarily high standards of research, documentation and conservation of collections, collaboration with the scholarly and scientific community, services to professional colleagues in America and abroad, significant publications, and serious pedagogy at the undergraduate, postgraduate, and teacher-training levels, while simultaneously seeking to broaden its base of public and community participation and support, to expand its role as a collaborative resource in public education at all levels, and to develop a full spectrum of high quality education, musical, and outreach programs and services that address popular as well as scholarly issues in a manner that is engaging and enlightening in the context of a pluralistic and culturally diverse potential constituency.

Developing an ear for language means being able to hear the voice in prose – others' voices and your own. Hearing good prose read aloud is invaluable for cultivating an ear for language, but learning to listen for voice can also be encouraged by the careful analysis of sentences.

      ∾ Here's a sentence composed by Rachel Carson, well-known both as a stylist and as a biologist and environmentalist:

The coelenterates, despite their simplicity, foreshadow the basic plan on which, with elaborations, all the more highly developed animals are formed.

1. If you're a good grammarian, carry out a grammatical

analysis. Identify the main subject and its verb and the subordinate clause. What's the referent of *which*? What part of speech is *despite*? Why is it where it is in the sentence?

2. Here's a model for the kind of rhetorical analysis you should learn to carry out on your own sentences as well as on complex statements you read.
a. Develop a mini-chaos by naming the *what*s:
coelenterates ... simplicity ... basic plan ... elaborations... highly developed animals
b. Develop oppositions:
coelenterates/highly developed animals
simplicity/ complexity
basic plan/ elaborated plan
c. Study how the two verbs articulate the spatial and temporal relationships.

3. Compose three interpretive paraphrases.
a. The development of animals later in evolution was based on the simple plan, exemplified by the coelenterates.
b. The simple coelenterates are the forerunners of all the animals which were to come.
c. Regardless of their simple form, the coelenterates exhibit the basic plan according to which later animals developed, elaborations and all.

These paraphrases are all unsatisfactory: each loses a point of emphasis or distorts the logic of the statement. But as an exercise, interpretation by paraphrase can be valuable precisely because it can help you determine just what makes the original sentence "work."

Here's a critique of the paraphrases:
a. The end of a sentence is what the reader carries in his mind to the next sentence; it's therefore a good place to put whatever you want to emphasize. Rachel Carson's *are formed* picks up the earlier *basic plan,* reminding us of the function of that plan. *Development, later,* and *evolution* all do the same work. The fact that the order of items is the opposite of the direction of development is not a fault, but it seems to have no purpose.
b. This paraphrase leaves out *plan* and the logic of *despite. Forerunners* has already done the work *were to come* is meant to do.

c. Here the role of *despite* is recognized, but by placing it first in the sentence, another sort of emphasis is created which may not work in the succession of sentences. This kind of decision can't be made without the passage which provides the context for the sentence. The end of the sentence also emphasizes *elaborations* rather than *formed;* that's not the clear purpose of the original.

Sometimes, of course, interpretive paraphrases can improve on the original, but when you have a sentence like this one, it's virtually impossible to change the elements around or substitute other terms without destroying an important point of logic or emphasis.

Along with reading aloud, rhetorical analysis, and memorizing, imitation can help develop an ear for language. The imitation of well-formed sentences is very old-fashioned. The traditional way of teaching composition was to set a certain theme or topic and require students to compose in the manner of a master stylist whose essay on the same topic had been painstakingly analyzed. Such practice has a lot in common with translation and it serves very well to slow down the process of composing sentences so that the interaction of syntax and meaning can be observed. The trouble was that the topics were generally banal or "irrelevant" and the distance between the student writer and Francis Bacon or Thomas Carlyle was often felt as a shameful fact. The exercise I'm proposing is closer to parody than old-fashioned imitation; it is, in any case, a lot more fun than other kinds of "model" composition. It's called *persona paraphrase* because what is being imitated is not the sense of the sentence but its style and rhetorical form and purpose.* You'll be attempting to "sound" like the person who wrote the original.

The procedure is as follows: you use a passage of prose as a model to guide you in constructing a sequence of sentences, each of which is as close syntactically to the model as you can make it, but the subject matter of your sentences is entirely different. The model acts to shape your sentences, somewhat the way an armature provides a framework when you are modeling a clay figure. There are two important requirements: (a) The logical relationship you are trying to articulate should be analogous to those the model articulates. You couldn't model the figure of a horse on an armature made for a bird in flight — or could you?

*For a full explanation, see Phyllis Brooks, "Mimesis: Grammar and the Echoing Voice," *College English* (35), 1973, 161-168.

Maybe a winged horse would result. The point is that you must observe the dialectic, letting the syntax of the model help determine what you are saying, up to a point. Any one model can't be appropriate to just any assertion. (b) You need to be deeply immersed in a problem, to have on hand a full lexicon of terms and well-developed concepts. It's because they are complex and strange that these models can be critically useful: they're like rest and recreation points from which you can return to your own sentences with renewed vigor and restored spirits; you can also bring back some ideas about articulation and emphasis.

In this demonstration, the individual sentences come from different sources; you can also practice persona paraphrase with extended passages. Try any selected paragraph in this book.

          ꔮ To begin, here's a sentence which forms a class and describes a member of that class – the green heron – with great particularity. Directly underneath the original is a paraphrase by a student from Italy, adept at translation and especially alert to English idiom. One of the benefits of persona paraphrase is that it transforms us into aliens: we begin to "hear" English more attentively. The other examples that follow are more or less successful – more so when they find language which matches the original both grammatically and rhetorically; less so when the new constructions seem to imitate the original but actually create an unidiomatic and ungrammatical sentence. Compare them with the original and see if you can find the points at which something goes especially well and where things go wrong. One thing they all get right is the point of "at once": how would you explain its function?

Like the black duck and the crow, the green heron
Like maccheroni and lasagne, wheat spaghetti

is at once a wary and venturesome bird,
is at once tasteful and nourishing pasta,

endowed with sufficient intelligence to discriminate between
   real and imaginary dangers
endowed with enough protein to ward off real and imaginary
   fears of becoming fat,

and often making itself at home in noisy, thickly settled
   neighborhoods

and often fitting comfortably in the menu of exotic and
  popular restaurants

where food is abundant and where it is not too much
  molested.
where food is appreciated and where pasta is not too
  much despised.

1. Like the Afghan and the Scottish Deerhound, the Borzoi
   is at once a beautiful and sturdy dog,
   bred for sufficient stamina to track large game
   and also outstanding in the modern show ring
   where judges appraise the quality of its coat
       and where it is appreciated for its elegance.

2. Like the lovely cove and the peninsula, the rocky island
   is at once an inviting and forbidding place,
   covered with enough vegetation to vacillate
       between stark and pristine appearance
   and forever making itself at home in crashing, white-
       washed waves
   where life is abundant and where it is not too carefully
       regarded.

3. Like the philosopher and the poet, the anthropologist
   is at once a subjective and an objective observer,
   endowed with sufficient training to discriminate
       between relative and absolute characteristics,
   and often taking up residence in the most far-flung and
       primitive villages
   where primary source data is directly available
       and where he has the time to correlate it.

                          ☙ Here are two student persona
paraphrases, modeled on sentences chosen from the
list that follows. Match the sample to the model and
explain why they are simpler than "Like the black
duck and the crow…"

1. A student involved in the composing process, in the
   initial chaotic state, can conjure or generate particulars
   to the number, as I have been told, of several millions,
   expecting, doubtless, that they will grow into future
   sentences and paragraphs; but for the want of a dialectic, and of that interpretive care which is always
   necessary and which will have to be taken from now on,

all the classification and conceptualization will be for nothing, and the paper is likely to continue blank.

2. Exhausted necessarily from the tensions and demands of the semester, we were happy to party now, but because we organized our lives by the demands of the various requirements of study – papers read in solitude, vacations missed regretfully, and schedules beginning at dawn, the noise of distraction, the sound of a television, and the great artistic voice of creation thinking and making and waiting in classrooms – the relaxing party meant only for enjoyment gave us a sense of pleasure that however much we enjoyed physically upset our study-geared minds with a lack of significance.

ॐ Try your own persona paraphrase using any of the following sentences as your model.

1. Sprung from the nomads of the Asiatic hinterland and for long dependent upon other nations for transport at sea, the Turks, when they had captured Constantinople, found it to their advantage to revive the commercial arrangements that had existed between Byzantium and the European states.

2. I must study politics and war, that my sons may have liberty to study mathematics and philosophy, geography, natural history and naval architecture, in order to give their children a right to study painting, poetry, music, architecture, tapestry, and porcelain.

3. Romanesque, too, is the conception of the figure with opposed directions of the head and body, a form that resembles a vital type in Greek art of the archaic period, when the painters and sculptors infused movement into the primitive figures by contrasting positions of the limbs, sharply turned from each other. It is an essential factor in the expressive force of the tympana and capitals of Vézelay and Autun.

4. I never saw a more beautiful country, nor more lively prospects, hills so raised here and there over the valleys, the river winding into diverse branches, the plains adjoining without bush or stubble, all fair green grass, the ground of hard sand easy to march on, either for

horse or foot, the deer crossing in every path, the birds towards the evening singing on every tree with a thousand several tunes, cranes and herons of white, crimson and carnation perching on the river's side, the air fresh with a gentle easterly wind, and every stone that we stooped to take up, promised either gold or silver by his complexion.

5. Sir James Macdonald, in part of the wastes of his territory, set or sowed trees, to the number, as I have been told, of several millions, expecting, doubtless, that they would grow up into future navies and cities; but for want of enclosure, and of that care which is always necessary, and will hardly ever be taken, all his cost and labor have been lost, and the ground is likely to continue a useless heath.

6. The thatched houses, so warm and safe in winter storms, have been condemned to extinction by an unimaginative authority which prefers two-storey wooden Swedish prefabricated houses planned for a totally different climate, the height of which exposes them to every gale that blows in Uist.

7. Washed up thankfully out of the swirl and buffet of the city, they were happy to lie there, but because they were accustomed to telling the time by their nerves' response to the different tensions of the city – children crying in flats, lorries going heavily, and bicycles jangling for early morning, skid of tyres, sound of frying, and the human insect noise of thousands talking and walking and eating at midday – the tensionless shore keyed only to the tide gave them a sense of timelessness that, however much they rejoiced mentally, troubled their habit-impressed bodies with a lack of pressure.

2. The Logic and Rhetoric of Paragraphs

Writers are concerned with statements, arguments, generalizations, classifications, etc. – all matters of logic. In a rhetorical perspective, they appear as sentences and paragraphs. Thought and language are inseparable as philosophical and psychological concepts, but they can be discussed in different terms. Here is one explanation of how logic and rhetoric supply those terms:

The writer attends to the logical connections between his statements – whether they make sense and hang together without contradicting each other – and he attends to their effect on others, those who hear and read him. In logic, he asks whether it is reasonable that one certain step follows another; in rhetoric, he asks whether it is effective for his purposes. In both, his grammar is a system which underlies and limits his choices; that is, he chooses constructions in words and syntax that will work together to take him where he wants to go.*

Rhetoricians are concerned about unity, coherence, emphasis; introductions, developments, conclusions; transitions, recapitulations, repetitions, and balance. Rhetoric is concerned fundamentally and continually with the relationship of language and thought: How does this way of putting it differ from that way? How does it change what is said? What changes in language affect my intention? And those questions in turn generate many others about the composition as a bundle of parts. In this section, we'll concentrate on the rhetorical aspects of those acts of mind by which we form and develop concepts.

A composition is a bundle of parts in which each element is both a part and a bundle; a sentence is both a bundle of grammatical parts and a part of the rhetorical bundle called a paragraph; a paragraph is both this bundle of sentences and a part of the whole composition. This dialectic of parts and bundles can be clarified by studying the structure of the paragraph.

The paragraph is a rhetorical form intermediary between the sentence and the whole composition, but it's not adequately described either as a super-sentence or as a mini-composition. There is no grammar of the paragraph and, though it is composed of syntactical units, it is itself not a syntactical unit. In some periods in the history of English prose there's a complete absence of what we would call paragraphs, but that doesn't mean that the compositions are disorderly; it only means that the chief rhetorical unit was the sentence. Sentences could be short or very long indeed, as in this example from the early seventeenth century:

*Josephine Miles, "English: A Colloquy; or, How What's What in the Language," *California English Journal*, 2 (1966), 3-14.

...It is an excellent observation which hath been made upon the answers of our Savior Christ to many of the questions which were propounded to him, how that they are impertinent to the state of the question demanded; the reason whereof is, because not being like man, which knows man's thoughts by his words, but knowing man's thoughts immediately, he never answered their words, but their thoughts: much in the like manner it is with the Scriptures, which being written to the thought of men, and to the succession of all ages, with a foresight of all heresies, contradictions, differing estates of the church, yea and particularly of the elect, are not to be interpreted only to the latitude of the proper sense of the place, and respectively towards that present occasion whereupon the words were uttered; or in precise congruity or contexture with the words before or after; or in contemplation of the principal scope of the place; but have in themselves, not only totally or collectively, but distributively in clauses and words, infinite springs and streams of doctrine to water the church in every part; and therefore as the literal sense is as it were the main stream or river; so the moral sense chiefly, and sometimes the allegorical or typical, are they whereof the church hath most use: not that I wish men to be bold in allegories, or indulgent or light in allusions; but that I do much condemn that interpretation of the Scripture which is only after the manner as men use to interpret a profane book.

Francis Bacon, *The Advancement of Learning*

We could very easily convert this passage, which is a single sentence, to a paragraph by changing the punctuation, and, indeed, one student of prose style, recognizing the relationship of punctuation and paragraphing, has defined the paragraph itself as a form of punctuation.

The conventional way of indicating a paragraph is to indent. That indentation is a signal to the eye, a convenience for the reader. In the days before printing, when all compositions were handwritten and the parchment or paper on which they were written was hard to come by, the scribes, instead of wasting valuable space by indentation, signaled the beginning of a new cluster of sentences by writing in the margin this sign: ¶. In proofreading and copyediting, this is still the conventional sign for a *paragraph,* a word that means literally *written alongside.* In other words, the paragraph is named after the sign which was written *alongside* it in the margin.

But paragraphing is not simply a matter of making some white space, though that is precisely what some newspapers use it for. Paragraphing is both an effect – it results from the way you have grouped your sentences – and a means, a form that bundles your sentences. A paragraph is the product of composing, but it is also a means of composing. Like concepts, paragraphs are gatherers and gatherings. They are often described metaphorically in terms of shape – funnels and pyramids, chiefly. A funnel paragraph begins with an assortment of particularizations that undergo classification and are finally narrowed down to a generalization, at which narrow point the paragraph ends. A pyramid paragraph begins with the assertion of a generalization that is then analyzed and demonstrated, given a foundation of fact and detail. There are variations, such as the hourglass, which combines funnel and pyramid. The gathering action of a paragraph might be explained by drawing an analogy with the triangular frame that organizes the balls for a game of pool. But none of these images can suggest the dialectic of the relationship of the structure and its parts. They are all faulty, since they concentrate on either the product (you can't build a pyramid from the top) or the producing (what happens to what goes through the funnel?) and thus do not adequately represent the way the sentences build the paragraph, which in turn shapes the sentences. If you think of the paragraph simply as a mold to pour sentences into, you lose the chance to learn its forming powers.

That's why it's useful to keep in mind that a paragraph gathers like a hand. Note that the gathering hand operates in different ways: the hand that holds a couple of eggs or tennis balls works differently from the hand that holds a bridle or a motorbike handle. When you measure out spaghetti by the handful, scoop up water by the handful, hold a load of books on your hip, knead bread, shape a stack of papers, build a sand castle, your hands move in different planes and with different motions, according to the nature of the material being gathered. But in any case, the hand can gather because of the *opposable* thumb. (The thumb of the human hand can be brought into *opposition* with the fingers.) A paragraph gathers by opposing a concept and the elements that develop and substantiate it. The kind of gathering a paragraph makes is thus dependent on both the kind of elements and the way in which they have been gathered.

Now, the way to use the paragraph as a rhetorical form that can gather and shape sentences – and form the substance of what you're saying – is to assure that there is an "opposable thumb." If you consider a certain cluster of sentences as parts that can be gathered together into a whole and if you then *name* that whole, you'll have a title for the proto-paragraph. We have been calling this title a *gloss.* Composed in the form of an opposition or of a shorthand sentence that identifies the *who* or *what* and the *does,* it will give you what journalists call a "lead" and the substance for what some English teachers and rhetoricians call a "topic sentence."

Composing a gloss is a way of stabilizing a cluster of sentences so that you can consider them collectively as well as individually. A gloss gives you a handle to pick up the bundle with; it's a way of seeing if you have the makings of a paragraph. Sometimes, the gloss will give you the bundle tie that your would-be paragraph has been missing; you can build the gloss back into the paragraph as the opening sentence or wherever else you think it fits. If you can't compose a gloss, it's a good indication that what seemed a cluster actually has no potential unity: the sentences may be too disparate or there may be too wide a range of detail to allow for generalization or there may be too many generalizations that remain undeveloped. Glossing lets you test the paragraph's grip. In short, composing a gloss is a critical means of reviewing the paragraph as a bundle of parts.

Another way of developing that critical skill is to read good paragraphs analytically, attending to how the parts are bundled. It's a misconception of the relationship of reading and writing in the study of composition to think that study of the patterns of sentences written by somebody else can teach you how to match your own sentence patterns to the shape of your thinking. But it's also a misconception to believe that you can learn to write complexly articulated sentences without studying such sentences. Critical reading is no panacea, but there's no substitute for its benefits.

The most important thing that the student of composition can learn from slowed-down reading is to appreciate the complexity of the relationship of topic and grammatical subject. *Topic* derives from the Greek word for *place** and refers both to the beginning and to the end: the topic is your point of departure and what you aim to develop. What, for instance, is the subject of the following sentence? What is the topic?

---

*Our word "commonplace" is a survival from rhetorical terminology: the "places" were carefully ordered and memorized, "common" to all students of rhetoric. The rhetorical term *place* occurs in Bacon's sentence, page 217.

There was no reachable post-office as yet; not even the rude little receptive box with lid and leather hinges, set up at convenient intervals on a stout stake along some solitary green way, affording a perch for birds, and which, later in the unintermitting advance of the frontier, would perhaps decay into a mossy monument, attesting yet another successive overleaped limit of civilized life; a life which in America can today hardly be said to have any western bound but the ocean that washes Asia.

Now, grammatically, the subject is *post-office* and the verb is *was* and yet the sentence is not "about" post-offices or even "about" the little box that wasn't there. The negative statement serves as the skeletal structure or framework for the topic. The paragraph opposes what was to happen with a time when these events had not yet occurred; note the phrases that establish this temporal structure: (*no*) *as yet....later...would decay...today.* The sentence is not "about" the nonexistent "reachable post-office" but the western movement that brought civilization to the shores of the Pacific.

As soon as we use language for purposes other than simple, direct reference — *The cat is on the mat* — or simple, direct expression — *Get that cat outta here!* — we have the problem of how to match thinking and language, of how to take advantage of the fact that linguistic forms discover ideas, as ideas find the forms of language. In conversation, we don't usually stop and figure out exactly what words we'll utter before we speak; everything happens at once. In reading, too, we let what's been said (read) help us read what's coming next. All reading skills are based on the dialectic of expectation and response; an efficient reader does not read word by word, but thought by word and word by thought. An efficient writer works the same way, letting form find form: letting syntactical structures — sentence patterns — help discover what's to be said; letting intention and purpose find the form by which it can be re-presented. The more critical reading you do, the more practice you have in writing by a dialectical method, the more continuous this mutual support of "saying" (writing) and thinking will be.

Nevertheless, you can listen in on the inner dialogue and come very close to re-presenting the process of forming a concept and still write incorrect, ungrammatical sentences. Why? Because the semantics of a sentence — the relationships it articulates, the oppositions it develops, the meanings it makes — are not necessarily identical with the base clause, the grammatical foundation provided by the subject and predicate. Because the linguistic structures you are using are subject not only to your *int*entions but to *con*ventions that have the force of law. If you disobey them, you will distract a reader who is aware of the correct form; if you disregard too many, you won't be making yourself clear. Word forms and syntax provide limits that you can learn to use to help you form statements, but they are not entirely flexible, any more than words are in their lexical definitions. You can learn to use the conventions of language to your advantage, conceiving of them as forms to find forms rather than as hurdles or roadblocks. Studying the structure of paragraphs is one way.

We've considered the Melville sentence as a bundle of parts. Now here it is as a part of a bundle:

> But a scene quite at variance with one's antecedents may yet prove suggestive of them. Hooped round by a level rim, the prairie was to John Marr a reminder of the ocean.
>
> With some of his former shipmates, chums on certain cruises, he had contrived, prior to this last and more remote removal, to keep up a little correspondence at odd intervals. But from tidings of anybody or any sort he, in common with the other settlers, was now cut off: quite cut off, except from such news as might be conveyed over the grassy billows by the last-arrived prairie-schooner – the vernacular term, in those parts and times, for the emigrant-wagon arched high over with sail-cloth, and voyaging across the vast champaign. There was no reachable post-office as yet; not even the rude little receptive box with lid and leather hinges, set up at convenient intervals along some solitary green way, affording a perch for birds, and which, later in the unintermitting advance of the frontier, would perhaps decay into a mossy monument, attesting yet another successive overleaped limit of civilized life; a life which in America can hardly be said to have any western bound but the ocean that washes Asia. Throughout these plains, now in places overpopulous with towns overpopulent; sweeping plains, elsewhere fenced off in every direction into flourishing farms – pale townsmen and hale farmers alike, in part, the descendants of the first sallow settlers; a region that half a century ago produced little for the sustenance of man, but today launching its superabundant wheat-harvest on the world; – of this prairie, now everywhere intersected with wire and rail, hardly can it be said that at the period here

written of there was so much as a traceable road. To the long-distance traveler the oak-groves, wide apart, and varying in compass and form; these, with recent settlements, yet more widely separate, offered some landmarks; but otherwise he steered by the sun. In the early midsummer, even going but from one log-encampment to the next, a journey it might be of hours or a good part of a day, travel was much like navigation. In some more enriched depressions between the long, green, graduated swells, smooth as those of ocean becalmed receiving and subduing to its own tranquillity the voluminous surge raised by some far-off hurricane of days previous, here one would catch the first indication of advancing strangers either in the distance, as a far sail at sea, by the glistening white canvas of the wagon, the wagon itself wading through the rank vegetation and hidden by it, or, failing that, when near to, in the ears of the team, peeking, if not above the tiger-lilies, yet above the yet taller green.

Luxuriant, this wilderness; but, to its denizen, a friend left behind anywhere in the world seemed not alone absent from sight, but an absentee from existence.

Though John Marr's shipmates could not all have departed life, yet as subjects of meditation, they were like phantoms of the dead. As the growing....

Herman Melville, John Marr

Thus, Melville, who in *Moby Dick* describes the whales as "mowing" through the ocean, in this sketch depicts the prairie in terms of the sea. That metaphor is the rhetorical binding agent for these intricately fashioned sentences, which, with their multitudinous details and melodramatic generalizations, would otherwise be very hard to follow. And you can see that the sentence we have studied takes its place in a passage whose purpose is to describe, define, compare, contrast; to assert, argue, and narrate – any rhetorical function you could name is performed by this passage.

Deciding when to start a new paragraph is an interesting task for the composer because the choices made (and remade) can illuminate obscurities and show up weaknesses. Paragraphing is partly a matter of logic and rhetoric, but it's also a matter of temperament: Mark Twain said he began a new paragraph when he felt like having a drink. A paragraph can consist of a single sentence, if you think the need for emphasis or a change of pace requires it. If you'll review the Melville passage, you'll see that one very long paragraph is followed by a paragraph of one sentence.

      ɞ In reading the following paragraph, decide where you think it could have been divided or trisected. What changes, if any, would you make in the course of reparagraphing? What advantages are there to having the passage as a single paragraph?

The dominant note which Navajo life strikes is joy, and buoyant confidence in the powers within the breast and in the world. And active happiness, positive health, are social duties among the Navajos. But equally, the Navajos do not entertain, and would scornfully reject, that view of life which is called "pangloss," or willful, fact-denying, sentimental optimism. Famine, war, drought, cold, and the dark storms that are within the human soul, they have always known, and have never tried to be oblivious towards them. Darkness and evil, not only light and love and joy, are indwelling deep within the nature of things, and their attempts to invade the soul are never-ending. Once, for a long cosmic interval, gigantism and darkness and evil predominated in the whole earth; then through a mighty effort the forces of beauty, love and joy subdued them, and scattered them afar, but never annihilated or sought to annihilate them; and to man then recreated or newly born, the Blessing Way was given, and many other symbols, precepts, rites and disciplines, and norms of conduct and feeling; and these as lived by man, are the City of God, but Darkness and active evil assail the City and invade it forevermore. Thus the cosmic and human drama is sustained by the Navajos, and the insecurity of things is wrought into a structure of beautiful security, a "dance over fire and water" whose rhythms are sometimes wildly impassioned but more often stately and gradual. And in these terms, Navajo religious art builds for eternity through building into the human and social tissue and soul, none the less for the fact that its material constructions* are demolished on the very day that they are completed.

        John Collier, *On the Gleaming Way*

---

*Sand paintings, "which are created as an element of the healing ceremonies and the ceremonies which renew the occult nature-man relationship."

❧ Here are 12 jumbled sentences in search of the paragraph they once were. Compose a paragraph with/for them.

1. Freedom is, I think, a mixed concept.
2. The true half of it is simply a name of an aspect of virtue concerned especially with the clarification of vision and the domination of selfish impulse.
3. It is in the context of such limitations that we should picture our freedom.
4. We behave well in the areas where this can be done fairly easily and let other areas of possible virtue remain undeveloped.
5. And can we, without improving ourselves, really see things clearly?
6. We are largely mechanical creatures, the slaves of relentlessly strong selfish forces, the nature of which we scarcely comprehend.
7. At best, as decent persons, we are usually very specialized.
8. There are few places where virtue plainly shines: great art, humble people who serve others.
9. There are perhaps in the case of every human being insuperable psychological barriers to goodness.
10. The false and more popular half is a name for the self-assertive movements of deluded selfish will, which because of our ignorance we take to be something.
11. The self is a divided thing and the whole of it cannot be redeemed any more than it can be known.
12. And if we look outside the self what we see are scattered intimations of *Good*.

❧ Revise this news release so that it has two paragraphs.

The Sol LeWitt exhibition of fifty drawings by the seminal figure in concept art will open to the public on March 4 through April 13 at the Museum of Art.

Born in Hartford, Connecticut in 1928, LeWitt received his B.F.A. at Syracuse University in 1949 and now lives in New York City.

LeWitt's work has been cited as the beginning of the movement called "Conceptual Art."

This is highly cerebral art, but in the graphic art of Sol LeWitt the ideas do produce work that while intellectual is generally quite beautiful and serene. In LeWitt's work, the concepts or ideas are not of great interest; they are actually quite simple. They do contain an element of games and humor which makes them all the more appealing.

In this exhibition there are working drawings for structures LeWitt has made, drawings that involve mathematical systems to explain the pieces. Also included are what LeWitt terms "mistake drawings," that is, drawings in which the logic was apparent but not real and so abandoned.

LeWitt has had a total of 36 selected one-man exhibitions since 1965, among which are Kunsthalle, Berne; The Dayton Art Institute, Dayton; Masschusetts Institute of Technology, Cambridge; The John Weber Gallery, New York; Lisson Gallery, London; Pasadena Art Museum, Pasadena.

He has been in a total of 91 selected group exhibitions since 1964. Much has been written about the artist in "Art Forum," "Arts Magazine," "Arts International," and "Art News."

          ∾ Write a press release about some activity of public interest. Suppose that you have a maximum of 250 words and proceed with the knowledge that the newspaper may cut the last 50 words.

A paragraph is analogous to any unit in other kinds of composition that is midway between the smaller parts and the whole. For instance, the *modular units* with which you can construct a house play a role like that of paragraphs, since each unit is made up of individual parts (wood and metal framing) and also constitutes, along with other units, a larger whole (a wall, for instance). If you consider a measure of music as analogous to a sentence, then the *section* – the series of measures set off by a double bar – would be analogous to the paragraph. It's instructive to try to identify a stage or a phase that is analogous to the paragraph in a process with which you're familiar. In that way, you form the concept of the paragraph as both a part and a whole.

          ∾ Pat wrote the following in response to an assignment to "form the concept of a place you know well." It's printed here without indentations so that you can practice editing for paragraphs.

Following the Depression, Grampy's farm in Maine no longer proved productive, so a new homestead had to be found for his family of nine. He chose the small mill town of Charlton, Massachusetts where jobs seemed available. The site was a knoll across from a dry riverbed on Southbridge Road, the main thoroughfare connecting Charlton with Southbridge. The road was sparsely populated, except at either end near the town centers. The spot Grampy chose was more like Maine than Massachusetts, halfway between the two town centers, isolated yet accessible, surrounded by open land with rolling hills as a backdrop. Grampy felt that the knoll would provide good drainage in heavy rains and protect the house from flooding. We all reaped the benefit of his foresight, when, in the 1950's, Hurricanes Carol and Edith caused the riverbed to flood over its banks and into the basement; this house withstood the onslaught while others were swept away. It took two years of back and forth between planting and harvesting seasons to complete the building. It was no modern architect's dream, just sound, simple living space with eight square rooms spread over two floors. By Maine farm standards, it was modern, with indoor plumbing and electric lights. Still, some of Maine remained – the "heat stove" in the parlor and a large grated vent in the ceiling to allow the warmth to penetrate the upstairs rooms, the hand pump outside "just in case," and the hen house, filled with his prized Rhode Island Reds and Plymouth Rocks. From the moment the last nail was driven and the paint had dried, the house was a sanctuary to those who travelled Southbridge Road. The door was hardly ever locked and if it was, everyone seemed to know that the key rested over the front door. Wayfarers inquiring at the local tavern might be told about the house down the road where they could rest for the night. In the 1940's many servicemen-in-transit helped themselves to a night's sleep in whatever space there was on the sofa, chairs or floor in the parlor. In the morning, after counting heads, Gram made breakfast and then sent them on their way. Once, in the dead of night, even an escaped German prisoner-of-war, tired, hungry and scared, dared to wander up seeking shelter and food. In spite of whatever fears may have prevailed, the man was not denied a hot meal at this kitchen table. The kitchen was the hearthstone where family and friends never ceased to congregate. From his chair by the kitchen window Grampy kept a protective eye on us grand-

children as we played, scurried and screamed in the backyard. Once, when the pony I was riding took off out the
yard, Grampy bolted through the house, out the front door
and caught the galloping steed on a dead run, though not
before I had been unceremoniously deposited on the wood-
pile. Unexpected visitors were the norm and every Sunday
was a family reunion with Grampy presiding from his chair
at the "big table." The meals were group efforts. We usually
brought some dessert or other, Aunt Ella some vegetables
and another dessert, and Gram prepared the roast. The old
gas stove became a bubbling cauldron of goodies. The room
seemed to grow just to accommodate us all. It was wall-to-
wall tables in order to seat all thirteen grandchildren; the
grown-ups, of course, ate at the "big table." Mealtime here
was a symphony of clatter, chatter and noise. After meals,
no matter what the season, we kids went out to play.
Sometimes we climbed the garage roof and slid down into
snow drifts or played king of the mountain atop the dog-
house. After a particularly cold and wet winter romp, the
opened oven door became a "fireplace" where mittens were
dried and small hands and feet regained their warmth. It
was always a joy sitting there in what felt like the center of
life and listening to the stories and legends float through
the air from around the "big table." In the nice weather we
kids busied ourselves, writing, directing, producing and
acting in what we were sure would be the hit of the "very off
Broadway" season. These productions usually took all of 15
minutes to prepare and we had the audacity to charge the
unheard of admission price of a penny a seat (bring your
own chair). When the masterpiece was ready, we invaded
the kitchen, collected our captive audience (and the penny
admission) and hustled them off, kitchen chairs in hand, to
the newly renovated Pony Pen Theatre. Needless to say,
every performance received a standing ovation and rave
reviews. The only one who didn't always participate in
these shenanigans was my older sister who was up to
something else. She had discovered that she could sit for
hours on the cross-ties of the "big table" and not be noticed.
In fact, she never was caught either by the adults or by us
kids. So under cover of the confusion of clearing meals and
children being hustled off to play, she took up her position
and totally absorbed all the family gossip. She was our
guru, being the oldest grandchild and two and one-half
years my senior, and led scavenger hunts into those parts of

the house where children didn't belong. When it was finally time for sleep, we kids were trundled off upstairs to sleep four and five together. We didn't really mind the crowded accommodations as the floor vents had been covered over and the more in a bed the warmer you slept. There huddled together under the covers, we talked and dreamed of the time when, according to Grampy's rule, "our belly buttons would come above the table," and we would finally be big enough to be granted the honor of sitting with the grown ups at the "big table" in Grampy's kitchen.

You can learn to use paragraphing as a way of expressing your own way of seeing relationships – the way you think. How your temperament leads you to employ logic and rhetoric determines style, but a sense of audience is essential if your style is to develop grace and power. A paragraph is a treat for the eye and an encouragement to the reader; it's like a pause in a formal speech. (Cicero warned students of oratory that interest would flag after the beginning of the oration but that it would pick up as soon as the audience felt that the end was in sight. The trick, then, was to keep beginning and to warn far ahead of time of the ending and thus virtually eliminate the middle of the discourse!) You can learn to use paragraphing in the interest of keeping your reader's attention: we all like to know where we are, what's happening, and when it will end. Studying paragraphs and paragraphing is one of the best ways to learn to strike a balance between the needs of your reader-audience and your own expressive needs.

〰 Using any of these definitions, compose a paragraph that defines a paragraph.

- A paragraph is a rhetorical form that gathers and sorts statements.
- A paragraph is both an effect and a cause, a gathering and a gatherer.
- A paragraph is a form of punctuation.
- A paragraph mediates between the sentence and the whole composition; it is an intermediary structural unit.
- A paragraph is a means of making meaning.
- A paragraph is half a page of elite type on an 8½ by 11 sheet with 1¼-inch margins.

3. Revising and Finishing

> The great thing about writing is its two stages: first trying to make yourself understand; then putting it to other people.
>
> Anthony Powell

> Writing and rewriting are a constant search for what it is one is saying.
>
> John Updike

Composing is like an organic process, not an assembly line on which some prefabricated parts are fitted together. However, plants and animals don't just "grow" mystically, developing from seed to flower and fully framed creatures, without plan or guidance or system. All organic processes are forms in action: the task of the composer is to find the forms that find forms; the structures that guide and encourage growth; the limits by means of which development can be shaped. The method of composing that we've been discussing and practicing is a way of making meaning by using the forms provided by language to re-present the relationships we see.

Composing by a dialectical method means that you write from the first; the final phase of composing is thus a matter not of going over an outline and "filling in the words" but of rewriting, which means taking another look at what you've written. Revision means a reseeing. That review is a continuation of what has been going on from the start—looking and taking another look. From chaos to oppositions; from statement to paraphrase; from definition to building the opposite case: at every stage you interpret what you're composing and those interpretations provide the ground, then, for further composing, further interpreting. Revision is a matter of interpreting your interpretations; it means hearing what you've had to say and deciding if you now know what you mean.

Revision is not the same thing as *correcting:* revising is an integral phase of composing; correcting is not. When you revise, you compose paragraphs. You write sentences; you rewrite paragraphs. It's only when you have several sentences – a paragraph in the process of formation—that it makes sense to try to rewrite any one sentence. When you're getting started and don't really know where you're going, one of the chief purposes of writing is to discover "what you want to say." Stopping to rewrite then is likely to curtail the exploration and to break the train of thought, once that's in progress. Even later, when you're developing concepts and definitions, too much fussiness over sentence structure or paragraphing can confuse the issue. Concentrating on correctness while you're composing sentences would be like polishing the handle before the door is hung.

André Gide, in a moment of reflecting on his habits of composing, put it this way: "Too often I wait for the sentence to take shape in my mind before setting it down. It is better to seize it by the end that first offers itself, head or foot, though not knowing the rest, then pull: the rest will follow along."

You compose sentences as forms that represent the way you see relationships; you revise sentences as elements of a larger form that is coming into being. In composing sentences, the dialectic is between saying and intending. In revising sentences, the dialectic is still between saying and intending – that never is finished – but it's now also between this saying and that saying, between this sentence and that one. *The sentences you compose by listening in on the inner dialogue form a sequence that becomes a paragraph when you revise those individual sentences as parts of a bundle.* Since fussing about correctness can interrupt this methodical circle, correcting will have to wait for a later phase.

Considering the relationship of any one sentence to the paragraph it helps to bring into existence is a bootstrap operation. In order to avoid the priority dilemma – which comes "first," the sentences or the paragraph? – you have to revise sentences and review/compose the paragraph simultaneously. The trick is to learn to use the paragraph as a form that guides the reforming of sentences; composing a gloss is the best way to do that because it lets you hear what you're saying. The gloss is like a garage door or a brick wall against which you can throw or hit a ball: the way the ball bounces tells you how you threw or hit it. Glossing is as useful in revising paragraphs as it is in composing them. It provides an excellent instrument for determining the structure of a paragraph – your own or someone else's. If you develop the opposition of the gloss, you'll have a summarizing statement; composing it can help you understand the logical and rhetorical structure of a paragraph in a way that passive underlining can't. You can then label as *A* or *B* each sentence or part of a sentence that moves toward one or the other term of the opposition. Sometimes a sentence that you haven't been able to follow will suddenly make sense when you work out this kind of schema.

In revision, paraphrasing serves the same function as chaos does earlier: it encourages choice, a sense of the alternatives.

When you paraphrase, you beat around the bush until you drive out the rabbit of intention. Restating is essential to concept formation; when it comes to sentence review, paraphrase is equally important, since it allows you a means of checking what you've written against what you think you mean. The paraphrase gives you a vantage point from which to assess the strengths and weaknesses of your sentences. It can help you to decide whether to cut, to mend, or to adjust; to amalgamate the sentence with others or to substitute the paraphrase, if it seems superior to the sentence under review.

And the third way to revise/compose a paragraph is to consider it the answer to a question. If you can't formulate the question to which your paragraph could be considered a response, then you probably don't have a paragraph.

The conventional criteria for judging a paragraph are *unity, coherence,* and *emphasis,* but you can't expect to discover if your paragraph is well-formed by asking, "Is it unified? coherent? emphatic?" You have to develop critical questions and it's in order to do so that you gloss or paraphrase or formulate the question the paragraph answers.

The *unity* of a paragraph can be easily tested by using the gloss: any sentence that does not state or support or illustrate the opposition you've developed in the gloss can be eliminated. (Don't cross it out too thoroughly, since this sentence might come in handy in another place.) In the following discussion, therefore, we'll concentrate on paragraph revision as a matter of assuring *coherence* and *emphasis.*

Coherence means "hanging together": you couldn't have coherence without unity, but unity without coherence is very common – the most common rhetorical fault. It's conceivable that you could have emphasis without coherence, but unified and coherent paragraphs frequently are written without any emphasis. You'll recognize this as characteristic of the style of many textbooks where the only means of emphasis used is to print topics in boldface type. In an incoherent paragraph, the sentences may all concern the same topic, but there will be no rationale for the order. One sentence will seem to call for further explanation or to promise examples, but then the next sentence will go on to something else. Many handbooks suggest that the way to make a paragraph cohere is to use road signs such as "for example..." or "on the other hand...." These little phrases can be valuable clues for your reader, but only if the relationships they signal are the ones that are indeed being set forth. If two sentences do not in fact present a contrast, then "on the other hand" won't help; if you aren't actually expressing a second thought or a reservation, then "however" won't make sense. It's a better policy to work out the logical relationships between sentences and *then* add the road signs, if you think they're needed.

A root cause of incoherence is frequently that you're working with sentences that present details and examples, but *of what* remains unclear. Composing the gloss can reveal the fact that you haven't developed a generalization that can unite particulars; in other words, it will be difficult to gloss the would-be paragraph. But if you can do so, the next step is simply to develop a sentence from the gloss and build it back into the paragraph, probably at the beginning.

Another root cause of incoherence is generalizations so vague that there isn't any clear way to decide what should come next; you have the feeling that you could as well read backwards as forwards. Vague generalizations are also likely to lead you into syntactical snarls; without substance to give them structure, articulations get fouled, like lines on a boat blowing loose. Checking your verbs can help test the substantiality of generalizations. The relationships in a sentence are articulated by means of the verb; if you check the verbs in successive sentences, you can more easily determine the relationships *between* the sentences. If most of them read *is* and *are,* you can do something about that right away by naming the relationships more precisely. And be warned: *contains* is generally an inadequate substitution. Letting *is* and *are* and *has been* etc. do all the work puts too great a strain on them; *is* is a very good cord for tying some bundles, but don't wear it out.

In reviewing a paragraph to see if it's coherent, you'll simultaneously be concerned with *emphasis:* getting sentences to cohere, getting a paragraph into shape, entails deciding what needs to be soft-pedaled or given second place. Subordination and emphasis are best considered together, since a choice concerning one will also concern the other. You subordinate in order to emphasize the main point, much as you build the opposite case in order to form a concept. Without subordinating, what you get is *parataxis* – and if that sounds like a disease, it is. Each element is given the same weight and assumes the same shape. The resulting paragraph is like a train of boxcars:

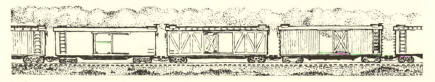

Paratactic order yields a paragraph like this one:

> The Yam Festivals are held each year before the harvest in Umofia. The purpose of the festivals is to honor Ani, the goddess of the earth and the source of all fertility. The land is very important to the farmers in the villages and this is why the festivals are the largest and most celebrated in Africa.
>
>   A great deal of preparation is made for this holiday and one is expected to have a big meal and many guests....

Note that the author here begins another paragraph when he comes to describing the preparation for the yam festivals. Now if the paper were entirely devoted to the yam festivals, a separate paragraph concerning preparation would be legitimate, since obviously there would be many facts and details to set forth and particulars to be developed; every aspect of the yam festivals would need to be discussed – origin, function, organization, etc. But the paragraph quoted appeared in a short paper on tribal customs in Africa and the topic of yam festivals is only one of many items. There's no reason for devoting to it more than one paragraph, which could include a description of preparation as well as comment on purpose, etc. Without subordination, there's no way to make the main point about the yam festivals in the larger context of a paper about social and religious institutions and celebrations.

   In finishing your paper, when you come across a series of boxcar sentences, it's a sign that your paragraph lacks emphasis. Unless you've subordinated, how will your reader be guided in identifying the main point?

   An alternative to judicious subordinating is to subordinate everything. James Thurber explains the dangers of that procedure in the following passage:

> What most people don't realize is that one "which" leads to another. Trying to cross a paragraph by leaping from "which" to "which" is like Eliza crossing the ice. The danger is in missing a "which" and falling in. A case in point is this: "He went up to a pew which was in the gallery, which brought him under a colored window which he loved and always quieted his spirit." The writer, worn out, missed the last "which" – the one that should come just before "always" in that sentence. But supposing he had got it in. We would have: "He went up to a pew which was in the

gallery, which brought him under a colored window which he loved and which always quieted his spirit." Your inveterate whicher in this way gives the effect of tweeting like a bird or walking with a crutch, and is not welcome in the best company.

It is well to remember that one "which" leads to two and that two "whiches" multiply like rabbits. You should never start out with the idea that you can get by with one "which." Suddenly they are all around you. Take a sentence like this: "It imposes a problem which we either solve, or perish." On a hot night, or after a hard day's work, a man often lets himself get by with a monstrosity like that, but suppose he dictates that sentence bright and early in the morning. It comes to him typed out by his stenographer and he instantly senses that something is the matter with it. He tries to reconstruct the sentence, still clinging to the "which," and gets something like this: "It imposes a problem which we either solve, or which, failing to solve, we must perish on account of." He goes to the water-cooler, gets a drink, sharpens his pencil, and grimly tries again. "It imposes a problem which we either solve or which we don't solve and..." He begins once more: "It imposes a problem which we either solve, or which we do not solve, and from which..." The way out is simple: "We must either solve this problem, or perish." Never monkey with "which." Nothing except getting tangled up in a typewriter ribbon is worse.

James Thurber, from "Ladies' and Gentlemen's Guide to Modern English Usage"

The chief subverters of emphasis are jargon and cliché. Jargon is terminology that is (or may be) appropriate and indeed essential in a particular field of study or activity, but that can be tiresome and misleading when it's used in other contexts. A biologist needs the word "viable" in describing experiments; when a politician uses it to mean "workable, in my opinion," he is attempting to sound "scientific." You can easily train yourself to spot jargon in your own writing and in what you read by paraphrasing and interpreting any statement that seems wordy:

The Institute is engaged in the design of experiments to identify parameters of creativity and to correlate those parameters of creativity with the characteristics and behavioral patterns of the creators.

Translation: The Institute will provide occasions for observing how creative people work – but if we don't make it sound complicated, we won't get our grant.

Clichés – and jargon terms quickly become clichés – are moribund metaphors, literary expressions, old proverbs, specialized expressions that have been used so frequently that they are no longer sharp or provocative. (*Cliché* is a French word, a printing term that refers to a kind of plate used in the nineteenth century to print photographs. After a few printing runs, such plates became worn and flattened so that the impressions they made were fuzzy or blurred.) A gifted public speaker can bring clichés to life. Dr. Martin Luther King, Jr. could preach a sermon that was fabricated mostly from clichés, but by the rhetorical arrangement and the cadences he composed, by the way he played them off against anecdotes from his own experience, he made them his own. Oratory in this style is like the art of quilting: it's not the scraps but the design and stitching that counts.

That said, it's better to avoid clichés. The most important point is to tune your ear so that you can recognize a cliché in your writing; then you can decide if you want to keep it. Seeing that you've written, say, "stark contrast" may remind you to review your statements to find if you've set things forth so that the contrast is indeed "stark." If it is, you may want to cut out the cliché; if not, you'll know that some further forming/finishing is called for.

☙ If you've ever worked for a governmental agency, this kind of prose won't be new to you. And, of course, we've all been on the receiving side of such language. Read the following:

The Department's approach and analysis seek first to deduce the management capacity within the existing organizational structure to determine what types of functional capacity exist and what planning and implementation configuration should be developed for the Department:

Management Capacity (as defined from a systems perspective) means an organizational configuration of functions juxtaposed in such a way so as to achieve an interdependent network of defined centers of responsibility and clusters of activities and tasks (with clearly defined parameters) allowing for the efficient, effective production of a service or a cluster of services to an eligible/needful population through a variety of deployment mechanisms.

Planning Functions include systems definition of resources development, allocation and utilization, systems development and systems operations for the purposes of rationalizing and making explicit the qualitative and quantitative characteristics and mechanisms of each system and subsystem so that all component sets of activities are defined and transmittable in either a manual (written procedures) or an automated mode of communication to cover all the basic functions and activities of policy development, planning, managing, administrating and financing of the local management systems.

What does it say?

The best thing to do with gobbledygook is to make fun of it, which is what Susan E. Russ (in the *Washington Post*) did with her "Bureaucrat's Guide to Chocolate Chip Cookies":

For those government employees and bureaucrats who have problems with standard recipes, here's one that should make the grade – a classic version of the chocolate chip cookie translated for easy reading.

Total Load Time: 35 minutes
Inputs:
    1 cup packed brown sugar
    ½ cup granulated sugar
    ½ cup softened butter
    ½ cup shortening
    2 eggs
    1½ teaspoons vanilla
    2½ cups all-purpose flour
    1 teaspoon baking soda
    ½ teaspoon salt
    12-ounce package semi-sweet chocolate pieces
    1 cup chopped walnuts or pecans
Guidance:
    After procurement actions, decontainerize inputs. Perform measurement tasks on a case-by-case basis. In a mixing type bowl, impact heavily on brown sugar, granu-

lated sugar, softened butter and shortening. Coordinate the interface of eggs and vanilla, avoiding an overrun scenario to the best of your abilities and skills.

At this point in time, leverage flour, baking soda and salt into a bowl and aggregate. Equalize with prior mixture and develop intense and continuous liaison among inputs until well-coordinated. Associate key chocolate and nut subsystems and execute stirring operations.

Prepare the heating environment for throughput by manually setting the oven baking unit by hand to a temperature of 375 degrees Fahrenheit (190 degrees Celsius). Drop mixture in an ongoing fashion from a teaspoon implement onto an ungreased cookie sheet at intervals sufficient enough apart to permit total and permanent separation of throughputs to the maximum extent practicable under operating conditions at this point in time.

Position cookie sheet in a bake situation and surveil for 8-10 minutes or until cooking action terminates. Initiate coordination of outputs with the cooling rack function. Containerize, wrap in red tape and disseminate to authorized personnel on a timely and expeditious basis.

❧ With *unity, coherence,* and *emphasis* as your criteria, evaluate these three paragraphs by different writers on the same topic, the idea of "community" as it emerges in a reading of the short stories of Sarah Orne Jewett.

1. The characters of *The Country of the Pointed Firs* lives seem to be very isolated from the rest of the world outside of their stomping grounds. The way in which they talked about another state seems as though it were another country. Their lives are built on mostly simple events. Their lives are so simple that they would appear boring out of context. Miss Jewett made beauty out of her characters with what little material made available to her. The characters didn't seem to reveal any real startling situations. But in context the excitement that arises from the coming of a yearly reunion is comparable to that of the excitement generated by that of the yearly Stanley Cup playoffs. The characters enjoy sitting around having a cup of tea and chatting as much as some people enjoy sitting around drinking a six-pack of beer and watching a Sunday football game.

2. The community of Dunnet Landing was that of father and son. It was said that everyone loved each other in that community. People would sing, dance, and play with each other until late at night. Some houses gave more beauty to the island because of their presence overlooking the sea. Sailors that arrived on the island would remark how close a relationship between the people of the island is. It gave the island a more attractive setting than other islands in eastern Maine.

3. Through lifetimes of self-sufficiency, Jewett's women of the Maine coast have become strong, indomitable characters. Their husbands die young fighting for an existence in a hostile world or spend their lives on distant seas. Women like Almiry Todd must learn to fend for themselves and meet life's crises with strength and courage. At best, life along the coast of Maine is difficult: Winters are harsh and long, desolate and lonely; spring is indeed welcome after the long winters and a time of reunion for families and friends. These women find happiness in the true and simple pleasures of life—each other and the beauties of nature. A yearly family reunion or a sail in the harbor are big events in their simple country lives. When life moves slowly and is regulated by nature, anything outside of the ordinary is exciting and topic for speculation among the village residents. The lives of these delightful women of the Maine coast reflect the beauty and the hardship of the landscape itself.

It's a lot easier, of course, to review somebody else's writing, but it's nonetheless good practice. As an editor, you should aim for being able to read what you've written as sentences and paragraphs constituting a discourse which your reader will be coming to, without privileged access to your inner dialogue. When you're your own editor, the dialogue is "outer": it's carried on between your "text"—and what you've written—and what a reader will think you have said.

One way to learn to edit your own writing is to remember that editing is a matter of interpretation: like medicine and law, editing is, we might say, a hermeneutic enterprise. We can discuss editorial procedures *in terms of* certain clinical practices. We can talk about "sick" paragraphs by analogy with sick creatures of any kind, including "dialectical animals," which is what we called definitions in Chapter IV. This metaphor of medical *diagnosis* (which is Greek for "knowing your knowledge") is useful because it underlines a fact about medical science that is analogous to any critical method. Once tests have been run and a diagnosis is completed, the treatment is simple, if not automatic. The doctor's skill is in recognizing symptoms and interpreting them in the context of the patient's history; then, once the diagnosis is made, the lowliest intern can look up the treatment plan and prescribe medication. The analogy with composing, revising, and correcting is that *recognizing* rhetorical and logical faults is more fundamental than knowing how to correct them; on the other hand, knowing what constitutes a healthy state of affairs provides important limits for interpreting the signs of disease. I've outlined a critical review procedure on the basis of this analogy.

A Procedural Guide to Paragraph Composition and Review

A. *Clinical techniques*

1. Gloss each paragraph.
2. Paraphrase any suspicious sentences.
3. Formulate the question to which the paragraph could be considered an answer.

B. *Diagnosis: a checklist of critical questions**

1. How is this sentence related to others? Does it define or qualify? generalize or interpret? assert or exemplify?
2. Should it be revised in order to clarify assumptions? to subordinate? to emphasize?
3. Would its role in the paragraph be strengthened if its position in the sentence sequence were changed? If it were amalgamated with other sentences? if it were rebundled? if it were eliminated – or moved to another paragraph? (Clinical procedure: Cover all but first sentence with a note card; formulate what you expect to be the substance of the next sentence;

*I have derived these questions from the following comment by Josephine Miles: "The major grammatical and rhetorical choice is the degree of predication, of assertion to be stressed or subordinated, or assumed."

check sentence as written against your supposition; then proceed with the questions concerning positions, etc.) Continue with the rest of the paragraph, sentence by sentence.

C. *Treatment plan: optional grammatical and rhetorical adjustments*

1. Develop generalization to gather particulars (Develop gloss into a statement and incorporate).
2. Substantiate generalizations.
3. Develop particular examples to support generalizations.
4. Name relationships more precisely than by writing "is."
5. Repeat yourself for emphasis (a phrase in apposition; grammatical transformation of key terms).
6. Add road signs where necessary to avoid confusion and to add emphasis.
7. Subordinate, amalgamate, eliminate; rearrange.

Archimedes, a Greek mathematician given to considering the problems of method, asserted that he could move the world – if he had a stick long enough and a place to stand. This is a principle that's centrally important to more than just mechanics: in revising a composition you have to establish some place "outside" the composition from which to regard it. That place can't be established by simply asking, "Am I being clear?" or "Is this paragraph coherent?" Rather, you will need critical questions that can establish a place from which to gain perspective; they will be dialectical in character: "If these sentences are to be a paragraph, what phrase would adequately name the topic they develop?" "If these three glosses in sequence come before that next sequence, what's the relationship between them?" "If the composition ends with a paragraph that can be glossed in such and such a way, does this gloss make sense when juxtaposed with the gloss of the opening paragraph?"

In the final stage of revision, when you have the whole composition before you, in order to take it all in, you need to see it from a distance, to get a perspective that lets you see everything at once. The more territory you have to survey, the higher up or the farther off you will have to be. You can consider the following suggestions as ways of providing Archimedean places.

1. First of all, copy out your paragraph glosses in sequence and number them. Read them through without checking the paragraphs and see if you can account for the order. Some rearrangement might be called for. After you've experimented, perhaps with new arrangements, give the sequence a title. This will be called the *supergloss* and it should include at least two terms from HDWDWW?

2. At another time – preferably another day – read through the entire composition and, without checking, write an *abstract,* a summary or condensed statement that presents the topic, the argument, and the chief support for the conclusions reached. Don't waste words by saying, "In this paper I have tried to show some of the more important influences on the development of one or two factors." Get directly to the topic and the points you make about it; explain yourself in as precise a manner as you can. (In France, *précis* writing forms the basis for the study of composition, as well as for critical reading and interpretation.) For a paper under 600 words, the abstract could be a single sentence; if the composition is 5,000 words (20 pages), the abstract should be not more than 250 words. Use these limits to give you a sense of how long an abstract should be. (You can get the hang of how to write an abstract by reading a dozen or so. The library will have various collections of abstracts appearing in scholarly journals.)

Preparing the abstract without having the composition in front of you means that you're working from what you think you've said. The abstract thus can represent your intentions, a checkpoint from which to review the individual paragraph glosses, what you've actually said. The abstract acts like a sieve: it should catch *all* the paragraph glosses, filtering out those that are trivial or irrelevant. Of course, if several paragraph glosses are not caught – that is, if some paragraphs are completely unrelated to the abstract – then you have trouble: either the paragraphs are indeed beside the point – or there is something the matter with the sieve. You can revise the paragraphs by reordering, amalgamating, or eliminating; the abstract can be repaired by checking it against the supergloss, the title of the paragraph sequence. If the abstract is too general, it won't function: you can't catch minnows in a crab net.

3. Another means of judging the integrity of the composition is to check the introduction against the conclusion, at which point you may discover that one or the other is missing! Some compositions can reach the final stage without a proper introduction, but that's easily supplied by composing a version of the supergloss. If the conclusion is missing, you can write a version of the introduction or adapt the abstract.

4. If you think of them as the limits within which you're working, the introduction and conclusion can help you with one of the most difficult tasks of composition, namely, the review of transitions: how did you get from beginning to end? by which routes? over what terrain? using what kind of map? stopping over where? how many detours? how many excursions off the beaten path?

Paragraphs are, in a certain sense, arbitrary; nevertheless, once you've indented, indicating thereby that you want your reader to consider a group of sentences as a whole, that paragraph should be clearly related to what has gone before and what follows. As you read one paragraph, can you say, without looking, what comes next? Can you name the relationship of paragraph A to paragraph B? C to D? and so on. Checking your paragraphs against the introductory and concluding paragraphs will help you to clarify the role of each in the sequence of paragraphs that makes up the whole composition. Number, or renumber, the paragraphs in the order you think best serves your argument or best preserves balance in the composition. (Don't waste time recopying. Writing out a single passage over and over is a habit some writers develop as a strategy to put off the hard task of articulating paragraphs.) Suppose you find that you have three paragraphs in succession that are devoted to particular cases; you might want to insert a short paragraph from earlier in the paper that deals with points more generally. You could indicate this change simply by numbering the paragraphs on whatever page they appear, in the sequence you think best. Now, once you've worked on another section of the paper, it might then appear that three particularizing paragraphs are exactly what's needed: the newly inserted paragraph is removed. Renumbering is a lot simpler than copying out once again, according to the new order. The trick is to work out ways of keeping your options open.

5. Once you have a sound sequence established, you'll then be in a position to check or compose the recapitulations that keep your readers informed of where they are in your discourse: recapitulations – the word means going back to the head *(cap)* or beginning – inform readers of the degree of generality that's been reached; the relationship of the opposite case to your explanation; the way the particular details specify and build context; etc. In reviewing recaps, watch for empty statements like this one:

Examples of how these philosophies can produce two completely different reactions to the action are easily found.

Ask HDWDWW? to remind you which terms need substantiating.

6. You can then check transitions against the paragraph glosses. If you work on transitions without first gaining an overall view of your composition, the temptation will be to shift paragraphs around aimlessly. Just as you should avoid re-writing sentences when you're getting started, so you should save the reordering of paragraphs until you have a clear view of the whole, an Archimedean point. Then you can decide what transition is called for by the gloss sequence and check to see what in fact you've written. This is the only way to alert yourself to overdependence on road signs, some of which may indicate transitions unrelated to what has been written.

A review of transitions will be unnecessary in a short paper, since the paragraph glosses will have revealed the gaps and holes in the structure, and it will be perfunctory for most paragraphs in a six- to ten-page paper. But it can be extremely useful in deciding the fate of a paragraph that could go anywhere or nowhere. Sometimes, adding a single sentence (the idea for which you might steal from the conclusion) can salvage a paragraph, putting it to work in a useful role in the composition. Finishing a paper in such instances is like finishing a jigsaw puzzle: getting the last pieces to fit is a lot easier than getting started, and what generally happens is that resolving one dilemma or solving one problem gives you the means of taking care of other troubles. Everything begins happening at once and that's a sign that the dialectic is in operation.

7. With transitions reviewed and paragraphs adjusted, you can revise the supergloss and then read through the whole composition in the light of that summary. At this point, you might well decide to compose a new title, since the composing process may have yielded a paper that has grown beyond its earlier limits. And with that, you're finished with the sorting and gathering that constitutes the concluding phase of the composing process.

Recapitulation

A dialectical method of composing can help you to do the following:

1. To cultivate a habit of "careful disorderliness."
2. To listen in on the inner dialogue and to make it sensible to others.

3. To make your own map of any territory you need to explore.
4. To generate chaos; to tolerate chaos; to learn the uses of chaos.
5. To develop contexts by naming from different perspectives.
6. To develop criteria for judging degree and kind of specification and to substantiate accordingly.
7. To define the presuppositions of a list; to develop the context of situation by interpreting a list.
8. To form oppositions and thus identify relationships.
9. To specify and substantiate the terms of relationships.
10. To articulate relationships and thus to make meanings.
11. To use the paragraph form to gather sentences.
12. To review paragraphs by glossing and paraphrasing them as answers to implied questions.
13. To revise in order to assure unity, coherence, and emphasis by considering beginnings and ends, generalizations and interpretations, definitions and articulations as dialectically related, thereby carrying out "a continuing audit of meanings."
14. To use the forms of language to find the forms of thought, the forms of thinking to find linguistic forms.

◆ Here's Charlotte's final draft. Gloss the paragraphs, carrying out a diagnosis of any which are difficult to gloss. Check transitions. Write out your recommendations, including matters which you — you're the instructor — would want to discuss in conference.

Be More Than You Can Be: Images of Women in American Advertising

Professional, compassionate, glamorous: American women must be more than they can be if they are to live up to the image of them presented by advertising in the media. A woman today is expected to be a professional (or at least to work), as one source, the *Wall Street Journal* shows, but another source, television advertising, makes a woman believe that her real achievements would be to stay home and master such chores as cleaning, child-care, cooking, and serious shopping. On top of these two role models, we have the magazines published just for women, and some of those, like *Vogue,* tell women that their primary role is to be socially stunning ("exciting," "brilliant," "unique"), which is impossible without a lot of money and extra time, luxuries which full-time jobs and families may not allow us to have. If Norman O. Douglas is right when he says that "You can tell the ideals of a nation by its advertisements," then women really do have to be more than they can be.

When looking at these three popular forms of advertising, you don't have to be brilliant to see that women have a burden that they can't live up to. All the time that we are worrying about getting our degrees and establishing ourselves in a career it seems, we are also supposed to be taking very good care of our families and staying gorgeous (finding "the real you underneath" the ugly you). What I see in American advertising is not the Helen Reddy version of a woman – "If I have to, I can do anything, I am strong, I am invincible, I am woman" – but a new slogan: "I have to work hard out of the home; I have to work hard in the home; and I have to work hard to be a social standout." It is obvious that we women have bought this slogan, because we buy the products and keep the ads coming, and we all know that "it pays to advertise." My argument, though, is that women should not let the American dream, or advertisements for it, interfere with their chance for happiness.

A female reader of the *Wall Street Journal,* for example, is probably flattered that women are treated just like men there, even if there are only one or two for every ten men. What I mean is that the women are never pointed out as women or as models for teachers or other female roles. They are just there in all the ads, whether for high-tech corporations like Xerox and Teledyne, or industries like Phillips Petroleum, or consulting and investing firms like Johnson and Higgins. All these ads have pictures of the executive staff, or some other important people, and there is at least one woman in them all. All the women are intelligent-looking, educated, dressed in suits and, as one ad says, "in-charge." Since my major is business, I am interested in these women, and I also know about the work they had to do to get through MBA degrees, master the technology, and climb the corporate ladder of success. I wonder how these women keep families going and what their social lives are like. I would guess that they are workaholics and not glamorous socialites or family-types in the old-fashioned sense. I can't picture Kay Knight Clarke, former Chairwoman of Templeton, Inc., a consulting firm, and newly-appointed Executive Vice-President for Marketing, Planning, and Development for McGraw-Hill, going to different stores searching for the latest mildew products, or fighting with her husband before work about what kind of soap kills the most germs. And I am sure that "Clarke," as the *Wall Street Journal* calls her, does not spend too much time trying to teach her "old hair new tricks" or finding a cream that will assume "new responsibility" for her face.

Just as "Clarke" is typical of the image of women in the *Wall Street Journal,* "Cindy" and "Alice" and "Honey" are typical of the image of women in TV advertising, which passes on the message that whatever else you do, your job as a woman is to be compassionate, to work hard for your family and keep those stains away. Women in TV ads do not seem to have outside jobs, even though they live in nice homes and can buy all the products on the market. I think that all women identify in some way with these TV models, however. They get to your heart. The one on Dubuque Hams says, "Welcome to Iowa," and goes on to point out that church and dinner and home are the important things, at least on Sunday. A pretty small town, with steeples and nice houses, is shown in the ad, and those of us who buy food will get hams that are made there, because they have to be good and good for our families. We will also buy the microwave fries made by Ore-Ida, because beautiful TV kids like them, and we will make Pillsbury Instant Chocolate Chip Cookies to keep our cute kids from running away. You look at these perfect, thin mothers and know that they don't eat those fries or cookies, but the myth lives on. The American woman should spend a lot of time in the kitchen and the rest of the time getting sweat stains out of her husband's shirts and underwear.

My favorite example of what TV ads do to create an image of women is the one for "Applause" by Kraft. It opens with a woman sitting at her kitchen table, looking mussed and exhausted. There is a closeup and she says to us: "I have 2009 ways to fix chicken but I need another one." The family will assault her if she fixes it tonight in one of those 2009 ways. An announcer from nowhere then tells her and us that Kraft has just come up with some "exciting new ways to fix chicken." As the story closes, the woman is at her kitchen table again, feeding her family and looking great (hair fixed, makeup on). The whole family is giving her a round of "applause" for coming up with a new chicken recipe. That new recipe was for barbecued chicken, which, I guess, was not in her first 2009 versions of how to fix chicken. The ad ends with the woman looking us in the face and smiling joyfully. She says: "Bring on number 2010." You would have thought that she had just passed her MBA exam or that one of her kids made the honor roll.

Women are not this stupid. Most of us are not highly-skilled professionals and millions of us don't have families that have stayed together or children that are totally attractive. We would all look for chicken recipes all day or paper towels with "greater absorbency" if we thought it would solve any major problems. My mom would love to get up one day and have only mildew to worry about.

But let's tell the truth. These advertisers know what they are doing. Today, most women do want to do something important outside the home, and they also want to be very good at home. It would be embarrassing to be a bad mother or wife, and it is not shameful to care about food, cleaning, and getting good products. I care a lot about these things and I think that it is a sign that I have *some* intelligence. What women don't know until it hits them, though, is that full-time jobs, no matter how you redefine them, are full-time jobs. Nobody can do two full-time jobs well. And now we know why heart attacks and other stress-related diseases are hitting as many women as men today. The advertisers are only reflecting the truth about burdens that women put on themselves.

Which brings me to the major cause of stress among women. The language of *Vogue* magazine tells it all. Women want to be more than good, clean, healthy, smart and nice; they want to be "stunning," "brilliant," "exciting," "fun," "burning," "unique." I call this the "fair sex pressure," because women have always had to be sexy, feminine, and gorgeous. I think they want to be. *Vogue* is written for "a whole new society of rich," according to Bill Blass, the designer, in the October, 1986, issue. It sells the middle class and upper class woman the idea that, to be a success, she must be "exquisite," not like "Clarke" or Alice and Cindy, but like very glamorous, middle-aged stars. This look is our goal. To be like Linda Evans and model Ultress Colourant Gel is to be the "ultimate" and to make everyone else seem "just plain ordinary." With this product, you can "be the best you've ever been." Also, you might give Elizabeth Taylor a run for the beauty award if you use her product called Passion. Liza Minnelli's Revlon ad sums it up: there are three glamorous pictures, each one representing a stage in a successful woman's life. In the first, she has a dreamy, far-away look like young Cinderella; then she is in a pose that says "New York, New York" I can take you on, as if she is bowing to an audience; in the last pose, she is "exquisite," a formed star and mature person, totally in control. Liza Minnelli is perfect here, because she tends to play homely girls who become successes. If she can become this fantastic glamor-girl, why can't the rest of us? Also, Revlon is one of only a few American products advertised. The rest have names like Dior, Lancome, and Cache, which are supposed to make us want to look or smell European, which, obviously, many of us do. The problem here, what causes the pressure, is that the people in *Vogue,* models and stars, have as their job the role of being beautiful. That's what they do. The rest of us have other jobs and not so much time or cash to "be all that we can be." That means that we are always trying to be more than we can be.

The fact that millions of us read the *Wall Street Journal* or *Vogue* shows that certain values are strong in this country. The *Journal* is very important to everybody in business and finance, and *Vogue* matters to all women who care about fashion and the latest in the cultural world. People who are able to watch daytime television probably also have certain values that the advertisers know about. I would not argue that women should give up their new roles in the professional world. I would never say that it is stupid to care about recipes, detergents, or even cleaning toilet bowls. And I care as much as anybody about being attractive. All I am saying is that the American dream, especially the one about what women should be, is a *dream* and that women should remember that.

4. Correcting Sentences: Some Common Errors

As you may have had occasion to discover, you can make sense of the explanation in a grammar workbook and complete the exercises there and still not be able to correct your own sentences. The reason is that when you're undistracted by the sentence's role in making meanings, you can more easily see/hear that there's something wrong with the way it is constructed. Real sentences, however, occur not in isolation but in the context of passages and paragraphs, books and papers, courses and lives. Since a faulty sentence can be recognized and corrected more readily when it's considered as a bundle of parts, you need some way of focusing on that "bundle" rather than on what you think you mean or what you wanted to say or what you think the sentence says.

Such a concentration can be encouraged, I think, by the simple technique of reading your paper backwards, a sentence at a time. This procedure creates an isolation that focuses attention on sound patterns, idioms, agreement, reference, and so forth. It can make your sentences sound alien, like those in a workbook, and for the purposes of correction, that's all to the good.

In the following pages you'll find examples of the kinds of errors that you can train yourself to locate by this technique of reading backwards. Remember that when you locate an error, you can sometimes correct it by rather simple adjustments, but that at other times you'll need to revise it; and that calls for returning it to the context provided by the paragraph.

We've included here only a handful of the possible errors that we all can get trapped by, but these seem to us to be among the most common and the most annoying to both reader and writer.

(*Note:* Corrected versions of faulty sentences are in **boldface type.**)

Word Trouble

Of course, all faulty sentences suffer "word trouble," but some errors can be fixed by simply cutting or adding a word or two, without getting into any heavy analysis. As a starter, here are some errors that can be corrected with minimal effort: they result from having (1) too many words, (2) too few words, or (3) the wrong words.

1. Simple redundancy: more words than you need in one sentence.

> *Example:* The woman in front of the roulette wheel stares at the wheel with an apparent disgusted look.

> You ought to be able to get rid of one *wheel,* and if she
> has a *disgusted* look, you don't need to say it's *apparent,*
> which means "the way it looks."

**The woman sits staring with disgust at the roulette
wheel in front of her.**
**The woman at the roulette table sits staring in dis-
gust at the wheel.**

What a sentence "needs" is problematic: you have to decide
whether each word pulls its weight. When Macbeth says that
he's "cabin'd, cribb'd, confin'd," he's repeating himself on purpose and that purpose is to express his growing anxiety that he's
not secure in his power. It's not repetition that's the problem in
redundancy, but *purposeless* repetition.

2. Short circuit: too few words to accommodate the needs of the
grammatical elements.

> *Example:* He is concerned with how society has, is, and may
> change.
>
> *Has, is,* and *may* do not in themselves carry the
> meaning; it's only when they are used with *change* that
> they can do that. The catch is that by grammatical conven-
> tion, the form of *change* is different in each instance: *has
> changed, is changing, may change.*

**He is concerned with how society has changed, is
changing [or being changed] and may change.**
**He is concerned with change in society, past, present,
and future.**

If you force a construction to carry more than it's designed to
handle, you overload the circuit, the sentence structure. When
you feel that adding the words needed to correct the grammatical
error makes the sentence seem long-winded, you may be right. In
that case, paraphrase and reconstruct.

3. Faulty diction: wrong words.

> *Example:* Let me first *extend* the symbolism of the potato.
>
> *Explore? develop? extend* it *to* other vegetables?

**Let me first explain the symbolism of the potato more
fully.**

You use the wrong word when you've confused two words or because you don't in fact know the dictionary definition of the word you've used. There's no way to catch these errors, except when they're due to simple carelessness rather than to ignorance. The more you read critically, the more reliable your ear will become. In most cases, faulty diction occurs when the writer is putting on a manner that's not her own.

Snarls: Verbal Confusions

What I'm calling "snarls" are syntactical errors that result from joining constructions that are at odds with one another linguistically, or failing to observe the conventions that govern the use of those grammatical elements that articulate the parts of the sentence. What the writer intends may be clear, but reading the sentence can make you dizzy.

Snarls result when you (1) mix metaphors, (2) mix constructions, or (3) confuse the terms of comparison and differentiation.

1. Mixed metaphor.

> *Example:* Miss Welty has dived into the realm of the balance between external forces in the world and the emotions of the individual.

> You can *dive* into all kinds of things, not just water; a *realm* is a kind of place, but it can refer figuratively to anything that can be said to be an "area" of thought or action; *balance* is both the name of a state of being and the name for a device used to measure an unknown thing against something of known weight. Each of these words can be used metaphorically to describe an action or concept, but when they're used together, each undercuts the other.

Miss Welty has explored the realms of emotion.
Miss Welty has examined the balance between personal emotion and...

Metaphor is central to the making of meaning. Metaphor, myth, and language itself all come from a single source, which is the human capacity to see the form of one thing in another. Bad teaching of poetry has led some students to believe that all images should be visualized, that the point of an image is to make you think in visual terms of what is being described. That's sometimes true of an image and sometimes not. Some metaphors present an image that brilliantly illuminates the visual character of what is being described; the prime function of other metaphors is to name indirectly a quality shared by two things or an idea and a thing, or two ideas. When Marvell wants to describe the meadows by a river just after they've been drained, he sketches this picture:

> For now the waves are fall'n and dried
> And now the meadows fresher dyed;
> Whose grass, with moister color dashed,
> Seems as green silks but newly washed.

On the other hand, when Gerard Manley Hopkins writes,

> Self yeast of spirit a dull dough sours

we're not meant to see the inside of a poorly run bakery.

Learning to read poetry is in part learning how metaphors work. That's why many teachers believe that composition students who study carefully the rhetorical forms of poems can learn something about creating rhetorical forms in prose, even in the unexciting, workaday prose of course papers.

Here are two rules about using metaphor:

- Don't use a metaphor unless you can use it to think with; don't use it as icing.
- If you do use a metaphor, trust it with the work you assign it. Don't explain it, don't draw it out at great length, and don't tack one metaphor onto another.

For an excellent – and very amusing – discussion of the rhetoric of metaphor, see H.W. Fowler, *Modern English Usage.*

2. Mixed constructions: fractured idioms and incongruously matched syntactic elements.

> *Example:* It's asking too great a drain on the writer.

> *Asking too much* or *it is too great a drain,* but not parts of each spliced together.

> **It's asking too much of the writer to require that... The demand you make is too great a drain on the writer.**

Mixing constructions, like mixing metaphors, loses the point of both. It's an error that comes from writing one phrase at a time without regard for the structure of the sentence: it results from assembling the parts without bundling them. As you sort things out and decide which construction you want to complete, you'll see that meanings shift; different ways of unsnarling will formulate different intentions. That's why it's a good idea to develop at least two different versions so that you can see which comes closest to what you intend to say.

3. Mangled comparisons and differentiations.

Many errors result not from getting lost in your argument but from losing your way in the structure of a sentence. Although the confusion in saying then becomes a confusion in meaning, in some cases the very elements that have caused the confusion can be used to straighten things out. The best way out of the mazes created by mismatched correlatives or incomplete idioms is patient paraphrasing and a sorting out of what goes on one "side" and what on the other.

Example: Their work is not much alike.

alike

Alike is a shorthand way of saying that two things are similar. It therefore can be used only when the subject is in the plural; a plural verb is thus required. Translating *alike* to mean *X is in the state of being like Y* can help you be sure that you have named both X and Y. That initial *a,* which in some other words is a sign of the negative (*a*moral, *a*pathetic, *a*symmetrical), here signals a state of being (cf. *a*maze, *a*but, *a*lign, *a*wake, *a*kin, and the beautiful archaic form, *a*borning). Note that when *a* signals a state instead of the negative it's never stressed in pronouncing the word.

Their paintings are not very much alike.

Example: In pre-revolutionary China, the status of women was much like those in other non-Westernized countries.

(much) like

Like signals a comparison of two subjects or objects — two things or concepts: X is like Y. But the X and the Y have to share the same degree of generality. (They have to both be vegetables or both be parsnips.) In its uncorrected form, this sentence states that the *status* is like *women. Like* can be qualified with *quite, much,* and *a lot. "Very like"* is archaic, but *very likely* is a common qualifier used about acts or events.

In pre-revolutionary China, the status of women was much like that [of women] in other non-Western countries.

In pre-revolutionary China, women had the same status as they did in other non-Westernized countries.

Example: It is this unity of perception that makes a reading of the two paragraphs together a more rewarding task than either of them separately.

more
(or less)
than

More and *less* are used with *than* to state comparisons formulated as measurements. *More* and *less* are quantitative terms, which by extension can be used of qualities as well. *Than* functions like the pivot or fulcrum of a balance.

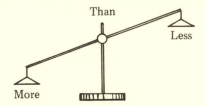

When you're reviewing a sentence with *than,* in order to be sure that you are weighing comparable items/ concepts/terms in the balance, you should check to see if you can restate exactly what is *more* (or *less*) *than* what. It's not the paragraphs that are being weighed but the task of reading them, singly or together.

It is this unity of perception that makes a reading of the two paragraphs together a more rewarding task than reading either of them separately.

Example: He reasons that man created God rather than God being the creator of man.

Rather is the comparative form of an adjective *(rath),* which has not survived in Modern English. It meant *first* or *early; rather,* therefore, originally meant "firster" or *earlier.* Like *than,* it is a temporal term,

rather
than

which by extension came to mean "first" in the sense of "preferable." To say "I would *rather* have this one than that one" is like saying "I would take this one *first, then* that." As is the case with *more than, rather than* can be separated, as in the example just given, but this usage should be avoided until you know what you're doing. The rule to follow is that whatever choices are being articulated, you should present them in parallel form: a certain grammatical element on one side of the balance must be matched on the other side.

He reasons that man created God rather than that God created man.

It's also a good idea to have on hand *instead of* and *whereas.* Here they are in revisions of faulty sentences using *rather than:*

Example: There is too much emphasis placed on discipline *rather than* education.

There is too much emphasis placed on discipline instead of education.

Example: The difference is that in a novel rather than a discourse we deal with the personal effort.

The difference is that in a novel we deal with the personal effort, whereas in a discourse, we do not.

Example: "The City and the Hive" deals with man's differences to the animal kingdom; the Gardners' study deals with our similarities.

different
from

similar
to

Stating differences and similarities causes less trouble if you refer to them as characteristics *"of X,"* rather than as *"X's";* don't make possessions out of similarities and differences. It's also useful to let the job of comparing and differentiating be done by the verbs *differ* and *resemble* (or *corresponds to, reminds us of, calls to mind, duplicates,* etc., according to context). If you do speak of differences, remember that they are *between* X and Y, not *to.* And don't undo the effect of your articulator by adding another: "The observer of American life and its accompanying values can see a marked difference between the appearance of a high-priced so-called luxury sedan *as opposed to* that of a more economically priced one." If you've written *difference between X and Y,* you don't also need *as opposed to.*

"The City and the Hive" deals primarily with the differences between man and the rest of the animal kingdom; the Gardners' study stresses the similarities.

Example: Simple acts like donning woolen sweaters instead of raising the thermostat and organizing car pools instead of one car wasting the fuel that four could use would enable us to postpone a long-term commitment to the plutonium economy.

instead of

Instead of means *in the place of:* X is where Y used to be or should be. It's a fulcrum that must weigh elements of the same grammatical kind. You can avoid many cases of "faulty parallelism" if you check out *what* is being placed where *what* was. Use your ears: in the case above, you'll know there has to be another *ing.*

Simple acts like donning sweaters instead of raising the thermostat and organizing car pools instead of wasting fuel in individual cars would enable us to postpone a long-term commitment to the plutonium economy.

Examples: Each is a means of communication and work on the principle of using waves.

Perhaps the illusion common to both Jake and Gatsby is their respective concepts of themselves.

In all phases of composition, you need to know how to single out and to form groups. When you use *one, each, self, other, everyone, anybody,* etc., to particularize you can avoid difficulties by remembering that they're all singular and all take singular verbs; likewise, when you group by means of terms like *both* and *others,* there's no problem, so long as you keep to the plural. So far, so good; confusions arise when you want to do two things at once – to group, but also to stress the single thing held in common; to differentiate, but not at the cost of disregarding commonality.

In the first sentence, *means,* which sounds plural because of the *s,* may have created static so that the writer didn't remember that *each* is her subject and that it requires a singular verb, *works.* Or she may have thought that after the *and* she could return to radio and television and refer to them in the plural. But once the sentence is started in a certain way, syntactical requirements can't be ignored: *Each is . . . and . . . works.* In the second sentence, the subject is singular — *the illusion* — and it's given the proper verb form, *is.* What's confusing is the shift to the plural in *their concepts* (even though it is not grammatically incorrect to have a singular subject and a plural subject complement); and "respective" doesn't really help. What's needed is a syntactic element that can allow a shift of emphasis from singularity *(the illusion)* to the matter of the two *concepts. Each* can clear things up:

Perhaps the illusion common to both Jake and Gatsby is that each believes he understands himself.

Perhaps the illusion common to both Jake and Gatsby is the concept each has of himself.

Another way to eliminate interference from a plural when you want to emphasize a singular, or from a singular when you want to be grouping, is to interrupt the syntax by means of punctuation.

Society plays a very large role when it comes to how each of us see our self.

Society plays a very large role when it comes to how we – each of us – see ourselves.

Using the pair of dashes allows you to interrupt the syntax momentarily for emphasis, but you return to the plural *we* and thus to a plural verb, *see,* and the plural *selves.* It's important to note that an interruption has to be carefully controlled.

Logical Confusions

These errors can be described in grammatical terms and they can be corrected by following "the rules," but they're difficult to recognize and to analyze in any but logical terms.

1. Pleonasm: logical redundancy.

This error is probably the most common rhetorical/logical fault in all sorts of composition. We could call it *"logical redundancy"* in order to differentiate it from the kind that's simply a matter of too many words. In rhetoric texts this error goes by the name of *pleonasm,* which is Greek for "too much of a muchness." The reason that pleonasm is harder to recognize than instances of simple redundancy is that the duplication can't be spotted just by seeing that there are more words than you need. But, fortunately, pleonasm is easier to correct than it is to explain. By paraphrasing you draw out the implications of each idiom or expression in order to see how to go about unsnarling. This is a case when it's especially useful to isolate a sentence by reading your paper backwards; you can suddenly hear the absurdity when you aren't attending to the role of the sentence in the paragraph.

Example: This growth has been paid for at the expense of the environment.

To say that something *has been paid for by* somebody else and that it has been *at the expense of* somebody else are two ways of saying the same thing: you can use either expression, but you can't use parts of each to make a third.

This growth has been paid for by our willingness to destroy the environment.

This growth has been at the expense of environmental quality.

Example: In pursuit of this quest he encountered many dangers.

The term *quest* includes the idea of a *pursuit* of a goal or trophy.

In his pursuit of X he encountered many dangers.

In this quest he encountered many dangers.

2. Classification errors.

This is the most common source of trouble in faulty sentences that do not suffer from grammatical weaknesses but that are, nevertheless, obscure or confusing because terms have been used inappropriately and concepts have been named with a degree of generality that is illogical for the context.

Example: The Reynolds portrait of Dr. Johnson couldn't have been painted in the 1500s.

Since neither the painter nor his subject lived in the sixteenth century, this statement is a truism, but of course the words do not accurately represent the writer's intention. Mistaking the particular for the specific – confusing an actual person/place/thing with a kind/sort/class – is especially common in writing about historical events and personages.

Options:

a. Use *such... as* in order to create a class to which you can then refer.

Such a portrait as that of Dr. Johnson could not have been painted in the sixteenth century.

b. Convert matter to manner by using "so―――――――a *way"* (or *manner* or *mode*). Convert noun to verb: *portrait* becomes *portrayed.*

A scholar of the sixteenth century would not have been portrayed in so direct and personal a way.

c. Rename the subject in specific terms by deciding which aspects you intend to discuss and then define by using the terms *class, type, kind, sort,* etc.

The style of Reynolds' portrait of Dr. Johnson is not typical of sixteenth century portraiture.

Example: The imagery Kleist uses is one of the most fundamental differences between himself and others.

Imagery here is limited and is defined as "the imagery Kleist uses"; it therefore can't refer to imagery other writers use, which is what this construction implies. Once a word is given a syntactical setting, it must function in that setting; if you need it in another sense or with another reference, you must create a new setting, develop another syntactical structure. In this case there are several options, each developing a meaning slightly different from the others.

Options:

a. You can name two specific kinds, both members of a class.

The imagery Kleist uses is fundamentally different from that found in the other writers we have studied.

b. You can change the focus.

It is his use of imagery that is the fundamental difference between Kleist and the others.

c. You can specify and make the specification the point of reference.

It is the dream-like quality of his imagery that distinguishes Kleist's style.

VII

ACADEMIC WRITING

Forming, thinking, writing are all ways of coming to understand how words work and how meanings are made. That is surely part of what it means to be an educated person. Such an understanding of language and thought is helpful to you in your academic work, and our assumption is that what you learn in studying this book will be helpful in your various courses. Although that's not to say that knowing how to carry out academic assignments is itself the most important purpose you could possibly have in studying writing, it may indeed be the most immediate purpose. We conclude, therefore, with a few comments about the psychology of writing in general and the particular difficulties of academic writing.

1. Writer's Block and Writer's Compulsion

Writing involves your feelings, no matter what the topic or circumstances; writing a term paper can involve you "emotionally" just as deeply as composing a sonnet could. Whatever else it is, writing is not a mechanical operation.

Writing certainly involves temperament. Some people can, for instance, carry on an inner dialogue without taking notes. They simply sit down, when the time comes to write, and pour it out, but the "it" has been invented and shaped and formed by means of language over a long period of time. The pouring out is not as mysterious as it seems; nevertheless, it's baffling to those whose temperament would not allow for that kind of intensity. Some writers compose at the typewriter or the word processor because they can type faster than they can write and because they can't think consecutively until they see what they're saying in type or on the screen. Others write by hand because they need to doodle; that kinetic activity acts as a kind of starter motor. Many writers can't start until they have the right pen, the right paper, the right chair, the right writing surface. This Goldilocks Complex, it's fair to say, is frequently a way of putting off the job. All of us are capable of using one or another obsession to forestall coming face to face with the blank piece of paper. On the other hand, a little compulsiveness never hurt any writer. If the search for the perfect pen can help you defuse some of the anxiety you may feel about writing, go right ahead with your collection; if you can write with greater ease on green-tinted legal paper without holes, go find a pack. Schiller, the great poet of German Romanticism, kept rotten apples in his desk: they provided an irritant for his restlessness to focus on so that the main channel of creative energy could be kept free. Tobacco serves the same function, but inhaling the aroma of rotten apples is better for your health.

Writer's Compulsion can help remove Writer's Block, insofar as that's a matter of rationalization about not getting to work. "Writer's Block" is a catch-all term used by nonwriters to keep themselves from examining their difficulties; occasionally, though, it names something very real, a resistance beyond the reach of games and harmless compulsions, beyond what a method of composing could cure. For every student who is unable to write because not-writing serves some psychological need, there are six who can learn the uses of chaos and how to search for limits. Not being able to write is a very real and upsetting experience, but it is not a supernatural affliction. You can learn to separate the hangups from genuine anxiety and thus decide if you need to talk to somebody about further remedies.

2. Working Rules

Many of the psychologically troubling aspects of composing can be dealt with by developing working habits, which can include giving in to harmless compulsions if they make you feel more comfortable. The way to develop such habits is to have the experience of seeing how they can save time and energy. The following "rules" can be useful in forming good working habits. They concern limits, schedules, and note-taking.

Working Rule No. 1: Work within the limits of the assignment. The method of composing this book teaches can help you find your own limits for any topic and to use them to make sound decisions about composition, but no method is reliable if it doesn't also keep you mindful of the limits set by the assignment itself. (Larry had a paper to write on the James-Lange theory of emotion. He wrote about how he disagreed with this theory and how very much superior he considered his own to be. He was astonished when his paper was returned marked "This doesn't follow the assignment. Unacceptable.") An efficient writer keeps in mind what's expected by the instructor. You should have on hand from the start a description of the assignment you've been given or the one you've worked out for yourself on the basis of an assigned topic. This descriptive statement should include a reminder of the relationship this paper bears to others in the course; specifications concerning the use of sources and the degree to which "your own ideas" are encouraged or welcomed; the date the paper is due; a definite indication of the minimum or maximum number of pages or words. If length has not been specified in the assignment, you must decide, since length of paper establishes an essential limit.

Understanding the limits is part of the composing process. A method of composing should help you make good use of them. I once saw the instruction sheet that a student had inadvertently turned in along with a bought paper. The student had prepared an explanation of how this paper fitted into the course; a description of what other papers he had written and what grades he'd received; how he wanted this paper focused, the texts he wanted cited, the quotations he wanted used. In short, the assignment was carefully interpreted, the ground carefully prepared. The next step should have been to set his own limits, and by that time the paper would have been half done! But the student wrongly thought that the "writing" would be the only work, and on the basis of that faulty notion, he rightly concluded that it could just as well be done by someone else. If you have, say, six weeks for writing a paper and your instructor doesn't ask for a progress report (or a first or second draft) at an earlier stage, then you should require it of yourself: one of the functions of this book is to teach you how to teach yourself how to write in circumstances in which no instruction is offered.

Working Rule No. 2: Establish a schedule that takes into account the time you need to produce a good, clean copy, ready to be handed in. The way you use your time when you compose is determined by your temperament, your other papers, your life. Some of these constraints are "necessary": they're not subject to your will or choosing. But you can learn to be honest about that and not confuse conditions that you can't really change and those to which you can adapt, to say nothing of those that you can radically change. We have taught students whose schedules are as complicated as our own. Most of them have jobs; some of them work fifteen or twenty hours a week. They don't have a lot of time to throw away; if they are to get their course reading done, their lab work done, their writing assignments done, they have to learn to plan their time. Even a short (five to six pages) paper should be composed over a period of two weeks, say, and not saved for a weekend or two successive weekends. Some aspects of composing require long stretches of time – revision, for instance. But there are various aspects of forming concepts and working out interpretations and generalizations that can be done in bits of time.

You can help yourself make hard decisions if you establish a target time and date and then work out a schedule from that point backwards. All writers benefit from one last overview of the whole composition. False deadlines are useful: if the paper is due Monday at 10 A.M., plan to have it ready for typing or print out by noon Saturday. This will give you time for the final review, which can make the difference between a "fairly good" paper and a "thoughtful, well-written" paper. After Chuck had experimented with this way of working out a backwards time frame, he remarked that he now understood what a former teacher had meant when he said that he "wrote" in the shower. Chuck learned very quickly how to use odd bits of time for thinking about his paper, learning how to compose it over a longer period of time than the weekend before it was due.

If you have a hard time starting (despite rotten apples in every drawer) or stopping, you can try giving yourself only fifteen minutes at a time for writing. Even if you're in high gear or even if you've written not a single word, don't let yourself go over the time allotted. If you equip yourself with a kitchen timer or a parking meter buzzer that can be set for five or ten minutes or any other fraction of an hour, that will be a more humane and a more productive method than one devised by Vittoria Alfieri, a writer of the Risorgimento period. When he was learning Greek, he had his servant tie his hair to the back of his chair, giving strict orders not to yield to his pleas to be untied short of the three hours he allotted himself. Once you've sharpened your sense of how long a time fifteen minutes (or five) is, you can know better how long a time you need for working at various phases of composing. It's a good idea to decide rather carefully what your next stint will be devoted to, before you close shop. Hemingway remarked that he never left his desk without taking one step toward the next job of writing, whether it was the next paragraph or the next chapter or the next novel.

Options should be kept open, but not wide open, and not for more than a third of your total working time. The novice writer spends two weeks of research on a topic, which she then decides is boring or too difficult. She pushes everything aside and starts over; the two weeks are simply lost, written off. The only way to avoid this waste of time is to define the options more carefully. Between the rigidity of the Formal Outline and a mindless looking around waiting for something to turn up is a method that can help you generate critical questions and thus establish a field in which your explorations can be carried out.

Working Rule No. 3: Work out a system of taking notes, but don't be a slave to it. A distinguished historian made the point in a lecture on research methods. "I use pink and blue cards, 3 × 5," she said. "The pink ones are for primary sources; the blue, for secondary sources. When I run out of blue cards, I take a pink card and write 'blue' at the top." Keep your method flexible and efficient so that note-taking can be a phase of the composing process.

Here are some suggestions: if you just fill out note cards and let it go at that, you're making a monumentally difficult job for yourself (unless you plan to fit the note cards, each with its own little "fact," into a prefabricated grid, in which case nothing in this book will be of interest to you). To keep from piling up the notecards without any notion of what kind of structure they could help to build, you can keep formulating what your paper is about, what you think you're doing. You can take notes on your notes; write questions and responses: don't save up the task of critical review. For every page of notes – or for every half dozen cards – you should write two or three sentences in which you note to yourself how those parts could be bundled with others. The best way to take notes is in a notebook like the one you've been using, with the right-hand side reserved for direct quotations from your reading and the left-hand margin for queries, statements of purpose, summaries, tentative amalgamations, bundleties of all sorts. Don't write on the back of the paper or note card except for a brief continuation of a quotation. Why? Because you may want to use the actual sheets of paper torn out or the note cards to represent a sequence. A pile of sheets or a little group of cards can be a proto-paragraph (*proto-* Greek, first of a series; earliest form). Dogs and cats and roommates are hazards, to say nothing of strong gusts of wind and two-year-olds, but a large flat surface in a still room provides one of the best devices for getting a composition together.

The principal reason that we warn students against the conventional prescriptions for note-taking and research – filling out notecards, developing a formal outline – is that these activities can mask the fact that the mind is not engaged and that the composing process has not even started.

Working Rule No. 4: Don't throw anything away until your paper is finally copied. Keep all the scribbles and notes and drafts of statements of purpose, lists of oppositions, etc. Since naming and defining continue right through to the very end, you should keep what you have on hand; it can afford the materials to help in all sorts of problems in the later stages of composing. (And, indeed, you could write another paper from the leftovers! Like making another film out of all the stuff on the cutting room floor.)

3. Complaints, Queries, and Suggestions

The following questions and answers might be a source of comfort, since they help define just what kinds of problems in composing are "universal"; they're typical of students of composition everywhere. The responses are not formulated as "rules," nor are they meant to be definitive; they're representative of the responses we make in conference.

1. *How can I write about something I'm not interested in?* Whenever a topic seems dull or difficult or vague, one way to approach it is to consider who might care, even if you don't. Or put it this way: to whose advantage is it that this subject remain dull? A little self-analysis won't hurt either: "Why am I uninterested in beet sugar manufacture? Why should I care about the Hundred Years War or the Putney Debates? the settlement of the Great Plains or the First Amendment? In what circumstances is it conceivable that I might care about the topography of the Iberian peninsula?" This suggestion is not meant to

encourage the strategy rediscovered annually by a million students, writing the theme about writing the theme, but only to remind you that if you think of composing for an audience that does have an interest, such a notion can provide useful limits to help in defining the topic.

"Writing from experience" is a favorite concept of many English teachers, but they don't always make clear just how learning to write an interesting account of a personal experience can have anything to do with writing a formal paper on, say, the development of modern Japan (to take a popular topic in introductory courses in economics, modern history, political science, etc.). If you write about what Emily Dickinson means to you, the reception your paper gets might be warm and enthusiastic; it might be contemptuous. A method of composing ought to free you from a dependence on your personal enthusiasms; otherwise, you'll be condemned to taking courses given by people who look kindly on whatever mode of writing you feel comfortable with. A method of composing ought to help you discover what bearing your experience has on what you're writing about, whether it's a narrowly defined topic ("The Use of Busing in Charlestown, pursuant to the orders of the Federal Court of Boston, September-October, 1975") or one very widely conceived ("Rituals").

First of all, "experience" must be interpreted to mean not just "what happened to me," but what you've thought about in your reading and in other areas of your life. Experience is the ground from which we depart; making your experience available as a resource in writing means learning to generalize so that you can discover what there is in common between what you know from experience and the topic. That doesn't mean that you write about how the space program reminds you of the summer your uncle decided to build a submarine in the garage; it means that in thinking about the personal experience, you discover some of the limits that will help you form the concepts necessary for a discussion of the public/science/political enterprise that is called "the space program."

2. *"My professor, when you ask him to explain, just puts it in other words; he doesn't explain."* Sometimes instructors are, in fact, confused about what they're asking for in an assignment. In such cases, your questions could help. On the other hand, if you haven't mastered the principal concepts of the course, you won't be able to understand the explanations. If an instructor offers study questions, use them; translate them; compose your own. At any stage of the composing process, you can develop your own study questions; they not only can guide critical

inquiry, but they can also help you decide where you are in your paper, what you think you're saying; they can help you to identify road blocks. (Finally, they can help you decide whether it's you or your instructor who's obtuse.)

Whatever the topic, you'll need a terminology. It may be simple or it may be highly technical. If it's ordinary, everyday language, you may need analogies to help freshen your sense of what the terms mean; if it's specialized language, you'll need either analogy or careful exemplifications in order to explain references. In most cases, it will be unnecessary to incorporate such explanations in your paper; the point is, rather, that *you* need to understand the range of reference and the uses of special terms. Here's a question from an exam in *Psychology 19: Human Sexual Behavior:*

> Give an example in which social class predicts differently for males and females in terms of premarital sex behavior, according to the Kinsey studies.

The jargon has to be understood: "predicts" is used in a way peculiar to statisticians; "in terms of" is used illogically and should be translated to read "with respect to." A student cannot usefully complain about barbaric language; the causes are much deeper than anything an individual instructor could control easily. It's up to the student to understand the use of terms peculiar to a subject. In this instance, the answer one student gave earned no credit and this comment from the instructor: "You should read the question more carefully."

3. *"You keep talking about how we should start writing right away, about chaos and all that. But I was always told not to start writing until I knew what I wanted to say. I thought you were supposed to have an outline before you could write."*

The composing process starts and stops and starts again; it goes in circles; it spirals; it can involve being "in the dark," though at other times, composing is like going over a well-worn path. In any case, you can't see where you've been until you get to where you're going. A method of composing that requires that you work out an outline before you start writing cannot possibly help you find the parts or guide you in bundling them: an outline is like a blueprint and, in the design of a building, drawing the blueprint is the final stage of the architect's work. You can't use an outline as a method to compose your paper unless you already know your topics, the line of argument or plan of presentation, the principal examples or supporting evidence – in which case, you won't need an outline!

One reason that students hold on to the formal outline as a kind of security blanket is the familiar fear that if they actually do start writing, there won't be more than a paragraph. The matching fear is that there's simply no way under heaven to bring any kind of order to what is on hand without writing at least forty-five pages. The fear that you have too little to say leads to tinkering with sentences, fussing over tiny details; the fear that you have too much leads, paradoxically, to further reading and writing, to heaping more on the pile in the hope that somehow it will sift down into manageable shape.

Cultivating a "careful disorderliness," learning the uses of chaos, can help you escape from this dilemma. Without a method, the chance is that you'll simply go to the other extreme of the formal outline, writing one sentence and then another. And another. The trouble with that non-method is that there's no way to get started again, once you get stalled. Here's a familiar sight: A student sits staring into space with a blank tablet of paper and a pen at the ready. A sentence gets written and then another. A long wait. Another sentence. A long wait followed by careful, loving rereading of The Three Sentences. More staring into space. A rereading of The Composition suddenly is brought to an end as the sheet of paper is ripped off the tablet, crumpled into a throwable ball. There's a long silence. Quickly, a sentence gets written, then another... and so on.

What's happening here is that the would-be composer has nothing to guide him but the sentence he's written down. There's no place to go where materials might be afforded and no other direction than the one indicated by the opener, vague as it might be. The result is generally about like this:

> One of the most important things about Chekhov's stories is his skillful characterization. For example, in "A Trifling Occurrence," he tells us that Bielyaiev is "a well-fed, pink young man." He also says that he is fond of the racetrack. We really feel that we know this character.

And with that remark, the composition comes to a full halt. There's no place to go except to another "example" – but of what? To speak of Chekhov's "skillful characterization" is like saying that water is wet. It leads nowhere except to the high school book report, the main purpose of which is to persuade the teacher that you've read the book.

One of the chief benefits of learning to look kindly on chaos is that it gives you some place to go when you're lost or provides new purposes to get you started again when your composition has come to a full halt.

4. *"It's all very well to talk about 'method' and I grant you that it can be very helpful in getting started, but I have to get this paper written and what I need for that is not a 'method' but a plan. I can't risk ending up completely disbelieving what I started out with."*

One reason for having a method is to know when and how to plan. Ending up somewhere other than the place you thought you were going when you started out may be to your advantage: if you don't proceed in such a way that that can happen, if you don't allow for the possibility of changing your mind, then it's a certainty that you'll learn nothing from writing the paper. A method of composing should help you understand what kind of process composition is. Any process can be broken down into three phases: beginning, middle, end. These phases or stages can be differentiated for the purpose of analysis, but that doesn't mean that you can say, "Right there is where the beginning ends; right here is the point at which the ending begins." In some processes, the stages follow one another very precisely, one step after another. When you bake a cake, you reach the point when the batter is at the right consistency and the oven is at the right temperature and you know it's time to put the cake in to bake. But composing is not that kind of process. All you can do to differentiate the three phases of composing is to say something like, "Right about here I can begin drawing things together.... Somewhere about now I could go back to the beginning and see how I can get it to match the conclusion." But there's nothing to say that you can't start off by working with the middle and figure out the beginning as the very last step. (Novelists I've talked with say that the first chapter is often written last.)

The most common problem is writing longish papers (fifteen or twenty pages) is how to balance the analysis of a set of themes, issues, events, or texts with a chronological account. We don't think you can decide on a strategy until you've reached the stage of gathering and sorting paragraphs, but once you're there and ready to rewrite, then you should decide – and stick with the decision. Composing alternate titles can help you determine which kind of format is best suited to the material you have on hand. You can write several introductions and conclusions, which can help you identify the conceptual issues that might have been disguised by the chronological account. Sometimes you will find that working out the chronology has served its purpose in helping you form and develop concepts and that it needn't be a structural element in the paper. You have to learn to differentiate the topic and the history of your attempt to deal with it: the discovery you make a week before the paper is due does not have to be part of the conclusion. Options can't really be identified and established until you've defined your purpose, though it's true that experimenting with options can help establish purposes. Deciding which options best serve which purposes is the composer's continuing task. Deciding them marks the beginning of the final phase of composing.

The relationship between organization and purpose can be seen if you consider this example. Suppose you are going to organize a series of programs featuring the cantatas of J. S. Bach. Here's how defining purposes would define the options for arrangement.

- To show the development of Bach's style in this form:

    Cantatas presented in order in which they were written with some skipping around to point up contrasts.

- To show Bach's mastery of the form and his influence:

    Cantatas representative of this mastery, juxtaposed with excerpts from works of other composers.

- To demonstrate range of style, kinds of treatment of texts:

    Cantatas presented according to the occasion for which they were written.

- To demonstrate the performing styles of contemporary choral directors and singers:

    Cantatas presented which best show off the performing styles of certain musicians.

There's a dialectic at work, of course: if you discovered that there is no "development" in Bach's cantata style, that he began complexly and kept it up, then that fact would limit the number of purposes and hence the number of rational arrangements.

5. *"I start out with what I want to say, but then I get a new idea and I can't fit it in, so I scratch out what I've written and start over again. I keep doing that."*

A sheepdog doesn't run in a straight line. Keep starting and keep beginning; just don't throw anything away. "In the realm of mind, to begin is to know one has the right to begin again" (Gaston Bachelard). Starting sentence composition too soon can stop the composing process before it has a chance to get started.

6. *"I didn't mark my book or take notes when I did the reading because I didn't know what to look for."* Learning to pose questions without answering them immediately is the essential critical skill and the essential power, too, of creativity. Underlining, even taking notes, is useless unless you're in a dialogue with what you're reading, and dialogue means posing questions. That felt pen that provides a yellow or pink background for important passages, which you carefully indicate by running the marker over the lines of print, is probably the most subversive of all the reading skills equipment on the market. Pages with rectangular pastel islands suggest anything but a careful reading, which depends on questions, paraphrases, transformations, glosses, abstracts, oppositions of all kinds. Remember that the process of construing – making sense of a text – involves the same acts of mind as constructing – creating a composition. Glossing paragraphs and writing a one-sentence abstract for each chapter – whether of a novel or a textbook – will yield greater dividends than highlighting the Important Passages.

7. *"In this paper, do you want us to be objective or can we say what we think?"* *Subjective* and *objective* are too problematic to be useful terms. By the time you explain what you mean by each, according to which context, you'd probably be better off with other terms altogether. It may be that within the context of a certain course, "objective" has been defined so that it can be critically useful, but I think that it's important for all writers to understand the premise that there's no such thing as context-free evaluation; that you cannot name without presuppositions; that the "objective" facts and figures you employ have been collected and arranged by a "subject"; that facts substantiate, not The Truth, but one's *judgment* of the truth. Language is not a veil between us and reality but our means of knowing reality. A means is always subject to objective evaluation, but the criteria have, in turn, been established by a subject. What we know, we know in terms of some form or other. The question properly should be about the kind of form required, not whether you're supposed to be "objective."

8. *"I don't like to read critical introductions; I'm afraid I'll plagiarize without knowing it."* Learning how to cite sources of acts and ideas and wording involves more than just learning correct footnote form, and there's no point in trying to get around it. Critical introductions to novels or standard works of any kind provide information that's in the public domain, simply gathered

and packaged in a convenient way. Particular insights and formulations should be cited – who said it where? – and credited or directly quoted. You'll need practice in deciding just what is a particular formulation. You should ask the teacher in any course requiring a formal paper for instructions about crediting sources if they haven't been provided. Studying carefully the kind of information cited in scholarly articles and critical studies in any one field can help you develop a sense of what's to be credited. I once knew an anthropologist who required her students to credit the sources for the information that the Eskimos are a circumpolar people. Learning how to determine what needs crediting can be a useful exercise in differentiating fact and opinion, which is, of course, an important aspect of forming concepts.

9. *"I don't know how to say what the author says without just quoting him."* One of the chief problems in critical writing is presenting the argument of a writer without misleading paraphrase or without depending on lengthy quotation. You can't solve this problem by varying the phrase "The author says." Consider John's discussion of George Orwell's views of socialism in the second half of *The Road to Wigan Pier*:

> Orwell paints an interesting picture of the English working class's lack of acceptance of the supposed virtues of socialism. He states that socialists, as a group, are their own worst advertisements. He goes on to explain that it is not only the Englishman's fear for what will happen to his Sunday trousers in a revolution that holds him back,* but his revulsion at the "fruit juice drinkers, nudists, sandal wearers, vegetarians" who seem to swell the ranks of socialists. This class consciousness was not seen in any other societies we read about and would seem to cast an unfavorable light on the relative importance of social mores and political ideology for the English working class. Orwell then seems to side with the workers in claiming that there are no artists or men of great imagination who are active socialists. He deplores this but does not find fault in socialism, only in the stereotypical socialist. But he does lament the fact that socialists have not given us a song worth singing.

*This is an allusion to Brecht's "The Buddha's Parable of the Burning House," pages 181-182.

Orwell goes on to talk about the relative merits of mechanization, condemning it while admitting that we can't live without it. He also strongly condemns those who fear for their trousers but who in reality possess Sunday best clothes only in their heads. He sees this false association with the upper class as a big stumbling block to the socialist cause, and one that has to be gotten over.

Once you firmly establish that you are paraphrasing, you can write without announcing the fact continually, as John does in the second and third sentences. When you come to a memorable phrase, quote it, as John does in his third sentence. When the subject changes, you can remind your readers that they are reading a *redaction,* an old-fashioned term meaning "reduction," a "boiled-down" version of the original. Of course, there will be times when you want to stress the fact that a writer is changing his mind or contradicting himself. In the last three sentences of the first paragraph, John is as interested in Orwell's ambivalence as in the attitudes themselves: *Orwell seems to side... deplores... also laments* are all ways of focusing on Orwell. But in the next paragraph, *Orwell goes on to talk... he also strongly condemns... he sees this* are phrases that could easily have been cut. ("Orwell condemns... while admitting...")

When you've reached the point at which you're ready to develop your own counter-argument, you'll have the same sort of problem with *"In my opinion..."* as you faced with *"He also says..."* Learning to set up a framework in which it's clear that what's being declared represents your ideas and is indeed the way you see things can save you from the use of such phrases as "Frankly,..." and "I definitely believe...," which are distracting. It takes a good deal of practice before you can differentiate pomposity from authority and judge when you have earned the right to declare your own opinion without more than one announcement.

10. *"I'm trying to build my vocabulary. I go to my thesaurus to find a fresh, pithy saying, but you mark it wrong."* Going to a word list to find The Right Word is as likely to turn your prose into gobbledygook as it is to help you get to your reader. Words that you *put in* will come across just that way — like raisins or cherries stuck into a dull box cake. Words work with other words and when you choose them without regard for their fellow-workers, you'll have labor problems. You'll create trouble for yourself because simply substituting one word for another often

wrecks an *idiom*. It's much safer to keep checking what you've written over against what you wanted to say. How? By writing another sentence, an interpretive paraphrase, asking "How does it change my meaning if I put it this way?"

11. *"I just tossed that off, but you liked it; what I really worked on – that was the one you didn't like."* "Really working" unfortunately bears no necessary relation to quality. What's "tossed off" is often better writing because it gives expression to concepts and feelings whose forms you've been familiar with and probably have a deep understanding of.

12. *"But that's what I meant! How can you say I didn't say it when you've just been able to explain what I meant?"* Learning to recognize the difference between what you think you've said and the meanings your language has made possible is a primary task in composing.

13. *"Am I doing the right thing?"* A writer who has learned to listen in on the inner dialogue will be able to be self-critical without putting herself down. Here's a note I had recently from an Advanced Composition student:

> Ann: In reflecting on our conference this afternoon and trying to figure out why I seem to be so limited in my thinking with this "stuff," I realize that *I* am restricting *myself* in not only this course but others as well. As a result of feeling completely overwhelmed with my demanding schedule, I think I'm approaching my assignments in too organized or rigid a style. In feeling the need to be *so* efficient, I don't think I'm spending enough time tossing ideas and concepts around in my head. I should be working through the assignments in a more relaxed and hopefully creative manner. Is this making sense?"

And then, after expressing thanks for extra conferences (and any teacher appreciates appreciation), she concludes:

> Your interest and enthusiasm is very encouraging at a time when I'm feeling quite frustrated with the material. I want very much to improve my skills, and intend to keep on keeping on, as they say. Thanks again – Kate."

There ain't no other way.

Index of Selected
Assisted Invitations